Lesbian Discourses

Routledge Studies in Linguistics

Lesbian Discourses

Images of a Community

Veronika Koller

Routledge
Taylor & Francis Group
New York   London

First published 2008
by Routledge
270 Madison Ave, New York, NY 10016

Simultaneously published in the UK
by Routledge
2 Park Square, Milton Park, Abingdon, Oxon OX14 4RN

Routledge is an imprint of the Taylor & Francis Group, an informa business

Transferred to Digital Printing 2010

Typeset in Sabon by IBT Global

Library of Congress Cataloging-in-Publication Data

Koller, Veronika, 1973–
    Lesbian discourses : images of a community / by Veronika Koller.
        p. cm. — (Routledge studies in linguistics ; 9)
    Includes bibliographical references and index.
    ISBN 978-0-415-96095-3
    1. Gay and lesbian studies.   2. Lesbianism.   3. Lesbian feminist theory.   I. Title.
HQ75.15.K64 2008
306.76'63091752109045—dc22   2007040961

ISBN10: 0-415-96095-9 (hbk)
ISBN10: 0-415-88389-X (pbk)
ISBN10: 0-203-92869-5 (ebk)

ISBN13: 978-0-415-96095-3 (hbk)
ISBN13: 978-0-415-88389-4 (pbk)
ISBN13: 978-0-203-92869-1 (ebk)

This book is dedicated to my mother, Brigitta Koldehoff. Without her unfaltering support and encouragement right from the word 'out', it would not even have occurred to me to write this book.

Contents

List of Tables and Figures

TABLES

FIGURES

Acknowledgments

This book grew out of my MA dissertation, submitted at the English Department at Vienna University in 1998. I returned to my postgraduate work when I joined the Department of Linguistics and English Language at Lancaster University (UK) in 2004. I am thankful to my colleagues there for many helpful suggestions, and especially to Paul Baker and Ruth Wodak for reading, and encouraging me to publish, my earlier work.

I am also grateful to all the women who granted me interviews, answered my questions and networked on my behalf. Further thanks is due to the authors and publishers of the texts analyzed in this book, particularly Ingrid E. Barnes, Lorna Gulston MBE, Lilian Mohin and Carol Ann Uszkurat.

I would like to thank all the friends I have been discussing this book with over the years. They are too numerous to mention, but I am particularly indebted to Bianca Rusu, Elisabeth Fischer and, above all, Ines Rieder. This book was conceived in her living room and our many nightly conversations about it have, I think, improved it considerably. Ines is truly the midwife and godmother of this book. Thanks also to Miriam Murtin and David Pearson for test-reading the glossary.

Finally, I would like to express my gratitude for the staff at Routledge in New York, research editor Max Novick and editorial assistant Elizabeth J. Levine. There was no problem to which they did not find a solution within a day.

A few sources used in this book were intended for a female/lesbian readership only by their authors. The material in question has been paraphrased instead of quoted and has been marked with an asterisk (*) in the citation and in the Bibliography.

Examples A and B (in Chapter 3) are reproduced with permission by the publisher. Examples C, E and H (in Chapters 4 and 5) are reproduced with permission by the authors. Example G (Chapter 6) is reproduced with permission by the editor. Figure 1.2 is reproduced with permission by H.A.F. Publishing. Figure 6.1 has been reproduced with permission by Club Munch (www.clubmunch.co.uk). Example F (Chapter 5) is from a source that is no longer traceable. The author did in no way intend to unjustly utilize materials at the expense of these individuals and organizations. Anyone who takes issue here should please contact the publisher for proper acknowledgment in subsequent releases of this book.

1 Introduction
Lesbian Discourses, Lesbian Texts

My life fits in with the decades quite well, because I was born at the beginning of a decade.

(interview with Vivienne Pearson)[1]

My first lesbian text was a slim paperback called *Women Without Men* written by a certain Jessica Simmons. Published in 1970, it must have been one of the last of the lesbian pulp novels so popular in the 1950s and 1960s, and accordingly, its cast is for the better part ailed by alcoholism, promiscuity, suicide and murder. Right at the end, however, a newly introduced character delivers a scathing diatribe riddled with revolutionary rhetoric about how the one truly powerful love, i.e., that between women, will topple capitalism and patriarchy alike. Whenever I have shown this book to friends in the past few years, reactions ranged from amusement to incredulity to the odd shriek of delight at this example of lesbian retro chic. Clearly, the book and its contents have gone from being outrageous to being all the rage.

This study traces that shift, looking at what images of a lesbian community self-identified lesbian authors in the US and Britain have communicated in non-fictional texts since 1970, how this change can be traced in texts such as pamphlets, magazine articles and blogs, and, finally, why this change has taken place. To put it in a nutshell, how and why did lesbian discourses, and the images of community that they transport, change from what we can see reflected in Figure 1.1 to what is conveyed by Figure 1.2? A close linguistic analysis of texts not only shows how change was effected, but also how particular historical narratives were constructed that do not necessarily reflect the complex reality of the times they refer to.

As the title of this book indicates, community is here understood as an 'imagined community' (Anderson 1983), i.e., as a model of a collective identity that shapes but ultimately supersedes local communities. The social constructionist view, according to which the 'subject is produced . . . across a multiplicity of discourses' (Fuss 1989, p. 97), holds true for

14402

The Woman Identified Woman

BY RADICALESBIANS

What is a lesbian? A lesbian is the rage of all women condensed to the point of explosion. She is the woman who, often beginning at an extremely early age, acts in accordance with her inner compulsion to be a more complete and freer human being than her society - perhaps then, but certainly later - cares to allow her. These needs and actions, over a period of years, bring her into painful conflict with people, situations, the accepted ways of thinking, feeling and behaving, until she is in a state of continual war with everything around her, and usually with her self. She may not be fully conscious of the political implications of what for her began as personal necessity, but on some level she has not been able to accept the limitations and oppression laid on her by the most basic role of her society--the female role. The turmoil she experiences tends to induce guilt proportional to the degree to which she feels she is not meeting social expectations, and/or eventually drives her to question and analyze what the rest of her society more or less accepts. She is forced to evolve her own life pattern, often living much of her life alone, learning usually much earlier than her "straight" (heterosexual) sisters about the essential aloneness of life (which the myth of marriage obscures) and about the reality of illusions. To the extent that she cannot expel the heavy socialization that goes with being female, she can never truly find peace with herself. For she is caught somewhere between accepting society's view of her - in which case she cannot accept herself - and coming to understand what this sexist society has done to her and why it is functional and necessary for it to do so. Those of us who work that through find ourselves on the other side of a tortuous journey through a night that may have been decades long. The perspective gained from that journey, the liberation of self, the inner peace, the real love of self and of all women, is something to be shared with all women - because we are all women.

It should first be understood that lesbianism, like male homosexuality, is a category of behavior possible only in a sexist society characterized by rigid sex roles and dominated by male supremacy. Those sex roles dehumanize women by defining us as a supportive/serving caste in relation to the master caste of men, and emotionally cripple men by demanding that they be alienated from their own bodies and emotions in order to perform their economic/political/military functions effectively. Homosexuality is a by-product of a particular way of setting up roles (or approved patterns of behavior) on the basis of sex; as such it is an inauthentic (not consonant with "reality") category. In a society in which men do not oppress women, and sexual expression is allowed to follow feelings, the categories of homosexuality and heterosexuality would disappear.

But lesbianism is also different from male homosexuality, and serves a different function in the society. "Dyke" is a different kind of put-down from "faggot", although both imply you are not play-

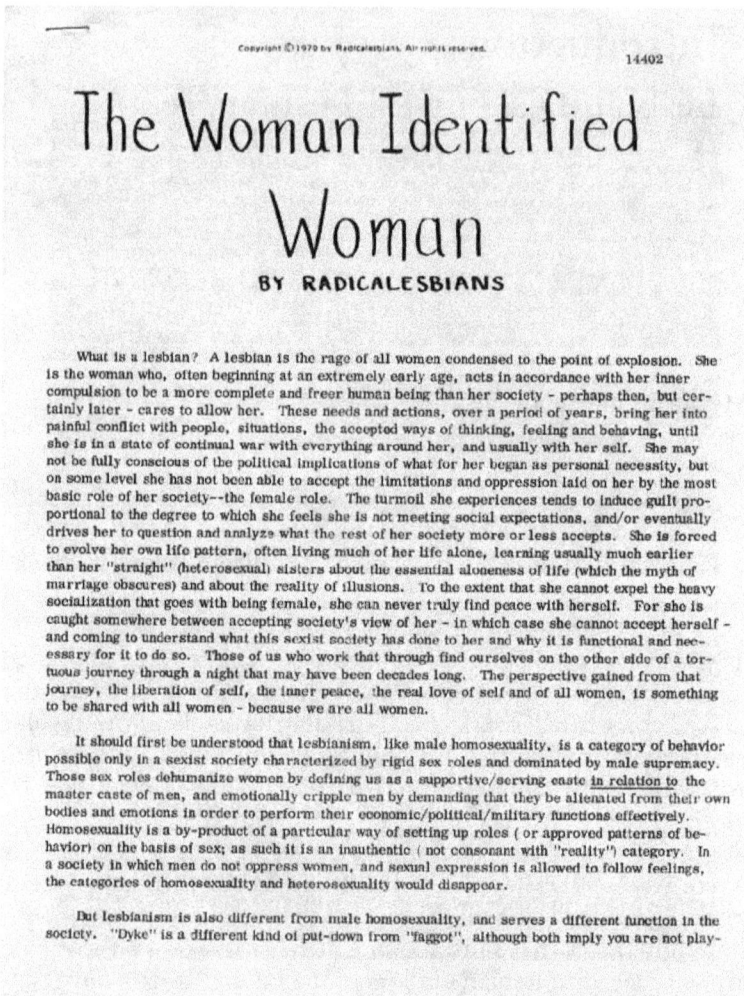

Figure 1.1   Original manifesto by the Radicalesbians, 1970 (see Example A in Chapter 3 of this volume).

the lesbian community as a collective actor as well. Images of such communities are largely, if not exclusively, an effect of discourse, i.e., accumulations of texts that particular people produce, distribute and receive in a particular way and as a form of social action. As such, any identity of discourse participants, including their collective identity as members of a community, is always preliminary, negotiable and open to change. For the

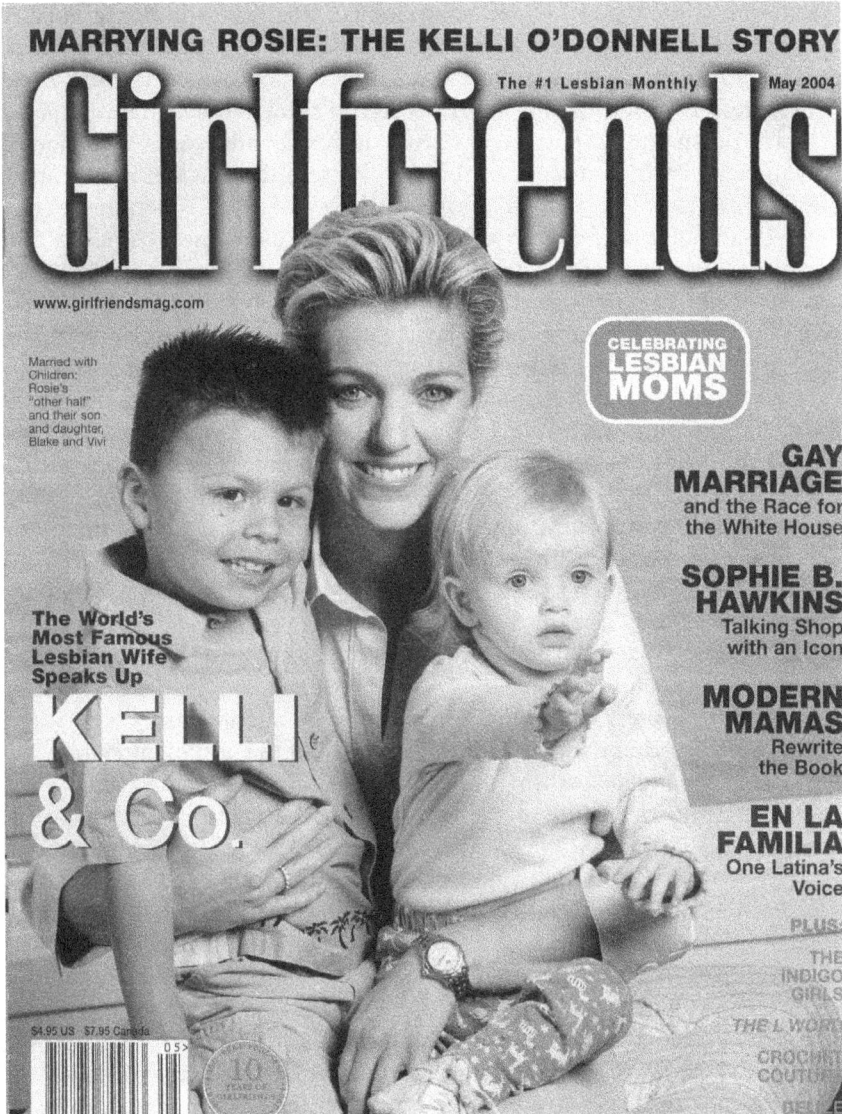

Figure 1.2 Cover of *Girlfriends* magazine, May 2004. Reproduced with kind permission by H.A.F. Publishing.

researcher who wants to find out about what images are constructed in discourse, and how this is achieved, it is logical then to turn to texts as the main source of data.

However, just as 'the search for an authentic women's speech overlooks the instability of gender divisions and the many differences between women'

(McIlvenny 2002b, p. 5), research into lesbian discourse will not reveal any typically lesbian way of using language. Rather, such research will uncover the discursive and cognitive repertoires drawn upon by self-identified lesbian writers at various points in history to construct and negotiate an image of lesbian community. Further, the study primarily addresses the image of lesbian community in discourses that involve self-identified lesbians, rather than the image of lesbians in mainstream discourse. This is despite the fact that lesbian notions of collective identity, and the discourses that effect and transport them, are not generated in a void, but influenced by the host culture in which they are embedded. Such influence may take the form of lesbians uncritically adopting society's view of them, as can be seen for many texts of the 1950s. Alternatively, lesbians may use texts to destabilize dominant views and establish a counter-model, as is the case in many instances of lesbian discourse from the 1970s. For various socio-economic reasons, lesbian and mainstream discourses have become more closely and explicitly linked since 1990 (see Chapters 5 and 6), with lesbian authors integrating features of mainstream discourses, and the images propagated in them, for the construction of their own models of community.

Although the attitudes with regard to both women and homosexuality have changed remarkably in both the US and the UK over the past three decades, this is not to say that lesbians as a social group, or indeed as individuals, have achieved full equality and freedom from discrimination. Sexual harassment and violence directed specifically against lesbians, discriminatory legislation, or just plain heteronormativity are still strong in both cultures, attempting to silence lesbians and make them invisible. As a marginalized social group, lesbians and their discourses are prime candidates for the academic field of critical discourse analysis (CDA), the aim of which it is to unveil, through linguistic analysis, the ideological underpinnings of discourses that lead to social injustice, and thereby lay the ground for political intervention. Yet, while a huge amount of literature can be found concerning questions of gender and ethnicity, comparatively little has been written on the subject of sexual identity from a CDA perspective (e.g., Higgins 1995; Morrish 1997; Livia 2002a; Baker 2005). While this study does not seek to unravel how 'heterosexual . . . power elites' (van Dijk 1993, p. 254) use textually mediated social action to marginalize lesbians by constructing a particular image of them, CDA, especially in its discourse-historical (Wodak 2001) and socio-cognitive varieties (Chilton 2005; van Dijk 2006a), still seems like a promising approach to the study of (written) texts by lesbian authors. CDA can contribute to this study in these ways:

- to establish how social change is reflected in, and produced by, texts,
- to link texts to textually mediated interaction, i.e., production, distribution and reception, as well as to wider socio-historical contexts, and
- to look at the (self-)representation of social groups and how it effects or challenges marginalization and power asymmetry within and between groups.

As such, the analytical model proposed in this book should prove useful for the diachronic study of the discursive construction and cognitive structure of collective identity in general.

CDA is interested in revealing the ideological underpinnings of discourse, including the discourse of the researcher herself. Accordingly, there can be no neutral academic account of the texts and discourses under investigation. Instead, 'critical discourse analysts ... take an explicit sociopolitical stance: they spell out their point of view, perspective, principles and aims' (van Dijk 1993, p. 252). Rejecting objectivity means realizing that 'communities are imagined on a number of levels, including the ways in which researchers themselves imagine the communities which they study' (Queen 1997, p. 237). An example of this is the study by Day and Morse (1981), who investigate conversations among long-term lesbian couples and find that 'lesbian communication patterns are characterized by ... symmetry' (p. 86), which in the authors' interpretation reflects the egalitarian nature of lesbian relationships as an alternative to heterosexual marriage. This interpretation reflects widely held views on lesbian relationships at the time and is therefore rather predictable. In the following analyses, I have tried to be as fair and represent as wide a range of views on lesbian collective identity as possible. However, a completely impartial stance seems impossible for any participant-observer, who is bound to be influenced by her own experiences with and in the community under investigation.

I have been a part of local lesbian communities since the early 1990s, be it as a member of grassroots political groups or lesbian and gay event organizations, as one node in a friendship network or as a researcher. Engaging with lesbians has been of varying importance to me over the years, in line with shifts in my own social, professional and sexual identity. In the ten years that I have intermittently been working on this book, my attitudes, values and beliefs have differentiated, partly as a result of engaging with a wide variety of lesbian texts and contexts. Consequently, my own politics have become increasingly eclectic, and I can now subscribe to at least some aspects of all the different views and images discussed in this book.

Any historical study runs the risk of imposing a false coherence on the past. For example, the early texts analyzed in Chapter 3 became iconic only retrospectively, through a historical narrative. One aim of the study is to show how this retrospective narrative informed later texts in their construction of community. Given the aforementioned impossibility of a neutral stance, however, the project to some extent continues a retrospective narrative. After all,

> [t]here is no story to be told about how one moves from feminist to queer ... [because] none of these stories are the past; these stories are continuing to happen in simultaneous and overlapping ways as we tell them. (Butler 2004, p. 4)

There are many stories which this book does not tell. The first concerns the focus on Anglo-American culture. It has been pointed out that 'the term "lesbian" is of European origin, yet woman-to-woman desire and love has origins, expressions, and terminologies that are grounded in various geographies and cultures' (Seif 1999, p. 34). It is therefore important to flag up the Anglo-American specificity of 'lesbian' as an identity label, to acknowledge traditions of desire between women in other cultures, and to address sexual identities as they are carved out through language in a globalized world, as scholars increasingly do (Leap & Boellstorff 2004; Sauntson & Kyratzis 2006b). If this book fails to do justice to lesbian life outside the Anglo-American world, it does so for reasons having to do with its development. The study originally started out as my MA dissertation, which I submitted at the English Department at Vienna University and which therefore required data from an English-speaking country. Britain proved the most practical and least costly choice for data collection, especially since I knew of several feminist and lesbian libraries and archives there. In the more advanced stages of the project, it became clear that despite cultural differences, lesbian discourses in the UK cannot be understood without recourse to some of their models in North American discourses, and the focus was therefore extended to include the US as well. Also, when I decided much later to publish a study on lesbian discourses with Routledge, one condition was that the book should also incorporate the US context, in order to tap that market. I eventually chose this publisher, rather than an independent one, because for political reasons, I wanted a book with 'lesbian' in the title to have maximum impact. Paradoxically, global distribution and—hopefully—reception only comes at the price of a narrowing in perspective.

The second gap is temporal rather than spatial. The present study starts with the Stonewall Riots as a more or less arbitrary cut-off point: on 28 June 1969, the police raided the gay bar Stonewall on New York City's Christopher Street. The ensuing street fighting continued for days and marks—under the name of Stonewall Riots—the beginning of the lesbian and gay movement. The annual Pride marches held in many cities around the world celebrate this event (Faderman 1991, pp. 194–5). Although the turn of the decade can be regarded as a watershed in lesbian history, it is of course true, as Stein (1997, p. 27) remarks, that 'lesbian life . . . did not begin in 1970.' It is further important to ask in how far a division into decades does justice to the development of lesbian discourses and their notions of community. Such a partitioning is of course to some extent arbitrary and was mainly adopted to provide an overall structure to the book. The goal of the discourse-historical approach that informs the project is to show the continuous development of images of community in lesbian discourses and to account for the reasons and processes of this change. The development is understood to be less than clear-cut, and is made even more complex by the only partial overlap between UK and US communities and discourses. Indeed, there are intertextual links between asynchronous texts, usually in that US texts impact on those produced in the UK. Whenever appropriate, these interrelations will be discussed and reference will be made not only to lesbian communities outside the US and the UK, but also to earlier lesbian discourses and their images of community. The same goes for other omissions, such as bisexual and transgender identities, and the interrelations between sexual identity, class and ethnicity.

What this book does encompass is structured as follows. The next chapter spells out the research questions in more detail and introduces relevant approaches to researching lesbian discourses, notably the discourse-historical and the socio-cognitive approaches within CDA. This further translates into a discussion of the linguistic parameters that are used in the analysis, and the reasons for employing them. Chapter 2 also presents the methods of data collection and provides a description of the data. Chapters 3 through 6 analyze and discuss two texts each from the 1970s, 1980s, 1990s and 2000s. These are considered paradigmatic, i.e., typical and/or influential, even if the images of community that they communicate are not representative of all lesbian lives at the time. The detailed linguistic analyses of these texts are preceded by an outline of the wider socio-political context each example is located in, as well as a discussion of how that context impacted on the production, distribution and reception of lesbian texts, and thus ultimately on the examples themselves. The conclusion to each analysis addresses how far the sample texts reflect these influences. Finally, Chapter 7 provides a contrastive summary of the analyses and briefly suggests further areas that researchers interested in sexual identity and critical discourse analysis might investigate. The book is rounded off by an index and a glossary explaining the technical terms used in the linguistic analysis.

Returning to the initial paperback narrating the trials and tribulations of 'women without men,' this study will take over where that novel ended, i.e., in the year 1970, which saw the emergence of a new image of lesbian community. Before that, however, I will introduce some theoretical and methodological considerations.

2 Approaches to Researching Lesbian Discourses

With any linguistics you can end up in funny places.

(interview with Laura Donne)

This chapter will first present the research questions guiding the present study and then unpack the title of the book to elaborate the meanings of, and interrelations between, the notions 'lesbian' and 'discourse,' 'image' and 'community.' This will include the different meanings that 'lesbian' has had for the authors of the texts analyzed in this book, as well as definitions of the central terms 'discourse,' 'genre' and 'text' (see also glossary). It will then provide an overview of the basic tenets of critical discourse analysis (CDA) as a threefold model of linguistic analysis which takes into account socio-political factors as well as the practices of production, distribution and reception that shape texts. After sketching the foundations of CDA, the focus will be on the discourse-historical model as developed by Ruth Wodak and her colleagues in Vienna (Wodak 2001; Reisigl & Wodak 2001). As for 'lesbian discourses,' this chapter will briefly outline how the main focus of relevant linguistic work has been on spoken texts and will position the present study as supplementary.

Concerning 'images of a community,' image will be defined as the socio-cognitive representation of an entity, an understanding which necessitates the application of the socio-cognitive approach to discourse analysis (van Dijk 2003, 2006a, 2006b). Individual and collective identities are understood as forms of mental representation, and the chapter will therefore outline the notion of community in socio-cognitive as well as political terms.

The remainder of the chapter will elaborate on the data as well as methods of their collection and analysis, introducing the eight texts that are analyzed in this book and discussing the conditions of their production, distribution and reception. Moreover, it will operationalize the initial research questions by detailing the linguistic parameters analyzed in the eight sample texts, and the reasons for focusing on those parameters. Finally, the chapter will provide details on the supplementary face-to-face and email interviews conducted in order to gain further background knowledge on lesbian communities and discourses in the 1970s and 1980s, and on the position of lesbian conservatives in contemporary communities in the US, respectively.

'LESBIAN' AND 'DISCOURSE'

The three overarching research questions guiding this study are the following:

- What images of a lesbian community have self-identified lesbian authors in the US and Britain communicated in non-fictional texts since 1970?
- How can this change be traced in non-fictional, lesbian-authored texts?
- Why has this change taken place?

Since Reisigl (2007) has rightly drawn attention to the pitfalls of naming discourses as either 'discourse on *X*,' '*X* discourse' or 'discourse of *X*' with no clear indication of the semantic differences between these labels, it should be made clear that 'lesbian discourse' here refers to ways of representing the world through written, spoken and multimodal texts of various genres whose authors self-identify as lesbians. The texts instantiating the discourse often represent creative genres such as fiction and poetry, films[1] and music, and as such continue to be very influential in lesbian discourse communities. However, the present study will focus on non-fictional written texts by self-identified lesbian authors. This in fact opens the next can of worms in that 'lesbian' has meant very different things to different authors throughout the decades, as reflected in the texts under investigation. Most authors see lesbianism as the defining characteristic of a community they identify with. In addition, texts from the 1970s and later ones adapting their central beliefs and features establish lesbianism as a political practice serving a radical feminist agenda (Examples A, B and F in Chapters 3 and 5 of this volume). Other authors see lesbianism primarily as a form of desire (Examples D, E and H, in Chapters 4, 5 and 6) whereas for yet others, identifying as a lesbian is closely linked to gender identity (Example C in Chapter 4). Self-identified lesbian authors—whatever meaning that aspect of themselves has for them—produce texts that can be grouped into certain genres and instantiate what we might call 'lesbian discourse.' In the following, a definition of the three central terms 'discourse,' 'genre' and 'text' will be given. This will lead into an outline of the basic tenets of critical discourse analysis (CDA).

Starting at the micro-level, texts can be seen as semantically coherent and syntactically cohesive units of written or spoken language. Their verbal elements are often combined with visual elements such as layout, images or gesture. (In fact, it is impossible for a written text not to have any layout.) That is to say, texts are instances of language use, the parts of which hang together to form a meaningful entity. Such textual entities are self-contained in that they can be processed as separate units, although understanding often requires background knowledge of the contexts of their production—e.g., the cultural or political background of the text producer—including other, previous texts that a text may and usually does refer back to, or any future texts it anticipates. For instance, Example C (see Chapter 4) alludes to the classic lesbian novel *The Well of Loneliness* (by Radclyffe Hall, 1928), and knowledge of at least the title of the book and its status in lesbian history is required to understand the ironic function that mentioning it serves at that particular point in Example C.

Typically produced, distributed and received in the context of social relations of some kind between text producer and text recipient, one of the main functions of texts is to mediate these relationships, through reinforcing, questioning or subverting them. From a critical perspective, these relationships are often characterized by the unequal distribution of power, so that the analytical aim is to uncover how power relationships are mediated through texts and how texts can contribute towards fairer distribution of power between individuals and groups. The focus on power and its mechanisms that we find in critical discourse analysis can be traced back to the political writings of Antonio Gramsci (1971). His concept of hegemony denotes a means of securing power through consent, rather than coercion, through naturalizing ideologies as common sense rather than through sheer force. Ideologies are here understood to be cognitive structures combining beliefs, values, norms and goals. From a discursive angle, ideology can be defined as a pseudo-causally connected set of propositions (personal communication Ruth Wodak, 15 November 2006). Because texts act as carriers for ideology, any hegemonic use of ideology is directly relevant to the study of language and power. We see power at play in many of the examples analyzed in this book, most notably in the way that many use linguistic devices at the micro-level to implement a discursive strategy of setting up an outgroup and constructing its members either as weak and insignificant or as morally and politically reprehensible.

In that they serve to negotiate relationships between text producers and receivers, texts can be regarded as instantiations of genres. As van Leeuwen (2008, p. 345) states, 'texts . . . embody particular types of interaction that come with particular relationships between the interactants . . . and with particular communicative functions.' Such communicative functions or purposes shape both the macro-structure of a text as well as its overall discursive strategy and the linguistic devices used at the micro-level to implement that strategy. To illustrate, Example E (see Chapter 5) is based on an interview and as such has a macro-structure that opens by narrating how the interview was arranged, employing temporal markers (e.g., 'next'). It then goes on to reproduce the interview in the form of direct, indirect and free indirect speech, and closes by directly addressing the reader through the second person pronoun ('you'). Following the basic genre categories established by Longacre (1974), the text thus combines narrative genre, whose function is to entertain, with expository genre, which seeks to explain an aspect of reality. The expository genre elements determine the overall strategy of the text, which is to demarcate different notions of lesbian community and identity, and the author uses linguistic devices like irony, ascribed linguistic behaviour of the interviewee and negative evaluation to do so.

So the communicative purpose of the genre(s) it represents shapes the structure and strategy of, and linguistic devices used in, a text. The functional approach to genre (Swales 1990; Bhatia 1993) maintains that texts are best categorized by identifying their shared communicative purpose rather than their similar formal features, not least because 'a purely formal approach soon runs up against the widespread uses in contemporary society of generic humor, impersonation, parody, pastiche and send-up' (Askehave & Swales 2001, p. 205). Such recontextualization of the formal characteristics of other genres can, e.g., be observed in Example B (see Chapter 3), which sarcastically draws on promotional language although its overall genre is expository, not persuasive. Since, however, the analyst can only infer, but rarely be sure of, the communicative purpose that the author sought to meet with her text, a comprehensive view of genre means that identifying a text as an instance of a particular genre also takes into account the discourse community that the text is embedded in, including its values, gaols, and material conditions as well as its genre repertoires and conventions (Askehave & Swales 2001, p. 208).

For present purposes, discourse is understood as textually mediated social action, doing ideological work by 'representing and constructing society' and by '[reproducing] unequal relations of power' (Wodak 1996, p. 18). Discourse thus serves both an ideational metafunction, by building and negotiating realities through texts, and an interpersonal metafunction. In short, discourse constitutes society and culture and is in turn constituted by them. Fairclough (2003, p. 206) distinguishes between the above sense of discourse as an uncountable noun on the one hand and as a countable noun on the other. The latter, e.g., 'lesbian discourses,' denotes the representation and construction of reality from a particular viewpoint. Discourses as 'ways of signifying experience from a particular perspective' (Fairclough 1995, p. 135) are ideologically invested in the sense that they attempt at gaining influence and power in the social world. They thereby become sites of ideological struggle. The interrelations between the linguistic and the social aspects of discourse are accounted for in a three-dimensional framework consisting of text, discourse practice and socio-political practice (Fairclough 1995, p. 9). Starting from a specific text as a form of social action, critical analysis of discourse allows for conclusions to be drawn regarding both the discursive and socio-cultural context determinant of, and reproduced in, the text.

The interrelatedness of text, context of production, distribution and reception, and wider socio-political context is mirrored in the linguistic analysis itself, which also works on three levels. In a data-driven approach, analysis starts out from observed linguistic features at the textual level, such as form and frequency of reference to social actors, evaluation, types of actions, modality, interdiscursivity or metaphoric expressions. The analysis then proceeds to the level of discursive practice and social institutions, accounting for the factors of setting, participants, genre, and text production, distribution and reception. Finally, the wider social formation determining these factors is also taken into consideration. Thus it becomes clear that each instance of text production is ultimately linked to a socio-political practice which is represented in social acts like speaking or writing, in social institutions providing the frame for social action and in the social formations in which institutions are located. Given that the three levels are embedded in each other, the analysis can be bottom-up, starting from the text, or, as in Chapters 3 through 6, top-down, i.e., first investigating the wider socio-political context of the time the text originates from, then looking at how that social formation impacts on the context of discourse production, distribution and reception, and finally analyzing the text itself in linguistic detail.

To illustrate, Example G (see Chapter 6) is a feature from a nationwide glossy magazine targeting a lesbian and bisexual female readership, mostly in the US. As a contemporary text published in 2004, in a particular cultural, political and economic formation, it has to be seen in the context of a lesbian community that enjoys considerable freedom of expression, although homophobic discrimination continues to exist in legislation and everyday life. It is also a community that has evolved and increasingly diversified for 35 years, if we take the Stonewall Riots of 1969 as a historical turnaround (see Chapter 1). Finally, it is a community that is embedded in a host culture characterized by consumer capitalism, wide-spread access to communication technology and an idealization of all things corporate. For the context of discourse production, distribution and reception this means that nationwide lesbian magazines are high-gloss publications produced for profit and relying on advertising money. They are also accompanied by websites that offer sponsored links to dating and shopping sites. Such publications are distributed through a wide network including bookstore chains and a decreasing number of independent outlets. They are thus relatively easily available, given that the would-be reader has the necessary money to spend and/or internet access. These contexts are in turn reflected in the text itself, which borrows from business magazines in presenting the '10 most powerful lesbians' and employs micro-strategies such as positive attribution and recontextualization of lesbian feminist discourses to celebrate the economic and professional success of individual lesbians.

The focus on textually mediated social interaction in CDA should not be mistaken for a 'discourse idealism' (Chouliaraki & Fairclough 1999, p. 6) which denies any pre-discursive reality. It is important to keep in mind that discourse participants live in particular material realities and engage in certain practices, including but not limited to discursive ones. As Wodak (2006, p. 106) notes, material and discursive practices may well be in conflict with each other; for lesbian discourses this often means that the images of lesbian identity and concomitant values and behaviours as purported in texts are at odds with sexual and sartorial practices on the ground. Ideal images can be communicated because some discourse participants, by dint of their social roles, are in the position to produce and distribute more or less influential texts. Apart from cultural capital such as literacy, control of the material means of text production and distribution, including money, technology and outlets, is largely determined by the social role of the discourse participants and the relative power it brings. Access to texts likewise relies on access to these cultural and material means. And of course, texts and discourses can have concrete material impacts, ranging from the (un)equal distribution of wealth to the creation and allocation of space to exclusion and even physical violence against objects and people.

Clearly, a view of discourse that integrates its material aspects, especially when it comes to means of production, is indebted to a Marxist tradition of political analysis. By contrast, other discourse theories draw more on the work of Michel Foucault (1972a, 1972b). In his genealogical work, he shows how modern societies are based on discourses as systems of knowledge which constitute and reproduce social identities and power relations. According to Foucault, the pervasiveness and ubiquity of discourse renders pre-discursive existence virtually impossible. This anti-essentialist notion was taken up by discursive psychology (see e.g., Edwards & Potter 2001), feminist post-structuralist discourse analysis (Baxter 2003) and queer theory, the proponents of which argue that (sexual) identity is socially and discursively constructed rather than an expression of a 'genuine' self. Butler (1990/1999) is credited with introducing the concept of performativity into theories of discourse and identity: Austin's (1962) and Searle's (1969) notion of performative speech acts says that particular utterances bring about what they proclaim (see, e.g., Chirrey's [2003] example, 'I hereby come out'). Drawing on Derrida, Butler extends the notion of performativity by understanding it to be less 'a singular or deliberate "act," but, rather, [a] reiterative and citational practice by which discourse produces the effect that it names' (Butler 1993, p. 2). For example, in queer theory, homosexuality is not considered an imperfect imitation of heterosexuality but rather 'heterosexuality is [seen as] an imitation that performatively constitutes itself as the original' (Butler 1991, p. 22).

Anti-essentialism, however, is not the same as discourse idealism. Indeed, when theorists influenced by Foucauldian notions of discourse maintain that there is no pre-discursive reality, this is not to say that they deny materiality. Rather, they claim that materiality is imbued with meaning only through discursive interaction. Indeed, Butler (1993, p. 8) herself notes that '[t]he point has never been that "everything is discursively constructed"; that point, when and where it is made, belongs to a kind of discursive monism or linguisticism that refuses the constitutive force of exclusion, erasure, violent foreclosure, abjection.' According to her (2004, pp. 198–9), performativity is not just a linguistic or discursive phenomenon but also involves bodily actions, which are ultimately beyond the confines of language. As a consequence of this modification, there are now attempts to end what may have been a rather artificial distinction between CDA and post-structuralism all along. Thus, CDA has been applied to feminist research projects, including those based on post-structuralist notions (Lazar 2005), while Kaur (forth-coming) has combined CDA with performativity theory to investigate gen-der construction in computer-mediated communication. The present study adopts the notion of discursively constructed (collective) identities, while also discussing the material foundations and consequences of discourse and discourse production.

It was mentioned that texts, while self-contained units, routinely inte-grate earlier and occasionally anticipate future texts. This metaphorical 'dialogicality,' to use Bakhtin's (1986) term, means that texts are always located in a historical context, including future contexts of reception, which are typically anticipated in asynchronous communication (e.g., the author of Example F anticipates the reader's reaction by stating 'You may be asking yourself, "why would I want to be a lesbian separatist?"', line 7). The same goes for the more abstract notion of discourse, which is historical in the sense that it is always connected to context, and to other discourses (Wodak 1996, p. 17). In this sense, 'discourse has a history that not only precedes but conditions its contemporary usages' (Butler 1993, p. 227). Since it is the aim of this book to trace the history of lesbian discourses in the UK and the US since 1970, it is necessary to briefly outline the so-called discourse historical approach within CDA (de Cillia, Reisigl & Wodak 1999; Reisigl & Wodak 2001, pp. 31–85; Wodak 2001; Wodak & Krzyżanowski 2008; Clarke, Kwon & Wodak forthcoming). Most notably, the approach is problem-ori-ented, starting from a specific social phenomenon that is brought into being, negotiated and reinforced through 'a complex bundle of simultaneous and sequential interrelated linguistic acts that manifest themselves as . . . texts' (Reisigl & Wodak 2001, p. 36), i.e., through discourse. What makes such a social phenomenon problematic from a critical standpoint is that it involves the unequal distribution of power between discourse participants, leading to marginalization and discrimination. The social phenomenon investigated in this book is the changing images of lesbian communities over a particular period of time; its problematic aspect lies in the fact that the marginalization of lesbians by societies structured around heterosexuality and dispropor-tionate male power often translates into the marginalization of particular groups within, or in direct contact with, the lesbian community. Turning discrimination on oneself lessens the chances of gaining more power vis-à-vis the outward discriminators.

As a problem-based approach, discourse-historical analysis is inherently interdisciplinary, drawing on an eclectic range of analytical methods, empir-ical data and background knowledge in an attempt to 'transcend the purely linguistic dimension and to include . . . the historical, political, sociological and/or psychological dimension in the analysis and interpretation of a spe-cific discursive occasion' (Reisigl & Wodak 2001, p. 35). As a consequence, discourse-historical research includes fieldwork and ethnography to study the phenomenon or problem from the inside (Wodak 2001, p. 89) and links textual analysis back to the contexts of discourse production, distribution and reception as well as the wider socio-political formation. The text under investigation is further analyzed for its links with other texts instantiating the same, or closely related, discourses. The discourse-historical approach postulates four levels of context:

- The immediate co-text for a particular linguistic feature found in the text, i.e., its embeddedness in the text as a whole.
- The other texts and discourses that the text draws upon.
- The conditions of text production, distribution and reception.
- The wider socio-political formation.

For each text that is analyzed in the following chapters, the current study draws on a variety of historical sources as well as on interviews conducted to provide additional background knowledge. On this basis, each chapter outlines the socio-political context as well as the contexts of production, distribution and reception that come to bear on the texts under investigation. In a variation of the discourse-historical approach, intertextuality and interdiscursivity—the second item in the list—are discussed as features of the text itself, while co-text is seen as different from context in that the latter is always external to the text. In the text analysis itself, the approach developed by Wodak and her colleagues focuses particularly on topics, the strategies used to elaborate on them for specific ends and the linguistic devices employed to realize these strategies (Clarke, Kwon & Wodak forthcoming). Since the topic of all eight sample texts in this study is largely the same, namely definitions and characteristics of lesbian collective identity, the focus will be on the strategies used to communicate such images of lesbian community, and in particular on the linguistic features these strategies translate into (e.g., evaluation and labelling used to construct an out-group from which the in-group can be differentiated).

The discourse-historical approach was originally developed to study the discursive construction of national identity, and while a case can be made for the similarities between this and other forms of collective identity such as particular communities (see below), applying the approach to the study of lesbian discourse means venturing into new territory. Moreover, what linguistic study there is of lesbians as a socio-linguistic group shows a focus on spoken language rather than the investigation of (non-fictional) written texts as instantiations of discourse (but see Sauntson 2006; for a comprehensive overview of research into gay and lesbian language and discourse, see Kulick 2000; Cameron & Kulick 2003, pp. 74–105). One of the earliest papers concerned with lesbian language use was Stanley's (1970; see also Gilliambardo 1966, pp. 204–13) account of lesbian slang. In line with Halliday's (1978) observation that, with regard to antilanguages, 'information usually comes to us in the form of word lists' (p. 164), we find a number of dictionaries of so-called 'homosexual argot' (e.g., Legman 1941; Cory 1965; Farrell 1972; Rodgers 1979). Yet, almost all the relevant work published before and after Stanley's account focuses on gay male slang and mentions lesbian language only as an afterthought, if at all. The advent of feminism and particularly lesbian feminism in the 1960s and 1970s changed the focus to the critique of patriarchally vested language (Penelope 1975, 1978; Spender 1980).[2] Attempts to develop a women's language were inspired by Irigaray's (1985) notion of 'phallogocentrism' as a signifying system in which women are always constructed as the Other. Rather than working towards representation as a subject under this system, so the argument went, women should establish their own semiotic system.

The research on language use by lesbians was given a new direction by the adoption of conversation analysis for the field of language, gender and sexual identity (e.g., Moonwomon 1986/1997, 1995; Fellegy 1995; Kitzinger & Wilkinson 1995; Maher & Pusch 1995; Moonwomon-Baird 1996; Liang 1999; Land & Kitzinger 2005). In its classical form, conversation analysis does not allow the researcher to draw inferences about the relevance of a speaker's sexual identity unless the speaker herself orients toward that facet of her personality. However, this dictum has been modified for the use of conversation analysis in the study of language, gender and sexual identity (Kitzinger 2002) so that gendered and sexual identities are now understood to be made relevant in implicit and indirect terms as well. Consequently, 'linguistic forms that index identity are more basically associated with interactional stances [i.e., the display of evaluative, affective, and epistemic orientations in discourse] . . . which in turn may come to be associated with particular social categories' (Bucholtz & Hall 2005, pp. 595–6; see also Barrett 2002, pp. 33–8). By being reiterated in texts, such stances 'accumulate into more durable structures of identity' (Bucholtz & Hall 2005, p. 596), a notion reflecting the concept of identity as a set of reiterable performative (speech) acts.

As far as it allows for identities to be indexed indirectly, conversation analysis is a prime tool for investigating the discursive construction of sexual identity in spoken texts and has also been adapted by researchers employing post-structuralist (Baxter 2003) and queer notions of the construction and communication of identity as a performative, repeatable practice. As McIlvenny (2002a, p. 141) observes, conversation analysis

> recommends that we avoid creating categories/subjects who talk in categorical ways. . . . Instead, look for local, reiterable, interactional practices. . . . Ask not "How do lesbians talk?," but "How do participants talk such that their lesbianness is made salient and consequential for their activities?"

The present study asks a version of the latter question when investigating what images of a lesbian community are constructed in non-fictional written texts by lesbian authors. More specifically, the question is what particular discursive strategies and associated linguistic features self-identified lesbian discourse producers employ to make lesbian collective identity relevant in textually mediated interaction. The focus is therefore less on the construction and negotiation of the individual sexual identities of discourse participants, although identification of the author as a lesbian is indexed in all texts, e.g., through out-group references such as 'our heterosexual feminist sisters' (Example B, line 3), or alignment of the first person plural pronoun with a group specifically marked in terms of sexual identity and sometimes desire (e.g., 'S/M lesbians have been accused repeatedly of being a threat to lesbian-feminism. . . . Why the concerted attempts to . . . politically neutralize us?,' Example D, lines 15–19). In fact, this self-identification of the author as a lesbian is a criterion for the text to be analyzed in the first place. However, the analysis then seeks to answer how sexual identity is defined and, crucially, used as a basis for changing models of collective identity. The fact that the authors take, or refuse to take, their individual sexual identity as a basis for a particular collective identity shows that the two forms are mutually dependent, with 'collective identities . . . constantly in a process of negotiation, affirmation or change through the individuals who identify with a given group . . . and act in their name' (Triandafyllidou & Wodak 2003, p. 211).

Although some texts explicitly link (collective) lesbian identity to desire (most notably Examples D and E), the focus of the study is on sexual identity rather than sexuality (for the latter, see Harvey & Shalom 1997; Cameron & Kulick 2003; Sauntson & Kyratzis 2006b; Morrish & Sauntson 2007). To demarcate, sexuality has been defined as 'the systems of mutually constituted ideologies, practices, and identities that give sociopolitical meaning to the body as an eroticized and/or reproductive site' (Bucholtz & Hall 2004, p. 470). To this it could be added that sexuality also encompasses desire and, potentially, sexual practice. Sexual identity, on the other hand, is that aspect of a person's self that is constructed, expressed and negotiated on the basis of sexuality (for a slightly different definition, see Sauntson & Kyratzis 2006a, p. 4). This is an important distinction, the more so since the conflation of sexuality and sexual identity—more specifically the reduction of sexual identity to sexual practice—is a homophobic discourse strategy. Given this difference between sexuality and sexual identity, 'linguistic acts of sexual identity may be wholly uninformative about the semiotics of sex' (Cameron & Kulick 2005, p. 120), and in fact the texts that are analyzed in the following chapters either do not index sexual desire and/or practice at all, or do so only as a basis for claims about group identity (Example D).

It should be clear from the above that the aim of this study is not to identify any specific use of language that is particular to lesbians, even if we limit this to lesbians living in Britain and the US in the latter half of the twentieth and early twenty-first centuries. Indeed, apart from the early compilations of homosexual slang, 'no researcher who studies [gay and lesbian]-centred language has ever claimed to be searching for [or having found] unique linguistic features' (Morrish & Leap 2006, p. 20), although debatable claims have been made that the self-identification of speakers somehow makes the topics they choose 'lesbian' (Morgan & Wood 1995). Trying to identify a specific lesbian language would be a futile endeavour anyway, because it would assume that there is a stable and homogeneous social group built on sexual identity. If this book is intended to show one thing, it is that notions of group identity and community differ vastly across time, as indeed do the linguistic features used to define and communicate such a community. Rather, the question guiding research into lesbian discourses is how particular linguistic features are significant in making sexual identity relevant to the context in which the text has to be seen. From a critical discourse analytical viewpoint, context also means the wider socio-political context (see Sauntson & Kyratzis 2006a, p. 3), although the context of interaction remains important; after all, every text is designed with a particular audience in mind.

By indexing sexual identity as a basis (or not) for imagined communities, the authors of the eight texts analyzed in this book use a broad range of linguistic devices, none of which is unique to lesbian language use. While features such as patterns of evaluation or metaphor use are distinct, they are available to other language users as well and are often transferred from other discourses. Such orders of discourse, i.e., the overlapping production, distribution and reception of discourses within and between discourse communities, make linguistic devices with particular affordances available to speakers and writers to use in specific actions and to specific ends (Jones 2006). For instance, the kinship term 'sister' is often used metaphorically in lesbian feminist discourse to construct a particular kind of community, to the extent that lesbian authors who purport a different image of community integrate the term into their texts in an ironic or even sarcastic way. The association between this particular expression and lesbian feminism has become so conventionalized in lesbian discourses that the word only needs to be quoted to index a particular group identity (see Bucholtz & Hall 2004, p. 478). Obviously, this particular linguistic resource is available to, and used by, members of other, overlapping social groups as well, e.g., by black speakers. The only 'lesbian' aspect of this and other linguistic devices is that self-identified lesbian authors have used it at particular moments in history in order to construct their image of a lesbian community.

Since images of a community as constructed and communicated in text and discourse are the focus of this study, it is worth exploring these two notions in more detail.

'IMAGE' AND 'COMMUNITY'

Obviously, lesbian discourses do not exist in a vacuum but are embedded within a host culture that is organized in diametrically opposed terms, i.e., around values and beliefs of heteronormativity and disproportionate male power. Similar to antilanguages (Halliday 1976), non-dominant discourses are interdiscursively linked to dominant ones as they respond to them, anticipate them, resist them and—directly or indirectly—quote from them. Most notably, non-dominant discourses are vehicles for establishing alternative realities, so that constructing an image of the alternative discourse community plays a central role in differentiating it from the host culture.

To borrow a term from social psychology, an image of a group can be seen as a socio-cognitive representation (Moscovici 2000). In contrast to relatively stable schemas, social representations, i.e., the cognitive structures jointly acquired, held and presupposed by members of a particular group, are theorized to be the subject of 'continual renegotiation . . . during the course of social interaction and communication' (Augoustinos & Walker 1995, p. 178). From a cognitive, discourse-analytical viewpoint, such renegotiation is effected through intertextual chains, in which the respective representations are recontextualized and possibly enforced in discourse. For instance, Example B draws heavily on the model of a lesbian community as a homogeneous group characterized by solidarity and the particular political beliefs and values that we can see in Example A. However, Example B, being published in Britain almost 10 years after the seminal US text, radicalizes those notions by defining the in-group more starkly against an out-group, thus adapting the collective identity model to a different time and a different cultural context. Further, social representations are said to provide a shared frame of reference so that communication can take place at all, i.e., they make available the assumed shared background knowledge that tends to become naturalized as 'common sense' in hegemonic discourses. Finally, social representations can be seen as establishing social identities and relationships by being communicated (Augoustinos & Walker 1995, pp. 178, 180), because '[s]haring a representation means that individual thinking is organized by principles that [a] person shares with other people' (Chryssochoou 2003, p. 227).

Since social representations such as images are constructed and negotiated in instances of language use, texts are also vehicles for their producers' cognitive models. Other discourse participants receive these texts, and doing so repeatedly under similar conditions of reception is likely to impact on their discursive and material practices, and indeed mental models. This impact may be one of the producers' main intentions with the text, preferably to align the recipients' mental models with their own and thus promote a particular image of community more widely and/or gain a position of defining power. As far as they are constructed and communicated to build, reinforce or challenge the unequal distribution of power in a discourse community, socio-cognitive representations such as models of a collective self are the building blocks of ideology. The link between text and society is therefore mediated by the particular ways in which texts producers convey their beliefs and ideologies and by the ways in which recipients infer meaning determined by their knowledge and attitudes. In this context,

Halliday's model of the ideational, interpersonal and textual metafunctions of language (Halliday & Matthiessen 2004, pp. 29–31) is of particular importance. From a critical cognitive viewpoint, we can state that the three metafunctions rely on the discourse participants'

- models of aspects of reality, such as the existence and definition of a lesbian community (ideational metafunction);
- textually mediated social relations, e.g., claiming or rejecting group membership for themselves or others (interpersonal metafunction);
- models and hence expectations of what a text in a particular genre will look like (textual metafunction).

In fact, ideational coherence and textual cohesion of a text would be impossible without mental models, while interpersonal discursive interaction depends on models involving intentions, roles, relationships and identities (van Dijk 2006b).

The interpersonal metafunction is especially salient for the formation of group identity through the construction and communication of socio-cognitive representations in discourse. By engaging in relational behaviour with each other, discourse participants (re-)produce 'a set of intercategory relationships, a set of . . . conditions . . . that are perceived to affect people because of their shared or different social category memberships' (Abrams 1999, p. 198). Bucholtz and Hall (2005) argue that identity, defined as 'the social positioning of self and other' is 'intersubjectively . . . produced and interactionally emergent' (pp. 586, 587). This concept of interactional identity is compatible with views of identity as a socio-cognitive representation that is negotiated between minds via the medium of text.

From a socio-cognitive perspective, then, collective identity is defined as a socio-cognitive representation that is in turn built on 'a socialized sense of individuality, an internal organization of self-perceptions concerning one's relationship to social categories' (Stein 1997, p. 211, n. 5).

As such, individual and collective identities are co-constructed and tie in with Anderson's (1983) famous concept of 'imagined communities,' which are 'imagined because members . . . will never know most of their fellow-members, meet them, or even hear of them, yet in the minds of each lives the image of their communion' (p. 15). Anderson's emphasis on literature and news publishing as 'technical means for "re-presenting" the . . . imagined community' (1983, p. 30) is reflected in the words of Lisa Ben, pseudonymical editor of the 1940s lesbian magazine *Vice Versa*: 'Even though my readers may actually never become acquainted with one another, they will find a sort of spiritual community through this little magazine' (quoted in Chasin 2000, p. 91). A corollary of the imagined community is that 'defining communities through any set of external criteria becomes irrelevant and effectively impossible' (Queen 1997, p. 235); rather, socio-cognitive representations of collective identity are produced, distributed and negotiated in and through discourse and may subsequently be enacted in material practices.

Anderson's (1983) work on imagined communities was originally developed for research into nations as providing and expressing collective identity. Communities built on facets of the self such as sexual identity are different from nations, but parallels and interrelations can still be observed. Thus, Chapter 6 of this book will describe how consumerist (Chasin 2000, pp. 118–25) and conservative lesbian discourses (Vanasco 2005) link lesbian identity to American identity. More importantly still, it could be argued that some socio-cognitive representations of a lesbian community are metaphorically structured by drawing on models of the nation. This is particularly the case in 1970s lesbian feminist texts, most notably in Jill Johnston's (1973) hugely influential autobiography-cum-manifesto, titled *Lesbian Nation*. Fuelled by a growth in lesbian publishing after 1969 (Chasin 2000, p. 159), 'rapidly growing numbers of people [were able] to think about themselves, and to relate themselves to others, in profoundly new ways' (Anderson 1983, p. 40), namely as a quasi-nation. Obviously, when a community is only being built, i.e., beginning to be imagined, the emphasis is very much on homogeneity in order to provide a relatively unproblematic model that will allow many people to identify with, and so garner support for, the emergent community. As Anderson remarks, 'regardless of the actual inequality and exploitation that may prevail in each, the nation is always conceived as a deep, horizontal comradeship' (1983, p. 16). This book traces the development from constructing an image of a homogeneous community to challenging that image, investigating its internal contradictions and current atomization, if not obliteration. In short, the following chapters will show how the mental construct that is the lesbian community is, like any other social identity, 'discursively . . . produced, reproduced, transformed and destructed' (de Cillia, Reisigl and Wodak 1999, p. 153).

Gellner (1997) has noted that the ideology of the nation 'is a phenomenon of *Gesellschaft* using the idiom *of Gemeinschaft:* a mobile anonymous society simulating a closed cosy community' (p. 74). The links between the two concepts are further underscored by definitions that decouple the nation from ideas of the nation state, such as the following:

A nation is a body of people who see at least part of their identity in terms of a single communal identity with some considerable historical continuity of union [and] with major elements of common culture . . . nations can exist despite extensive dispersion geographically. (Robertson 1985, p. 223).

In fact, broad definitions such as the preceding one make 'nation' almost synonymous with 'community' and throw up the question in how far the model of a 'lesbian nation' is actually a metaphoric one. Surely, a lesbian community can, like a nation, be seen as 'mental construct, as an imaginary complex of ideas that consists of collective unity and equality, boundaries and autonomy' (Georgalou 2006, p. 7) and predisposes its self-identified members towards certain emotions, values, beliefs and behaviours. Rather than indicating different denotative meanings, differences in terminology would then become linguistic devices to realize political goals, such as preferring 'nation' over 'community' because the former carries more political clout (McKee 2002).

The connotative associations, rather than denotative meanings, of the term 'community' are also likely to have contributed to its increased usage in lesbian feminist discourse (Creet 1991, p. 142). Although there have been, and continue to be, local communities in the social network sense—now mirrored in online communities—it is the imagined community as mental model and ideological construct that is most important for the formation of alternative social relationships and realities (Wolf 1979, p. 169). As for the different meanings that Lemon and Patton (1997, p. 18) give for community, the imagined community seems to hold together local social networks and their institutional base in organizations, places and groups rather than being a result of them.

A discourse-historical analysis of the socio-cognitive representation that is the lesbian community shows that what in particular the model entails has changed significantly over the past four decades. In these processes of discursive change, 'those who are able to communicate their views most widely, most insistently and most early will have an obvious advantage' (Reicher & Hopkins 2001, p. 23) when it comes to establishing new meanings. It follows that the discourses that are identified as paradigmatic in the following chapters are just that, typical and often influential, but not representative of the beliefs, values and practices of all lesbians at the time, or indeed any time. Nevertheless, certain common denominators can be established for the notion of community which have proved surprisingly resilient. According to Muniz and O'Guinn (2001, p. 413), communities are held together by:

- Shared consciousness, i.e., 'the intrinsic connection that members feel toward one another, and the collective sense of difference from others not in the community,' e.g., through the 1970s discursive practice of consciousness-raising.
- Shared rituals and traditions, e.g., women's music festivals or annual Pride parades.
- A sense of moral 'duty or obligation to the community as a whole, and to its individual members,' e.g., the creation of women's spaces or the socialization of young lesbians into both a local and an imagined community.

Against the backdrop of these persistent defining characteristics, the emphasis in the discursive construction of lesbian communities has shifted from homogeneity and occasional border patrol, where 'a small but extremely loyal group . . . desires to keep the infidels out' (Muniz & O'Guinn 2001, p. 419) to a more heterogeneous model that allows for intra-group differences as long as members stay within the—shifting—boundaries of lesbian identity. Currently, the socio-cognitive representation of the lesbian community in the UK and the US incorporates 'a relatively hedonistic and liberatory ethos, where pleasure is more sanctioned than restricted, and where bounded individuality is celebrated' (Muniz & O'Guinn 2001, p. 427). An instance of changing values combined with persistent characteristics is the image of lesbian community as constructed in Example G, where the professional success of individual women is celebrated as long as they 'give some of their success back to the community' (lines 8–9).

To sum up, the analyses in this book investigate the ways how, and reasons why, images of a lesbian community have changed in non-fictional texts published after 1970 by self-identified lesbian authors in the UK and the US. In doing so, the following chapters draw on an analytical framework that combines the discourse-historical with the socio-cognitive approach to discourse. As a consequence, texts are seen in the context of their production, distribution and reception, as well as against the background of the socio-political formation at the time. Analysis of textual material is supplemented by interview data and other texts that are linked to the examples in question. It aims to uncover what discursive strategies the respective authors follow to construct and communicate their image of a lesbian community, and what linguistic devices they employ to implement those strategies. Finally, collective identity is understood as a socio-cognitive representation, with texts acting as the carriers and creators of that mental model. Both the discourse-historical and the socio-cognitive approach not only influence the interpretation of results from the analyses, but also determine the linguistic parameters investigated. The next section will spell these out in more detail, after introducing the data used in this study.

DATA DESCRIPTION AND METHODS OF ANALYSIS

The choice of sample texts is based on extensive reading of primary texts from and across the respective historical periods, which made it possible to identify them as central in their impact on later texts and/or incorporating typical features of lesbian discourse at a particular moment. At eight texts, the sample is relatively small but a close analysis of a limited number of texts seemed more amenable to answering the research questions than expanding the corpus at the risk of missing out on analytical detail. Obviously, not all pieces of lesbian non-fiction constitute valid data for the representation of community. They do so only insofar as they are either explicitly programmatic or set one model of lesbian community and identity off against another, presupposed one. The sample texts were chosen for these criteria.

The eight texts analyzed in Chapters 3 through 6 are the following:

- Example A: 'The Woman Identified Woman,' a text authored by the New York-based Radicalesbians collective, first distributed at a feminist conference and later reprinted in book form (1970/1988).
- Example B: 'Political Lesbianism,' a text by the Leeds Revolutionary Feminists, first presented as a conference paper and later reprinted in a magazine and also in book form (1979/1981).
- Example C: 'Butch,' a text by Lorna Gulston, published in the now defunct British lesbian feminist magazine *Sequel* (1980).
- Example D: 'What We Fear We Try to Keep Contained,' a text by Katherine Davis, written on behalf of the lesbian feminist S/M group Samois and published as the introduction to an anthology edited by the San Francisco-based group (1981).
- Example E: 'The Lesbian Heresy,' an interview with Sheila Jeffreys, conducted by Carol Ann Uszkurat and published in the now defunct British lesbian magazine *Lip* (1994).
- Example F: 'Finding Your Inner Lesbian Separatist,' a text by Corynn Hanson, published on the US author's website (1998).
- Example G: 'The 10 Most Powerful Lesbians,' a text by Julia Bloch, published in the US lesbian magazine *Curve* (2004).
- Example H: 'I Feel Left Out,' a text by Ingrid E. Barnes, published on the now defunct blog of the New York-based author (2002).

To keep the analyses succinct, almost all of these texts, with the exception of Example H, are reproduced in extracts. To make sure that the extracts are representative, the whole texts were analyzed for a set of parameters, and extracts showing typical features were identified.

The eight texts are all different, if often similar, with regard to genre. Following Longacre's (1974) functional approach, we can classify them according to their overall purpose. In that they more or less explicitly construct an image of a lesbian community, all texts are expository, seeking to describe, explain and interpret an aspect of reality and thereby fulfil the ideational metafunction. However, the texts differ in what secondary functions they have. Thus, Examples B, C, D and F also have a strong hortatory component—and therefore meet the interpersonal metafunction—in that they aim to persuade the reader of the author's idea of what a lesbian community should look like and what values and behaviours are appropriate for its members. Examples F and H further show the interpersonal metafunction by incorporating a procedural aspect that seeks to instruct either the reader (Example F) or another group (Example H) to adopt a certain goal-oriented behaviour. The last genre category, narrative, is the most problematic one, and it could be argued that narrative is not a genre so much as a linguistic device. Examples A, C, E, G and H all include story-telling, but in Examples A and H at least, it is doubtful whether the aim really is to entertain the reader.

Given the proviso that analysts cannot know for certain what the author's aim was, let us re-classify the texts according to their different forms of production, distribution and reception. As for the conditions of production, it is noteworthy that the first two texts were written by collective authors, while all others are single-authored. (Example D represents a hybrid, being authored by an individual on behalf of a group.) The first two texts also started out as ephemera, being typed and duplicated as pamphlets (Example A) or conference papers (Example B) and only later reprinted as part of a book. Again, Example D has a middle position in that the texts in the anthology, if not the introduction itself, were based on a pamphlet. Although they represent two different discourses that are paradigmatic of different decades, Text B and Texts C and D, respectively, were published around the same time. For their production, this means they were all typed and duplicated; we have to go to Example E to find the first printed text in a magazine. While the relevant publication's non-commercial approach meant a dearth of funds and hence black-and-white printing only, 10 years later, magazines are run for profit, relying heavily on sales and advertising money, featuring high-gloss paper and full colour (Example G). As instances of desktop publishing, Examples F and H were again produced with minimum funding and expertise. While this makes them similar to the early examples, as a website text and a blog entry, respectively, their distribution affords a much wider impact.

In line with increasing commercialization, decreasing marginalization and the subsequent move of many lesbian communities toward the mainstream, the eight texts show an ever wider circulation as time progresses. Examples A and B were first distributed at conferences, i.e., at specific venues and one-off occasions. Their subsequent circulation through informal networks such as consciousness-raising groups (see Chapter 3) made them influential enough to be reprinted in books. The distribution of Example C was also restricted, since the magazine in which the text was published was available through subscription only and relied almost exclusively on word-of-mouth in order to sell at all. A different kind of limited distribution is at stake for Example D; its topic, sado-masochism as a sexual practice among women, was so controversial at the time that only a small range of gay and women's bookshops agreed to stock the Samois anthology, most feminist bookstores deciding to censor the book by refusing to distribute it. As a publication from the early 1990s, the magazine in which Example E was published shows mixed distribution channels, being circulated through subscription and independent specialist bookshops. The increasing de-marginalization of lesbians for commercial purposes means that the magazine featuring Example G is distributed via commercial bookshops and high-street stationers, while technological advances make the web-based Examples F and H potentially available on a global scale and at minimum effort (although specific literacy skills are still required).

Finally, reception of all texts is intentional, i.e., most readers will deliberately seek out the texts. (A partial exception to this is Example A, which was first distributed by the authors literally gate-crashing a feminist conference and handing out their pamphlets.) Reception can also be accidental, e.g., for customers browsing magazines at a bookstore and chancing upon the publication including Example G, or for internet users landing on the websites featuring Examples F and H by following a series of hyperlinks that may take them further from what they originally looked for. Especially Examples A and B were widely received, triggering a large amount of discussion, intertextual referencing and also academic study (not only in this book but, for Example A, also in Nogle 1981; Shugar 1995, pp. 25–34). The anthology introduced by Example D even triggered another book in response (Linden et al. 1982), while Examples C, E, G and H potentially prompted letters and comments from readers/users. When Example B was reprinted in the feminist magazine *Wires,* the increased reception led to a deluge of letters to the editor, a selection of which were published, along with the text and authors' comments, in book form. Together, the texts' production, distribution and reception thus mirror socio-political and technological changes over the past four decades.

In a final classificatory move, the eight texts can be located in what Malešević (2006), writing on ideologies of the nation, has called the normative and the operative realm. According to her, the normative realm 'is built around principles outlining fundamental goals and values as well as providing a blueprint for the realization of these goals. . . . The normative layer of ideology is most often deduced from authoritative texts,' such as scriptures, manifestos, constitutions etc. (2006, p. 309). Clearly, Examples A, B and D fall into the normative domain of ideology, constructing as they do a model of the lesbian community, its genesis, characteristics and the ideal norms, values and practices of its members. The fact that Example B is noticeably influenced by Example A, and that D challenges the ideology communicated in both of them, does not change the fact that all three are indeed normative. However, 'the success of a particular normative doctrine lies in the process of its "translation" into its operative counterpart' (Malešević 2006, p. 317), meaning that the ideal-type models constructed in normative texts are recontextualized as routine practices and in texts relying on 'simplified concepts, language and images with popular appeal,' often using 'emotional and instrumental' language (Malešević 2006, p. 310). Text types in which normative ideals are inculcated at the operative level include textbooks, tabloids, specific websites, advertisements and political speeches. For the present data, Examples C, E, G and H can be categorized as operative, the more so given the likely additional purpose of the first three to entertain the reader. Example F (see Chapter 5) cuts across both the normative and the operative realm, combining the construction of an ideal lesbian community (expository genre) with concrete steps for how to implement it (procedural genre). It is perhaps no surprise that the earlier texts tend to be normative, while later ones are more operative; this reflects the top-down way in which discourse participants with symbolic capital such as education and concomitant discourse access constructed images of the lesbian community early on, which were later implemented, contested and rejected in texts of a different nature.

Despite the variety of genres, however categorized, that the eight texts show, their comparability is guaranteed by the fact that the different sample texts relate to each other intertextually and interdiscursively. This is particularly noticeable in the samples from the 1990s and 2000s, which show a high degree of hybridity with regard to genre, including typical features from previous samples. A diachronic study will necessarily rely on different genres and media, as we can witness a change in favoured text types and outlets due to new technologies like the internet, and to channels of communication, such as radio and television, that have become widely available for lesbian discourse participants only over the past 15 years or so.

The overall purpose of a text translates into a discursive strategy it seeks to implement, i.e., a 'more or less intentional plan of practices . . . adopted to achieve a particular social [or] political . . . aim' (Wodak 2001, p. 73). As all eight texts more or less explicitly construct, negotiate or reject socio-cognitive representations in the form of collective identity, it is safe to assume that their overarching discursive strategy is to bring into being an in-group ('us'), mostly in demarcation to an out-group ('them'; Wodak 2001, p. 73). Strategies of 'us vs. them,' used to communicate images of a community, can be constructive (Example A), preservative or reproductive (Examples B, F and C, although C seeks to preserve a different kind of community than the other two), transformative (Examples D and G) or destructive (Example H; Wodak 2001, pp. 71–2). If we accept that 'identification [is] inherently relational' (Bucholtz & Hall 2004, p. 494), strategies of 'us vs. them' distinction are indeed centrally important. Apart from being constructive, preservative/reproductive, transformative or destructive, such strategies can be further divided into assimilation or the construction of intra-group sameness on one hand, and dissimilation, i.e., the construction of inter-group differences, on the other (de Cillia, Reisigl and Wodak 1999, p. 151). In the context of lesbian discourses this can not only mean that the lesbian community is contrasted with the heterosexual, male-dominated host culture (Examples A and F); most of the texts starting with Example B actually construct an ever narrower in-group that is set off from other parts of the lesbian community, until the idea of collective identity is rejected altogether (Example H). Also, it should be noted that many of the texts focus on out-group vilification at the expense of constructing a positive in-group image.

Knowledge of the eight texts as well as texts related to them, and of texts constructing collective identities in general, makes it possible to draw up a list of linguistic parameters that can be used as devices to implement a discursive strategy of 'us vs. them' distinction. This set of parameters will be applied consistently across the texts. At the same time, it will be handled flexibly enough to allow for supplementary and corroborative devices that are relevant in a given text, e.g., irony, forms of reported speech or narrative. When looking at the 'us vs. them' distinction, the most obvious parameter is that of social actor representation.

As a linguistic parameter, social actor representation tells us what individuals and groups are represented in what role in a text. Formally, social actor representation can be effected through personal pronouns and other deictic devices. In his 'sociosemantic inventory of how social actors can be represented,' van Leeuwen (1996, p. 32) points out that social actors do not necessarily map onto grammatical actors; for instance, impersonalized actors can be non-human entities that are still represented as engaged in particular actions, be it as active actor or as passive goal. An example would be the statement, taken from Example B, that '"pleasure" is created by fantasy, memory and experience' (lines 16–17), where both the actors ('fantasy, memory and experience') and the goal of the action ('pleasure') are abstract grammatical actors. However, since they are not human, they are not social actors. The following analysis will concentrate on human social actors, both groups and individuals. Agency, be it by social or grammatical actors, is not only realized in the formula 'X did Y (to Z),' but can also surface in possessive pronouns (e.g., 'our heterosexual feminist sisters,' Example B, line 3, which could be traced back to 'heterosexual women are our sisters') and in prepositional phrases such as 'we resent being used by heterosexual feminists' (Example B, lines 38–9). The following analyses will focus on instances where social actors are actually named, thus also disregarding backgrounded and suppressed actors (van Leeuwen 1996, pp. 38–42). However, what is of importance for the research questions underlying this study is generic/assimilated and specific/individualized actors, i.e., actors referred to as categories of people or as individuals (van Leeuwen 1996, pp. 46–50). Genericization in particular can be reinforced through absolute quantifiers such as 'every' and 'all.' In the context of constructing an image of a community, social actor representation helps to indicate who is part of the in-group, what degree of individuality is accounted for, and how detailed a model of social actors is represented. Typically ambiguous in its referential range, the first person plural pronoun 'we' occupies the middle ground in that it is a generic reference to a group of people envisaged as homogeneous (van Leeuwen 1996, p. 50) but at the same time refers to a group including the individual author. This 'we' is typically differentiated from the 'other,' realizing the 'us vs. them' distinction as a discursive strategy. Given the nature of lesbian communities, it can also be expected that the 'we'—and indeed the 'they' in texts which establish sub-groups within an imagined lesbian community—refers to a group of actors classified along socially sanctioned demographic markers such as gender and sexual identity (van Leeuwen 1996, p. 54). The question of how social actors are referred to is treated in the discourse-historical approach as a referential or nominational device, which can be further broken down into parameters such as labelling, euphemisms or pronoun usage (Wodak 2006, p. 114; Khosra-viNik 2007).

Van Leeuwen's (1996) taxonomy combines different linguistic parameters such as reference itself, transitivity (see below) and metaphor. However, in the following analysis, social actors, actions and metaphor are treated under separate headings. The reasons for this are partly practical, i.e., dividing the analysis into sub-sections to make it more readable, and partly theoretical, in that the definition of metaphor used in this book (see below) goes beyond an understanding of it as merely a rhetorical figure. Nevertheless, social actor representation is analyzed first because in texts constructing and nego-tiating collective identity, this device is obviously of paramount importance and in fact, other parameters can be seen as feeding into it.

Social actor representation is closely linked to evaluation, in that social actors are not only referred to in more or less generic terms but differ-ent individual and collective social actors are also differentiated from one another. The socio-cognitive notion of in-group bias predicts that the mental representation of the social actor group that the speaker identifies with is more detailed and incorporates more positive values than the out-group model. Listed under the heading of 'predication' in the discourse-historical approach (Wodak 2006, p. 114), this device can include categorical gener-alization and stereotyping (Teo 2000; Flowerdew, Li & Tran 2002). More concretely, evaluation may involve explicit attribution through adjectives (e.g., 'the good work that our heterosexual feminist sisters do,' Example B, line 3), relational process types (e.g., '[m]en are the enemy,' Example B, line 2; see below) or the connotations accruing to a word (e.g., '[h]eterosexual women are *collaborators* with the enemy,' Example B, lines 2–3; emphasis added). Furthermore, positive aspects of the out-group may be modified, given low prominence or attributed to context rather than to an inherently good personality (van Dijk 1995). Evaluation is likely to be of both the social actors themselves as well as their actions.

Social actors and their actions are combined in the grammatical concept of transitivity, which basically captures 'how participants are labelled and what processes they are involved in' (Thompson 1996, p. 78). A crucial question in this context is what individuals and groups are represented as the actors[3] and what other individuals and groups are at the receiving end of the action, and in what kinds of actions who takes which role. (Note that the analysis will concentrate on verbs to express actions and disre-gard nominalizations.) This kind of role allocation renders particular social actors relatively active or passive and thereby constructs them as more or less powerful vis-à-vis each other (van Leeuwen 1996, pp. 42–5).

Functional approaches to grammar traditionally distinguish between three main kinds of action, or process types, namely material, mental and relational ones. Three more process types—behavioural, verbal and existen-tial—are located at the interfaces between them (Halliday & Matthiessen 2004, pp. 170–259). Material processes '[construe] a . . . change in the flow of events . . . through some input of energy' (p. 179). Participants in material processes are the actor and goal in transitive clauses, where the actor engages in an action that impacts on the goal, e.g., '[w]e must reexamine our politics of sex and power' (Example D, line 28). According to Halliday, material processes can also take an intransitive form (e.g., 'the lion sprang'), where the change affects only the actor. However, since the aim of the following analyses is to ascertain which social actors are constructed as having the power to impact on others, intransitive material processes will be analyzed as behavioural processes. These capture a behaver's physical and psychological behaviour which does not impact on a goal, e.g., '[s]ocial and political costs run very high' (Example D, line 3). (Incidentally, this example shows that via personification as a special form of metaphor, abstract and non-animate entities can also function as behavers.) While material processes are about an action impacting on an outward entity and behavioural processes capture both bodily and psychological actions, a mental process 'construes a . . . change in the flow of events taking place in our own consciousness' (Halliday & Matthiessen 2004, p. 197). Mental process types therefore comprise perception, cognition, desire and emotion (p. 208) and involve a typically human-like, conscious senser and the phenomenon that is perceived. An example is the title of Example D, 'what we fear we try to keep contained.' Moving on, verbal processes comprise 'symbolic relationships constructed in human consciousness and enacted in . . . language' (p. 171) and as such involve a sayer and possibly a target or addressee. It should be noted that 'saying' here extends to 'any kind of symbolic exchange of meaning' (p. 253). An example is '[w]e must talk about what we do' (Example D, line 32).

Perhaps the most problematic category in the system is that of relational processes. These 'construe change as unfolding . . . without an input of energy' (Halliday & Matthiessen 2004, p. 211) and thus capture processes of being, becoming and having. However, they also seem to shade into mental processes of perception, cognition and desire (p. 238). In the interest of disambiguation, the analysis will restrict itself to processes expressed by forms of the verbs 'to be,' 'to become' and 'to have.' Relational processes can be further subdivided into attributive and identifying ones, where the former characterize somebody through ascribing an attribute and the latter identify somebody by allocating a value. Table 2.1 illustrates the different kinds of relational processes.

Relational process types are important for the analysis because '[c]lass membership is construed by attributive clauses and identity by identifying ones' (p. 214), and these two discursive strategies are obviously at the centre of constructing and communicating images of a community. The final process type identified by Halliday is existential processes. These are infrequent in texts—Halliday and Matthiessen (2004, p. 257) give a figure of about 3 or 4 percent of all clauses—and the point has been made (Ryder 2007) that pragmatically, speakers rarely if ever refer to the mere existence of an

Table 2.1 Examples of Relational Processes

	attributive	*identifying*
being	Is S/M good or evil? (Example D, lines 11–12)	She is the woman who . . . acts in accordance with her inner compulsion (Example A, lines 2–3)
becoming	We become heretics (Example D, line 26)	You will emerge into your new identity (Example F, lines 5–6)
having	We must have precisely the same dialogues (Example D, line 36–7)	There you have us for what we are worth (Example C, line 57)

Note: As for the possessive sub-type of relational processes, the same clause ('the piano is Peter's') is cross-classified as both attributive and identifying by Halliday and Matthiessen (2004, pp. 249–50). It seems that the two are not clearly distinguishable.

entity without their utterance carrying any implicature. Thus, the first part of the slogan 'we're here, we're queer, get used to it' does not simply denote the existence of a group but implies that others will have to arrange themselves with the fact of its existence (as spelled out in the slogan's latter half). Therefore, the analysis will follow Ryder's (2007) suggestion and conflate existential with relational processes.

The system of process types includes fuzzy boundaries and overlaps between the different types (Halliday & Matthiessen 2004, p. 172). Beyond that, the inherent contradiction in Halliday's model resides in the fact that it was devised to describe semantic categories but relies on linguistic surface structures to do so. One consequence is that metaphoric expressions lead to functional misallocations. For instance, judging by its surface structure, a clause such as '[w]e must have precisely the same dialogues' (Example D, lines 36–7) expresses a relational process but actually refers to a verbal process. As a way around this problem, such instances will be doubly coded as overt and covert process types.

In sum, an analysis of process types tells us more about the model of social actors, including groups and communities, which the author seeks to convey. In particular, process types show how certain social actors tend to be represented as relatively active or passive and engaged in one set of processes rather than another. This device potentially makes in-group members look more active, more impacting on their environment, or more differentiated in terms of their thoughts and feelings, thus helping to implement and flesh out the 'us vs. them' strategy.

Images of a community are ideological in that they incorporate socio-cognitive representations of identity, combined with beliefs, values and attitudes toward the community. Of these, beliefs and values are encoded by the linguistic feature of modality. This can be sub-divided into deontic and epistemic modality. Deontic modality conveys degrees of obligation and thereby transports the values of the author with regard to the behaviour and characteristics of a community and its members (e.g., '[w]e must all ask and answer these questions,' Example D, lines 39–40). Epistemic modality, on the other hand, conveys degrees of certainty and thus acts as a carrier for beliefs about individual and collective development (e.g., the metaphorical 'night that may have been decades long' in Example A, lines 24–5). Both forms of modality can be expressed by modal verbs, as in the preceding examples, but also through adverbs (e.g., '[s]urely you've heard of the really big power lesbians,' Example G, line 4) and attributes in relational processes (e.g., 'I am not sure I want to do this now' as a polite, because mitigated way of declining).

To proceed, intertextuality and interdiscursivity are key for a discourse-historical analysis, because these two devices show what other texts and discourses the author draws on and thus what models she aligns herself with or distances herself from. The notion of intertextuality refers to the integration of bits of other texts into the present text by means of reported speech and other forms of quotation. As such, it goes back to Bakhtin's discussion of utterances as 'link[s] in a very complexly organized chain of other utterances' (1986, p. 69), which was taken up by Kristeva (1986) in her work on intertextuality. In the Bakhtinian framework, this understanding leads to the notion of dialogicality, where texts have to be seen in the historical contexts of other texts they draw on. Intertextual quotations can be either from the same or from different genres (Cook 2001, p. 193), the latter giving us the concept of interdiscursivity as a hybrid mixture of different discourses and genres in a given text. The preceding classification of each of the eight texts as integrating different genres is a case in point. Interdiscursivity can be established through lexical traces, e.g., the use of words and phrases linked to particular discourses in the speaker's mind. An example is the religious discourse drawn upon in Example F ('your route to lesbianism is to become enlightened,' line 39). Kress (1989) maintains that '[t]here are preferred conjunctions of discourses and genres, and prohibitions on other conjunctions' (p. 20) and while this is certainly the case, it should be noted that at times of great social change, texts can be remarkably hybrid, combining past with present discourses in an often iconoclastic way.

One means of achieving interdiscursivity is through the use of metaphor. This study employs the cognitive semantic theory of metaphor (Lakoff & Johnson 1980; Lakoff 1993; Kövecses 2002; Cameron 2003; Koller 2004, pp. 8–42), which posits that metaphor is first and foremost a cognitive phenomenon and as such a way of structuring mental models. In essence, metaphor at the cognitive level conceptualizes one thing in terms of another, e.g., coming-out as a journey (in fact, this example is a variation of the pervasive metaphor LIFE IS A JOURNEY).[4] The entity thus conceptualized is known as the target domain (e.g., coming-out), while the entity it is conceptualized as is called the source domain (e.g., journey). It should be noted that so-called mappings from the source to the target domain are only ever partial, the semantic features which are mapped being known as the ground of the metaphor. For instance, coming-out is conceived as a journey by drawing on the semantic feature of goal-oriented movement from one place to another; however, other, more specific semantic features of the journey domain, such as lost luggage or late-running trains, remain unmapped. As a cognitive phenomenon, metaphor finds its surface level reflection as metaphoric expression in language and other semiotic modes, e.g., '[we] find ourselves on the other side of a tortuous [sic] journey' (Example A, lines 23–4). This example combines a primary spatial metaphor ('on the other side'; see Grady 1997) with the more complex JOURNEY metaphor ('a tortuous [sic] journey'). Complex metaphors can be regarded as further developments of primary metaphors; thus, COMING-OUT IS A JOURNEY can be seen as a further development of a so-called event structure metaphor (Lakoff 1993), PURSUING A PURPOSE IS MOVING TOWARDS A DESTINATION. Complex metaphors are gained by combining primary ones, broadening the cognitive resources available to a discourse community. This pool of resources can be enlarged by adding new complex metaphors, and the ones already in it can, moreover, be recombined in secondary and further assembling processes. Apart from metaphoric hybridization on the interdiscursive level, metaphoric shifts may also occur within the boundaries of a discourse. As a result, we find a complex network of both internal and cross-boundary metaphoric mixing, active at the level of not only discourse, but also of genre and text.

Metaphor lends itself to a critical analysis of discourses on collective identity, because '[i]n linguistically [and cognitively] constructing imagined communities and collective subjects . . . metaphors serve to create difference-levelling sameness and [in-group] cohesion' (Reisigl & Wodak 2001 p. 56). In fact, metaphor is akin to discourse in that it fulfills ideational, interpersonal and textual metafunctions (Koller 2003). As for the ideational metafunction, Lakoff and Johnson (1980, p. 156) observe that

> metaphors . . . highlight and make coherent certain aspects of our experience . . . metaphors may create realities for us, especially social realities. A metaphor may thus be a guide for future action . . . this will, in turn, reinforce the power of the metaphor to make experience coherent. In this sense metaphors can be self-fulfilling prophecies.

This quotation in fact applies metaphor to one of the central claims of CDA, namely that discourse is embedded in socio-political practice, that it constructs this context from a particular perspective and is, in turn, constructed by it. Further, Lakoff and Johnson state that such selective representation is motivated by intentions, in the sense that 'people in power get to impose their metaphors' (1980, p. 157). If we consider discourse and, by extension, metaphor as constitutive of socio-political relations (interpersonal metafunction), one of the clearest manifestations of power is the possibility to control discourse and hence cognition, e.g. by 'a coherent network of [metaphoric] entailments that highlight some features of reality and hide others' (Lakoff & Johnson 1980, p. 157). As it is realized in surface-level metaphoric expressions, metaphor also links discourse and its manifestation in text. At the micro-level, texts are structured by the metaphoric expressions deriving from the conceptual metaphors prevailing in the discourse that the text instantiates (textual metafunction). As such, metaphoric expressions may help to reify cognitive models governing discourse, and underlying metaphors may partly determine the surface structure of text.

Together, the linguistic parameters of social actors, evaluation, actions and process types, modality, intertextuality and interdiscursivity, and metaphor implement the 'us vs. them' strategy that looms large whenever texts are used to construct, reinforce, negotiate or reject particular mental models of (collective) identity. In most texts, these devices will link to each other in an accumulative way, although they can on occasion also contradict each other, possibly indicating a hybrid, changing image of community. On the whole, such micro-level analysis of text helps uncover how particular historical myths where created and how out-groups are constructed. In Chapters 3–6, the analysis is related to the context of its production, distribution and reception, which is in turn seen as influenced by the wider socio-political context of the time.

Knowledge about that wider context was gleaned both from sociological and historical accounts, including oral histories (Faderman 1991; Neild & Pearson 1992; Hamer 1996; Stein 1997). Such accounts were particularly important for the 1970s and 1980s, while for the 1990s and 2000s, I could in addition rely on knowledge gained as a member of lesbian communities in Germany, Austria and Britain. Published historical accounts were supplemented by a small number of interviews I conducted with self-identified lesbian women born between 1931 and 1957. Since the book is based on textual analysis, the interviews are not intended as an empirical data base. In fact, they could not serve as such because the sample is not large enough, comprising only six individual and one group interview. Also, the sample is far from representative; since interview partners were found through friendship and other social networks, the group of women may reflect the experience of lesbians in Austria and the UK, as well as the US, where one interviewee used to live, but is homogeneous in terms of ethnicity and class. Rather than seeking corroboration for historical generalizations, then, the interviews are intended to balance the inevitable bias in a researcher of another generation. As such, the interviews provided valuable background information, albeit only from the point of view of white, middle-class lesbians. Two of the interviews were translated from German, and all but one were conducted at the women's homes. In accordance with good practice in Applied Linguistics (BAAL 2007), pseudonyms are used throughout the book. All interviewees gave their written consent to be recorded and quoted, and, where possible, have seen and agreed to the context in which quotes from the interviews with them appear. The nine interviewees are listed in Table 2.2.

Table 2.2 Interviewees

Name	Date of birth	Interview date and place
Lola di Marco	1942	23 November 2006, Manchester/UK
Laura Donne	1949	23 November 2006, Manchester/UK
Gillian Eastham	1958	23 November 2006, Manchester/UK
Ina Feder	1954	19 July 1997, Vienna/Austria
Erica Jones	1948	11 September 1997, London/UK
Paula Kingsley	1955	12 April 2006, Doncaster/UK
Vivienne Pearson	1931	17 February 2006, Manchester/UK
Pam Taylor	1937	15 September 1997, London/UK
Vera Vaizek	1956	29 August 1997, Vienna/Austria

Note: All names are pseudonyms.

The interviews lasted about one hour each and were semi-structured around the following sequence of topics: preliminaries (name and date of birth, consent form), coming-out, media, terms for self-reference, separatism and lesbian feminism, self-image in the 1970s/1980s and now. The recordings were transcribed using conversation analytical methods to capture as much detail as possible, although this is not reproduced in the quotes.

A second set of five interviews was conducted by email, in order to gain background knowledge about lesbian conservatives in the US. The interviewees are again referred to by pseudonyms (except for Ingrid E. Barnes, who is also the author of Example H). They are: Ingrid E. Barnes, Tessa Borrodaile, Rachel D'Amico, Andrea Houghton and Sarah Weber. All women were or still are members of the Log Cabin Republicans, a gay and lesbian lobbying group within the US Republican Party. They were initially contacted through the group's website and asked to snowball a list of questions comprising political background and political beliefs, experiences with and characterization of lesbian women of other political beliefs, gender imbalance at the Log Cabin Republicans and any specifically lesbian issues, as well as published writings by conservative lesbians. The email interviews were conducted between March and June 2005.

To close this chapter, let us recapture the research questions against their theoretical background, and their operationalization for the sake of analysis: How and why have images of a lesbian community changed in lesbian discourses after 1970 in Britain and the United States? This question relies on an understanding of images of a community as socio-cognitive representations of collective identity which are constructed, reinforced, negotiated and rejected in and through texts. Texts are seen as instantiations of a discourse, i.e., representations of reality from a particular perspective, here those of authors who self-identify as lesbians, with that identity having different meanings across time and contexts. Texts are moreover shaped by the conditions of their production, distribution and reception, as well as by the wider socio-political context. The historical aspect necessitates the texts under investigation to be linked to other texts that they draw on explicitly or implicitly and also requires additional background information to be gathered through fieldwork.

Further, how can this change be traced in non-fictional, lesbian-authored texts? In investigating non-fictional written texts, this study supplements the body of research conducted on conversation among lesbians. The analysis looks at the overall discursive strategies of the texts, most notably the 'us vs. them' distinction made to construct collective identity and, based on close knowledge of the present and related texts, further employs a set of linguistic devices that are theorized to implement that strategy. These devices are:

- Social actor representation: What groups and individuals are referred to and how?
- Evaluation: What qualities are associated with the group and individuals
- Actions: Are social actors are allocated more active or more passive roles? What kinds of actions are ascribed to them?
- Modality: What values does the author has with regard to the community? What beliefs does she have about its development?
- Intertextuality and interdiscursivity: What other texts and discourses does the author align with or refute?
- Metaphor: What conceptualizations of the community are observable in the texts? How does metaphor structure the representation of social groups, and of the relations within and between them?

After the relevant theoretical and analytical approaches to researching lesbian discourses have thus been outlined, the next chapter will begin the analyses of images of a community as constructed in lesbian discourses, starting in 1970.

3 Creating a Community
The 1970s

> If you make a revolution ... you create, at least for some time, this
> sense of belonging.
>
> (interview with Ina Feder)

This chapter traces the development in the image of a lesbian community in
the UK and the US from around 1970 to the end of the decade. Taking the
Stonewall Riots of 1969 as the starting point of the modern lesbian and gay
movement (see Chapter 1), it is shown how lesbian existence as a political
category can be traced back to sources such as the New Left, second-wave
feminism and gay liberation. The first paradigmatic text chosen for analysis
is the Radicalesbians' 1970 manifesto 'The Woman Identified Woman.' In
the analysis, it is argued that its opening stretches can be read as a paradigmatic coming-out narrative that is related to genres such as the *bildungsroman* and the picaresque tale, especially in its use of the JOURNEY metaphor.
This sees the paradigmatic lesbian transform from troubled individual in a
hostile world to part of a benevolent community conceptualized in quasi-
religious terms. Here, the development of a lesbian feminist worldview
can be, and has been, compared to a conversion experience (Wolf 1979, p.
67). The community-building nature of the text is further realized through
attributive processes and positive evaluation of the emergent in-group.

Moreover, the chapter discusses how a political definition of lesbianism was at odds with pre-Stonewall notions of lesbian life, which rather
centred on desire and lifestyle. In the discursive formation of the 1970s,
this latter notion was gradually backgrounded by politicized voices gaining
preferred discourse access. In this sense, the two texts that I analyze are not
representative of 'the' lesbian community at the time, which was varied and
segregated along dimensions of class, race and political beliefs (Wolf 1979,
p. 71). They are, however, paradigmatic in that they, while not uncon-
troversial, were important in constructing and disseminating a particular
ideal notion of community that in later years came to be seen as central to
1970s lesbian culture. Throughout the decade, there were attempts to conflate lesbianism, i.e., love and desire between women, with feminism as the
political struggle for equal rights for women, giving rise to a harsh critique

of heterosexual feminists. This is exemplified by the Leeds Revolutionary Feminists' 1979 manifesto 'Political lesbianism.' This later text relates back to the earlier one in its use of declarative statements and absolute quantifiers, but focuses on a WAR rather than JOURNEY metaphor. Organized in a debate format, the later text transports an image of the lesbian community that is defined by demarcation against a discursively reconstructed Other who is evaluated in negative terms.

SOCIO-POLITICAL BACKGROUND: ISSUES AND ARGUMENTS

Whereas lesbian existence in Europe and North America in the 1950s and 1960s was defined mostly from outside, in criminal and psychiatric terms, the 1970s saw an internal redefinition of 'lesbian' as a political programme. While the 1960s had seen the New Left and hippie culture spread across and beyond the US, these counter-cultures showed themselves to be as sexist as mainstream 1950s society (Faderman 1991, pp. 203–4) and ultimately gave rise to second-wave feminism. On one hand, political lesbianism has its roots in the women's movement of the 1960s and indeed, the first national lesbian convention in the US was held as early as 1960, hosted by the Daughters of Bilitis in San Francisco (Wolf 1979, p. 53). The gay liberation movement emerged from the 1950s homophile organizations such as the Mattachine Society (founded in 1951) and the Daughters of Bilitis (founded in 1955) in the US (Faderman 1991, pp. 148–50 and 190) as well as the Minorities Research Group (founded in 1963) in the UK (Pointing 1997) and was another basis for politically active lesbians. Early optimistic views saw a chance that lesbians would bring about a united gay/feminist movement (Johnston 1973, p. 183). However, by the mid-seventies lesbians in both the UK and the US had announced the need to split off from a gay liberation movement which they increasingly saw as reproducing male privilege and oppression, and as irreconcilable with the view of lesbianism as anti-patriarchal (Stein 1997, p. 37). Another bone of contention was sexual politics; due to different experiences and socialization, 'many men were talking of sex as a tool of liberation, [while] many women were talking about it as a source of oppression' (Valocchi 1999, p. 67). (It was not before the 1980s that lesbian discourses would incorporate the notion of sexuality as a radical way to emancipation; see Chapter 4). Lesbian feminists therefore sought to articulate lesbian demands in the women's movement. There was initial, albeit never undivided, support for lesbians on part of feminist groups such as the National Organization for Women (Faderman 1991, p. 212), and lesbians certainly supported women's issues, e.g., pro-choice campaigns. Nevertheless, their specific demands were often not acknowledged by heterosexual women who feared to lose any chance of acceptance if they became associated with lesbianism. Referred to as a 'lavender menace' and as 'lesbian chauvinists' (Johnston 1973, p. 148) by fractions of the women's movement, lesbians were at the same time underrepresented in the gay male movement, where political work tended to focus on gay male issues (e.g., the age of consent), while specific lesbian issues (e.g., child custody) were once more disregarded.[1]

> I think that's been the crux of the matter, this split between heterosexuals and lesbians. Lesbians felt they put their heart and soul in. They've supported heterosexual women . . . but whenever we've asked for help, suddenly they've scurried away and you never see no one. We've always been stood there on our own ultimately. (quoted in Hall Carpenter Archives 1989, p. 116)

Lesbians reacted to this dilemma of being 'the stepchildren of two movements' (Kasindorf 1993, p. 32) by leaving and establishing their own movement. This declaration of independence can be traced back to as early as 1971 in the US (Stein 1997, p. 113) and 1972 in Britain (Hamer 1996, p. 197) and marks the beginnings of what later became lesbian separatism (see Chapter 5). Yet the split was not effected by all politically active lesbians. While some chose radical or revolutionary feminism, others stayed with socialist feminism or co-operated with men in the gay liberation movement—a decision they were continuously reproached for by the more radical groups.[2]

The emerging movement established various institutions, the most important ones being consciousness-raising (CR) groups (see later in this chapter), collectives formed by political activists and events like summer schools, camps and music festivals (the most famous one of which is undoubtedly the still-running Michigan Womyn's Music Festival). It goes without saying that within this network of quasi-institutions a number of discourses and discursive practices were generated. In socio-cognitive terms, these discourses constituted a mental model for a community by providing definitions 'that emphasized members' common interests, experiences, and solidarity,' by developing 'interpretive frameworks [and] drawing lines that separated insiders from outsiders.' In short, lesbian feminist texts of the time met the ideational metafunction of discourse in that they 'redefined the ways their members saw the world' (Stein 1997, p. 14).

Concerning the image of community as constructed in the paradigmatic discourses of the early 1970s, the identity construct of the politically conscious lesbian feminist prevailed, and in later accounts of the decade, lesbianism and feminism are described as inextricably linked. This belief is built upon a stock element of shared textual knowledge, namely the misquotation of a saying by Ti-Grace Atkinson. While Atkinson actually maintained that '[l]esbianism is a "sexual" position, whereas feminism is a "political" position' (1974, p. 83), it was later ascribed to her to have said that 'feminism is the theory, lesbianism is the practice' (see Brunet & Turcotte 1986, p. 48, for one example of many misquoting Atkinson). Thus Atkinson's dictum, which set lesbianism in contrast to feminism, was reversed to denote the opposite.[3] In its new form, the phrase captured the dominant ideal of the lesbian as part of the feminist avant-garde, the greatest threat to patriarchy. According to this concept, lesbianism was less regarded as a sexual (and/or emotional) preference, or a lifestyle based on it, but rather as a form of political resistance that came up with 'a "transcendent" definition of sexuality where lesbianism . . . came to be seen as the practice of feminism' (Hollibaugh & Moraga 1981, p. 58). In view of this, it is not surprising that the expression 'politically correct' was, albeit erroneously, traced back to a lesbian coinage of the 1970s.[4] In her much-discussed and influential paper 'Compulsory heterosexuality and lesbian existence,' Rich identified a 'lesbian continuum to include a range . . . of women-identified experience' (1980, p. 647), a concept in which actual sexual experience was no longer a constitutive element. As such, Rich's text is indebted to the linguistic features found in Example A and to the ideas they express. Likewise, Johnston had already in the early 1970s defined 'lesbian' as 'a generic term signifying activism and resistance and the envisioned goal of a woman committed state' (1973, p. 278). Both Johnston's and later Rich's texts were soon included in the canon of lesbian discourse.[5] Toning down the sexual element of lesbian identity was a common thread, as evidenced by Johnston's claim that 'sexuality is not central to the political definition of a lesbian woman' (1975, p. 86). This found its most extreme form in Atkinson advancing that 'lesbianism, in fact *all* sex, is reactionary, and . . . feminism is revolutionary' (1974, p. 86). This latter quotation supports the assumption that Atkinson, at least in some of her texts, never really saw a connection between lesbianism and feminism in the sense that the former was the practice of the latter.

Downplaying sexuality as a defining feature of the prototypical lesbian may have reflected negative experiences with straight sex and sexuality in general. Politically, this discursive move counters the exaggerated sexualization of lesbians in both turn-of-the-century sexology and pornography aimed at straight men. In addition, a focus on the political can be used strategically to make lesbianism more palatable to straight feminists.[6] In any case, and despite the phenomenon of celibate 'political lesbians' (Faderman 1991, p. 208), desexualized definitions of lesbian life seem to have been a feature of lesbian discourse rather than a reflection of actual practices. It is certainly true that 1970s lesbian discourse saw lesbian existence as political rather than sexual. Nevertheless, '[t]o say that lesbianism is not only genital sex is not say that lesbianism is not sex at all' (Thompson 1993, p. 171). The notion that lesbian culture was desexualized has to be regarded as a myth. After all, a particular discourse need not mirror the culture in which it is generated. Rather, it conveys a particular perspective on that culture, and oral accounts indeed draw a picture that is quite different from the one 'officially' constructed and passed on: 'We fucked a lot of women, we had fucking great parties and took a lot of drugs' (quoted in Doyle 1996, p. 187). Even Johnston's (1973) landmark lesbian feminist text shows no shortage of raunchy detail throughout.

The outspoken and articulate nature of a discourse largely sustained by (white) college or university-educated women tends to obscure the fact that the majority of lesbian lives in the early 1970s were only marginally affected by lesbian feminism. Women of colour, working-class butch-femme couples and many closeted and/or older lesbians did not usually form part of it (Faderman 1991, pp. 217–18). Further, older lesbians from both middle-class and working-class backgrounds who had come out before the advent of lesbian feminism found the new radicalism alienating (Faderman 1991, p. 197). This is corroborated by one of my interview partners:

> There was a whole group of women who joined the feminist movement and found lesbianism via feminism but I was already a lesbian before that. And not only did I not have any entrée into lesbian groups I did not have any entrée into feminist groups either. . . . I think most of the women who found their sexuality via those groups, perhaps they were only 10 years younger than me. . . . Women of my age tended to go to [places] feminist women didn't go to, they were more involved with political things. And women of my age went to the few clubs there were—or didn't go anywhere. (interview with Pam Taylor)

Nevertheless, lesbian feminism surely was the paradigmatic discourse of the 1970s and was given iconic status by later historic accounts of the era.

In the course of the decade, a utopian movement fuelled by revolutionary energy and enthusiasm had to realize that 'the process of developing a new social self, new kinds of personal relationships, and a community based on these was slower and more frustrating than had been originally proposed' (Wolf 1979, p. 9, recounting her observations in San Francisco in 1974). In some cases, this frustration could lead to an increasingly dogmatic approach to the 'correct' politics of lesbian feminism and concomitant infighting across ideological battle lines (Faderman 1991, pp. 230–5). As the revolution took its time and the heterosexual order proved more resilient than anticipated, the aggression generated by living as lesbians in a patriarchal system and by the frustration about that system's seemingly unassailable nature turned inward to the next available target. Outer appearance, sexual behaviour and language use all became hotly debated issues. The pressure to conform—politically, linguistically, sartorially and sexually—developed into a downward spiral; the more lesbian feminists saw themselves ridiculed, attacked or ignored by straight and gay men, heterosexual feminists and other lesbians alike, the greater became the need for in-group cohesion. The original ideal of equality as an alternative to heterosexual reality became a call for conformity, leading to ever more rigid rules of conduct, and, consequently, an ever smaller core group. While this in-group continued to provide strength and a sense of belonging to its members, other women referred to it by a variety of metaphoric expressions from politics and religion, such as 'the lesbian intelligentsia' (Califia 1981, p. 78), 'crusaders' (Stein 1999, p. 57) or 'the Stalinist element' (quoted in Doyle

1996, p. 187). The often aggressive pressure for cohesion is perhaps best sum-marized by the following quote from one of my interview partners:

> You can't have a pure lesbian line and be part of the world, maybe that's it. You can have a little cult over there, there are lots of cults all over the place and they sort of agree with each other. But [radical lesbian femi-nists] were trying to change the world. And when you're losing you get very aggressive. . . . The image I get is like in the West, all the wagons drawn up in a circle because you're under attack. So what you have to do when you're in the circle, you can't be too outrageous, you have to fit in. (interview with Erica Jones)

Defining an in-group and community-building in general requires massive discursive-cognitive resources and strategies. Given the adverse conditions under which the fledgling lesbian community existed in the 1970s, it is remarkable what resources it could mobilize. However, the next section also shows how discourse access was not equally distributed across the lesbian population, with particular sub-groups gaining disproportionate influence.

PRODUCTION, DISTRIBUTION AND RECEPTION OF TEXTS

Lesbian life as a topic was—at least in its written form—largely restricted to the literary genre until the twentieth century. Oral accounts point out the continuing importance of lesbian fiction and poetry, especially from the 1970s onwards, when more positive depictions of lesbian life began to be published. The history of lesbian non-fiction writing in formats like the magazine or the pamphlet is intermittent throughout the twentieth century. After the first wave of publications in the 1920s—Goldstein (2003, p. 25) mentions 'more than two dozen [gay and lesbian] publications' in the Berlin of the Weimar Republic—there was a long interval in which enforced cen-sorship prevented any lesbian publishing. The first underground magazines appeared again in the late 1940s to mid-1950s: *Vice Versa,* a short-lived journal published and distributed privately—and under a pseudonym—in Los Angeles between 1947 and 1948 (Shugar 1995, p. 189; Chasin 2000, p. 62), and *The Ladder,* which was published monthly by the US organization Daughters of Bilitis between 1956 and 1972. For the UK, there was *Arena Three* (published between 1964 and 1971). Editors in the 1950s and 1960s, and no doubt later as well, were at the receiving end of male harassment and threats, as related by Diana Chapman, co-editor of *Arena Three:*

> We hadn't realized that there was this interest in lesbianism as por-nography. . . . We'd have men knocking at the door or ringing up . . . we wouldn't send it out to any married woman who didn't have her

husband's approval because I think we had one or two letters from raving husbands more or less threatening to sue us for alienation of affection. (quoted in Hall Carpenter Archives 1989, p. 53)

Given the restricted space for lesbian voices in the homophobic atmosphere of the 1950s and 1960s, the magazines often acted as lifelines, and subscribers showed a keen interest by writing letters and donating money (Neild & Pearson 1992, p. 39). Financial help was made possible by a largely middle-class readership (Faderman 1991, p. 341, n. 31; Hamer 1996, p. 176). In the absence of advertising income, private donations and revenues remained the only funding for these early publications. However, to be the only source of information about and, crucially, by lesbians, guaranteed readers' loyalty. For some readers, learning about other lesbians even made them change their life by moving from the country to urban centres to end their isolation and turn an imagined community into a local one (Wolf 1979, p. 53; Neild & Pearson 1992, p. 102; see also Bright 2004, p. 30).

Moving on to the 1970s, the UK saw a short-lived magazine entitled *Artemis* (later *Artemis and Gay Girl*) at the beginning of the decade and, between 1972 and 1981, *Sappho:*

> The first magazine I ever read was a lesbian magazine called *Arena Three,* and then that became a magazine called *Gay Girl.* And then that folded around 1971, 1972. . . . And then there was *Sappho* and *Spare Rib,* which had a lesbian interest. You had to subscribe to *Arena Three, Gay Girl* and *Sappho,* but not to *Spare Rib.* You could buy that in newsagents. I learned about them because I had joined the Campaign for Homosexual Equality . . . and I may have seen an ad in the *Gay Times.* . . . I remember [*Arena Three*] as really dreary. I mean it was good to have it at the time . . . but it was full of this terrible poetry about people being lonely and unhappy. (interview with Paula Kingsley)

The editors of these magazines often provided physical discourse space as well, by organizing meetings and discos, which sometimes spawned into regional and special-interest groups (Neild & Pearson 1992, pp. 40, 67, 93–4, 101; Hamer 1996, pp. 180, 182–3). Production conditions were dire, relying on make-shift technology employed by a small group of dedicated contributors:

> [Magazines like *Arena Three* were] very low key, they looked as if they had been run off on people's presses. They were put together with paper clips, you know . . . and poor quality paper and poor quality print. . . . Yes, they were underground. (interview with Pam Taylor)

Production conditions continued to be low-budget until well into the 1980s:

> I do remember quite an intense period in the mid-1980s where things like the *Red Rag Feminist Newsletter* and *Wires* and those sort of things [were] very cheaply produced, duplicated newsletters with very limited circulation and really cutting-edge politics . . . the *Manchester Women's Liberation Newsletter* . . . was all done by volunteers, it came out once a month and the circulation was about 500 . . . it was done on a duplicating machine, you typed onto stencils, duplicated it and collated it. It was all produced at something called the Manchester Area Resource Centre. (interview with Gillian Eastham)

Distribution was equally fraught with problems since it was almost impossible to be granted advertising space in mainstream publications. As a consequence, the newsletters had to rely on word-of-mouth (Neild & Pearson 1992, pp. 100–1). The magazines were circulated by subscription only, since selling lesbian-themed magazines to the general British public put the producers and distributors at risk of being sued for 'corrupting public morals' (Hamer 1996, p. 168).

Nevertheless, in the first years after the Stonewall Riots in 1969, genres and media that were available or adapted for lesbian discourses diversified considerably. Written texts like articles, books and pamphlets began to be produced and distributed, often under arduous conditions,[7] and contributed to the great importance of lesbian publishing in the 1970s (Forster 1984; Sutton 1999). In line with the communal stance of 1970s feminist politics, the publications were often launched by publishing collectives. Thus, the early UK magazine *Arena Three* had been very influenced by the personality of its founder Esmé Langley, whereas its successor, *Sappho,* was published collectively (Neild & Pearson 1992, p. 96; Hamer 1996, pp. 166–90). The women had often specifically learned to print in order to make their voices heard (Faderman 1991, p. 224), and the magazines were distributed by subscription, through women's bookshops and benefit discos or even by street sale (Stein 1997, p. 96). Like production, distribution also relied heavily on volunteer work:

> There were quite a few independent bookshops [then], far more than there are now and people who had cars or had friends who lived in the outlying parts of Greater Manchester used to distribute them. The [*Manchester Women's Liberation Newsletter*] had quite a big subscription base and [was] sold at benefit discos. (interview with Gillian Eastham)

As noted earlier, the outward appearance of the publications clearly marked them as underground newspapers (Neild & Pearson 1992, p. 40; Hamer 1996, p. 168):

> In the 1970s was the start really of things being published; it started very much with just articles, though, through the 1970s there had been some magazines, very much the sort of duplicated things. Basically, yes, just

newsletters in London, from the London's Women's Centre the *London Women's Liberation Newsletter,* which was tight single-spaced, duplicated double-sided and wrapped very tightly. Basically they published just about everything, anything that was sent in by women and you had to subscribe to it. (interview with Erica Jones)

According to lesbian feminist ideals of inclusion and anti-capitalism, the publications were either free or priced on a sliding scale.

Spoken texts have always played a vital role in lesbian discourse practice. Like any other marginalized people excluded from dominant discourse, lesbians (still) rely heavily on oral tradition, gossip and chat for the formation of their individual and collective identity. In this context, gossip and chat are to be understood in a non-pejorative sense, as forms of informal conversation providing information and helping to establish networks between otherwise dissociated individuals. This understanding of the terms also appears in the analysis of Higgins (1995, p. 127): 'In retelling events and commenting on them, a marginalized social group reinforces its internal solidarity and underscores its separate identity.' Gossip can be regarded as 'a female cultural event which springs from ... the restriction of the female role' (Jones 1990, p. 243). The genre of gossip is indeed so central to lesbian discourse that a quarterly journal for lesbian feminist ethics in the 1980s was called *Gossip.* In a collection of essays originally published in the journal, Livia (1996, pp. 1, 3) points out the central role of gossip to non-dominant discourses: 'gossip [is] part of knowing we belong to a lesbian community ... lesbian histories are encapsulated in gossip.' Oral genres became quasi-institutionalized through the discourse generated in consciousness-raising and other political groups. Since the 1970s, however, written texts have gained considerable importance for the construction and negotiation of images of a community as socio-cognitive representations. The exploding number of written texts on lesbian feminism also provided the grounds for the production of spoken ones, e.g., when pamphlets were distributed and discussed in group meetings. As one of Stein's informants recalls the early 1970s (1997, p. 51):

[The people at the meeting] were distributing mimeographed copies of 'The Woman Identified Woman.' ... Things were happening very fast; every time you turned around there was more going on, more stuff being written, more things to read and talk about.

Groups were often comprised of friends who were interested in consciousness-raising (CR). This genre was developed as a strategy for the lesbian feminist struggle to change existing power relations. The belief that women first had to become aware of their oppression and its structural reasons and mechanisms before they could take direct political action led to the creation of space in the form of CR groups where discourse could be generated. The discursive event of a CR session was very flexible, ranging from the highly regulated, with each woman narrating her experiences in turn and the whole group drawing generalizations afterwards (*Aspen 1979), to the very informal:

> I joined a group for consciousness-raising and with one exception, all the women there were lesbians and we were all feminists. We would meet once a week in someone's house, it was usually the same place, somebody would offer her house. We would generally have a topic we would discuss then or something we had agreed on and we would just sit there talking. There was no structure really, no formal, hierarchical thing. It was at the same time a social group, we would be friends. (interview with Paula Kingsley; see also Hall Carpenter Archives 1989, p. 84)

In any case, drawing generalizations from personal narratives was meant to show the structural (read: patriarchal) foundations of the women's experiences of oppression and raise their consciousness of them (hence the name).

An important part of the CR group format was the coming-out story (Stein 1997, pp. 55, 61, 69). In linguistic terms, the practice of coming-out has been discussed as a conversational turn (Kitzinger 2002) and as a performative speech act (Chirrey 2003), in which one declares one's homosexuality and thereby contributes to the 'cultural and political meaning of what it is to be homosexual' (Butler 1993, p. 107). The coming-out story represents a narrative genre that is interdiscursively related to the spiritual autobiography, the quest novel and the *bildungsroman* (see below). In CR it was recontextualized to illustrate the central feminist claim of the personal being political, i.e., of private circumstances and experiences reflecting structural conditions.

The political significance of CR is corroborated by one of my interview partners:

> Consciousness-raising was a revolutionary means and the women really thought if we find ourselves, everything will change because we will suffer no more violence against us and no state and no capitalism and no men and no patriarchy. Generally speaking, coming together in small groups to experience what consciousness-raising might be and to find a language for that—that was the feminism of the early 1970s. . . . We still believed then that if only we were to do enough consciousness-raising, we would see the truth . . . of what being a woman was about. (interview with Vera Vaizek)

Other retrospective looks at CR show considerable disillusionment and criticize the practice for assuming that the experiences of white middle-class women can represent the lifeworld of all women (Fuss 1989, p. 68). Some views are even cynical: '[The term "CR"] is extremely effective in implying that the somewhat Neanderthal tendencies of your opposition can be corrected by some feminist equivalent of a Maoist rehabilitation centre for intellectuals' (Cunningham 1996, p. 42). Dismissals on other grounds are no less scathing: 'Women's consciousness-raising groups drew the really ill-dressed, unclassy women, who regurgitated their personal feelings in small groups' (quoted in Stein 1997, p. 144). Nevertheless, CR groups can be seen as a paradigmatic space where lesbian feminist discourse was generated, distributed and received during the 1970s, while also giving rise to a particular format in which different genres could be recontextualized and combined.

Taking matters a step further meant activists forming political pressure groups. The women in those groups did political work such as organizing social and cultural events like lesbian dances, concerts and readings as well as establishing women's centres, cafés and switchboards. Geographical constraints made it necessary to go beyond oral communication and produce and distribute texts in the form of numerous newsletters and pamphlets. Discourse access became a vital issue as 'those with the capability to distribute their materials nationally often became recognized leaders in the movement' (Shugar 1995, p. 4). Since the need for the development of a network was recognized by a vast number of lesbians, there was a high degree of intertextuality with articles being referred to and reprinted from other newsletters and magazines, further reinforcing the influence of particular opinions. Another link between oral and written discourse practice was established by single events like discussions, camps and summer schools being accounted for in the media, often word by word:

> *Off our backs* really was the journal of the movement. . . . What they did was that they reported on all the things that happened in the community with admirable love of detail. Often verbatim. When you had an argument somewhere, a discussion, they really transcribed what *A* had said, what *B* had said, what *C* had said. (interview with Ina Feder)

The events thus became part of the shared knowledge of a lesbian (discourse) community. Especially conferences and camps were organized to intensify and elaborate networks, discuss political strategies and also, in the words of an event organization team, 'to have fun together and renew ourselves and our bonds' (Ayres & Saxe 1988, p. 109). Some of those events also functioned as fund-raisers for other lesbian projects.

Then as now lesbian texts came in a variety of media. Apart from print media, independent films and recordings of lesbian-written and produced music served a crucial role in building a lesbian community and providing an outlet for lesbian discourse in the 1970s. They were shown at, and distributed by, independent cinemas and labels as well as at film and music festivals such as the Michigan Womyn's Music Festival. Occasionally, they even made it into mainstream distribution outlets such as record stores and radio stations (Faderman 1991, pp. 220–4; Stein 1997, pp. 110–11).

The fact that lesbian feminists, while downwardly mobile, tended to be university-educated granted them the intellectual and sometimes financial background to engage in theorizing and publishing in the first place. In the lesbian publications of the period, 'their image of lesbianism [consequently] dominated the 1970s, since they felt freer than the other women to present themselves through the media' (Faderman 1991, p. 218). Still, it is worth keeping in mind that proponents of political lesbianism at no time represented the majority of lesbians but rather a vocal minority that reached paradigmatic status.

Let us now first look at a seminal text from the beginning of the decade: the 'most famous of lesbian feminist manifestos' (Jeffreys 1990, p. 290), the Radicalesbians' *Woman Identified Woman* (1970/1988). The text was chosen for its early date as much as for the influence it had on later texts and indeed on lesbian communities in Britain and the US for years, if not decades, to come. It should be noted that the opening paragraph reproduced is not necessarily representative of the remainder of the text, although words and phrases introduced at the beginning are echoed throughout. While the opening represents a narrative, the other six paragraphs elaborate on the political implications of that narrative. However, the extract contains those ideas in a nutshell and can therefore be regarded as a summary of the whole text that combines the overall expository with narrative genre elements. The following analysis will uncover how the authors use certain linguistic devices to implement their overall strategy of constructing an emergent in-group and thereby communicate a cognitive representation of a group identity. The reader is referred back to Chapter 2, as well as to the glossary, for the explanation of technical linguistic terms.

EXAMPLE A: 'THE WOMAN IDENTIFIED WOMAN' (RADICALESBIANS 1970/1988) (EXTRACT)

Reproduced with kind permission by the publisher.

 1   What is a lesbian? A lesbian is the rage of all women condensed to the point
 2   of explosion. She is the woman who, often beginning at an extremely early
 3   age, acts in accordance with her inner compulsion to be a more complete
 4   and freer human being than her society—perhaps then but certainly later—
 5   cares to allow her. These needs and actions, over a period of years, bring her
 6   into painful conflict with people, situations, the accepted ways of thinking,
 7   feeling and behaving, until she is in a state of continual war with everything
 8   around her, and usually with herself. She may not be fully conscious of the
 9   political implications of what for her began as personal necessity, but on
10   some level she has not been able to accept the limitations and oppression
11   laid on her by the most basic role of her society—the female role. The turmoil
12   she experiences tends to induce guilt proportional to the degree to which she
13   feels she is not meeting social expectations, and/or eventually drives her to
14   question and analyze what the rest of her society more or less accepts. She
15   is forced to evolve her own life pattern, often living much of her life alone,
16   learning usually much earlier than her 'straight' (heterosexual) sisters about
17   the essential aloneness of life (which the myth of marriage obscures) and

18   about the reality of illusions. To the extent that she cannot expel the heavy
19   socialization that goes with being female, she can never truly find peace with
20   herself. For she is caught somewhere between accepting society's view of
21   her—in which case she cannot accept herself—and coming to understand
22   what this sexist society has done to her and why it is functional and necessary
23   for it to do so. Those of us who work that through find ourselves on the
24   other side of a tortuous [sic] journey through a night that may have been
25   decades long. The perspective gained from that journey, the liberation of the
26   self, the inner peace, the real love of self and of all women, is something to
27   be shared with all women—because we are all women.

Reprinted numerous times, this text was first presented at the Second Congress to Unite Women in 1970, where it was staged in a coup to interrupt the conference (Thompson 1993, pp. 173–4; Katz 1996, pp. 140–1). This ephemeral mode of text distribution was typical of the late 1960s and early 1970s (Chasin 2000, pp. 69–70), with only the most influential texts being transferred into print. The manifesto was later published in *Notes from the Third Year*, a collection of writings edited by members of Radicalesbians, a New York-based group of lesbian feminists. In its original version, it was printed on low-quality paper and stapled, with the title and name of the authoring collective added in handwriting (see Figure 1.1). As the 'first statement of an autonomous lesbian feminist politic, [the] essay circulated widely among young radical feminists and achieved enormous influence' (Stein 1997, p. 35). By the mid-seventies, the pamphlet had become 'the credo' (Shulman 1983, p. 53), its title was used for self-reference and it triggered a number of texts contributing to the discursive construction of the so-called political lesbian. A decade after the Radicalesbians' 'powerful text' (Johnston 1973, p. 148), the concept of the 'woman identified woman' was still a central term in lesbian politics (Rich 1980). Indeed, the manifesto's role in persuading women to identify with and pursue the aims of lesbian feminism was considerable, as evidenced by Leck's (1995, p. 319) acknowledgement that it 'contained for me one of the most profound sets of ideas I had encountered to that time' (see Nogle 1981, p. 261, for further appreciations of the text). As noted previously, the extract constituting Example A is the opening paragraph of the manifesto.

Social Actors

Looking at social actors, we can see that these are first and foremost the paradigmatic 'lesbian' (line 1), in whom the complexity of lesbian existence is scaled down to a singular figure. Clearly, the opening of the text 'plac[es] an individual into an imagined social category and [thereby] establishes the imagined category itself' (Barrett 2002, p. 33). The prototypical in-group member is given prominence by being headlined and defined as a 'woman identified woman,' which signals a reversal of the sexologist pre-Stonewall notion that lesbians were 'inverts,' i.e., women harbouring masculine feelings in a female body (Sedgwick 1990, p. 84). In lines 2–23 of the text, the 'lesbian' is further characterized by being contrasted with the collective actor 'society.' The actions of this second social actor are nominalized in 'social expectations' (line 13) and 'socialization' (line 19). In lines 6–7, the collective actor 'society' is broken up into 'people, situations, the accepted ways of thinking, feeling and behaving,' in short 'everything around her' (lines 7–8). However, this enumeration does not make the actor any more concrete; in fact, its most specific representation is the social collective of 'her "straight" (heterosexual) sisters' (line 16). Thus, while the total of all lesbians is compressed to, and genericized in, a single paradigmatic figure, the counterpart is depersonalized as the collective actor 'society.' Both, however, have in common that they are positioned in an ahistorical and decontextualized eternal present, as indicated by the use of present simple tense throughout (e.g., 'she is the woman,' 'turmoil she experiences' in lines 2 and 11–12). By employing simple present in concord with social actors who are stripped of their complexity by being either compressed to a single individual or augmented to a uniform collective, the authors endow their texts with an aura of factuality and eternal truth, a characteristic feature of manifestos.

The overall discursive strategy of this programmatic text is to construct the mental model of an in-group. This is introduced towards the end of the above extract, when the collective 'we' is first mentioned (line 23). While this 'we' clearly follows on from 'a lesbian,' it should be noted that the two are not conflated; the paradigmatic 'lesbian' does not unproblematically stand for the group as a whole. Rather, the 'we' is limited to 'those of us who work that through' (line 23); it is only a particular sub-group consisting of the authors and the women they address, namely those who have made the metaphorical journey from internalized misogyny and homophobia to a raised consciousness about the misogynist and homophobic foundations of patriarchal society. The final lines (25–6) of the extract spell out the results of such a raised consciousness, namely 'the liberation of self, the inner peace, the real love of self and all women.' The collective social actor 'all women' is repeated three times in short succession (lines 26–7). It not only incorporates the generalizing quantifier 'all' but further presupposes women to be a homogeneous group unified by a common gender, a notion that glosses over the complexity of lesbian genders (see Chapter 4). So we are again dealing with simplification and compression of social groups, a rhetorical strategy that renders complexity more comprehensible for the reader.

It is moreover crucial that the implicit augmentation of the paradigmatic 'everywoman' to a whole social group has the words 'lesbian' and 'woman' collapse into each other: the extract's final lines do not feature 'all lesbians' but 'all women.' Likewise, the state of the lesbian in society is problematic not because of any non-conformist desire she may experience but because she cannot 'accept the limitations and oppression laid on her by . . . the female role' (lines 10–11). Lesbian identity thus hinges on rejecting gender stereotypes and identifying with the essential, uncorrupted womanhood that the text constructs. Its central rhetorical move is to redefine lesbians as woman-identified women spearheading a revolutionary political movement. This substitution of same-sex desire with gender identification proved an excellent recruitment strategy for the lesbian cause, enabling straight feminists to identify as lesbian on political grounds, without actually having to have sex with other women. By rendering 'lesbian' a category that potentially every woman can place herself in, women's energy is redirected from men, and from identification with a male worldview, to woman identification. This ultimately gives rise to the separatist theory that withdrawal from men would topple patriarchal structures (Faderman 1991, p. 206; Shugar 1995, pp. 25–33; see also Chapter 5, this volume).

Evaluation

The likely persuasive intention of the text, i.e., to convince women of the benefits of identifying with the opened-up category 'lesbian,' could not be met without the appropriate evaluation of the different social actors. As elaborated previously, the three main social actors in the text are 'a lesbian,' 'society' and 'we,' with the 'lesbian' first finding herself in 'society' but gradually emancipating herself from its beliefs and expectations to become a member of 'we,' the in-group of woman-identified women in which individuality dissolves. The paradigmatic lesbian is said to be determined by an inherent 'inner compulsion to be a more complete and freer human being' (lines 3–4). The comparative form of the positively connoted attributes 'free' and 'complete' is explained by the social restrictions that the unemancipated lesbian confronts when living in 'society.' This 'society' itself is given the attribute 'sexist' (line 22) and is said to emanate 'limitations and oppression' (line 10). The contradiction between the lesbian's inner needs and the outward forces acting upon her lead to a negatively evaluated split existence, a 'painful conflict' (line 6). Thus, the lesbian's potential to lead a positive life is turned into its opposite, i.e., into 'a state of continual war' (line 7), 'turmoil' (line 11) and 'guilt' (line 12), for as long as she still identifies with heterosexist social norms.

As pointed out earlier, overcoming the split existence of 'lesbian in society' involves realizing that the society in question is based on gender stereotypes that are detrimental to women. The gradual development of leaving the heterosexual matrix and its values is evaluated in strongly negative terms as 'a tortuous [sic] journey through a night' (line 24). By contrast, the state after this metaphorical journey is evaluated positively as 'liberation of the self' (lines 25–6); the potential of the lesbian for full personhood has been realized, and her 'inner compulsion' (line 3) has reached its goal. Likewise, the negatively connoted 'state of continual war' (line 7) has been replaced with the 'inner peace' (line 26) that was already anticipated as 'peace with herself' (lines 19–20). Moreover, the inability to accept oneself (line 21) has given way to 'real love of self and of all women' (line 26). Due to allegedly sharing the same gender identity with other women, love of oneself automatically translates into love for other women, which further underscores the shift from third person singular ('she') to first person plural ('we'), from individual strife to communal bliss. The attribute 'real' here reflects an essentialist belief in a 'true' lesbian nature. This attribution thus reinforces the factuality and timeless validity indicated by the present tense.

Actions

This flavour of eternal truth is further brought about by what actions the social actors engage in. If we look at the social actor that is at the centre of lines 1–23, 'a lesbian,' it becomes clear that where she is acting herself, it is mostly relational processes she is engaged in, i.e., she carries particular attributes, identifies in particular ways and exists in particular circumstances. Thus, the text opens with a relational process in question form ('What is a lesbian,' line 1) to which it provides the answer by the attribution of a lesbian as 'the rage of all women condensed to the point of explosion' (lines 1–2). The concentration of relational processes in the opening stretches of the manifesto (lines 2–3, 7) contributes to the programmatic nature of a text that offers models for identification, establishes an in-group and naturalizes these constructs as expressions of a true self. The two other relational processes are '[s]he may not be fully conscious' (line 8) and 'she has not been able to accept' (line 10). The attribution in those two sentences, though, points towards mental states of limited consciousness and lack of acceptance, respectively, which are corollaries of living as a lesbian in a heterosexist society. Overtly mental processes are 'the turmoil she experiences' (lines 11–12) and 'she feels she is not meeting social expectations' (lines 12–13). Here, mental processes are employed to represent the action they govern as subjective experience rather than objective fact.

Mental states are also captured by overtly material processes, in which the actor acts upon a goal. Thus, 'she can never truly find peace' (line 19) and 'she cannot accept herself' (line 21) are ultimately statements about mental conditions. The two other overtly material processes are the metaphorical 'she cannot expel the heavy socialization' (lines 18–19), which again points towards a mental development, and 'she is not meeting social expectations' (line 13). We can see, then, that where 'a lesbian' functions as the source of a process, it is mostly relational and mental processes she engages in, some of which are encoded as overtly material processes. This focus on the relational and mental is very much in line with the text's manifesto character, the genre-specific purpose of which is to establish and define categories that the readers can identify with.

Where the lesbian as social actor is found in a passive position, i.e., as the goal of a process, it is exclusively material, albeit metaphorical, processes that are enacted upon her. These are performed by abstract or backgrounded actors, e.g., 'the limitations and oppression laid on her by . . . the female role' (lines 10–11) and '[s]he is forced to evolve her own life pattern' (lines 14–15). Where the lesbian grammatically engages in overtly material actions upon society and its aspects, these processes are negated ('she is not meeting social expectations,' 'she cannot expel the heavy socialization' in lines 13 and 18–19). Society, by contrast, acts directly upon her, featuring as an actor in material, or a senser in mental processes. Thus, we find 'what the rest of her society . . . accepts' (line 14), which points to a covertly mental process. Reversely, the overtly mental process of 'society cares to allow her' (lines 4–5) indicates a covert material process, such as restricting movement or sanctioning particular clothing styles. Overt and covert processes coincide in the material 'what this sexist society has done to her' (line 22), which clearly shows the top-down flow of power between society and the lesbian. Nevertheless, the focus is still on the latter; 'lesbian' features 18 times as a social actor. Compared to that, the text features only three statements that include 'society' as a collective social actor.

As indicated previously, the focus shifts from the individual to the community in line 23. The 'we' is engaged mostly in material actions, e.g., 'those of us who work that through' (line 23). As a backgrounded actor, which is not present in the phrase but can be inferred from the co-text, 'we' is implicit in '[t]he perspective gained from that journey' (line 25; a covertly mental process) as well as in '[this] is something to be shared' (lines 26–7). The text ends as it begins, with an attributive relational process—'we are all women' (line 27)—that sees the object of such a definition shift from the individual lesbian to the whole community. By starting out with a definition of the third person singular and closing with one of the first person plural, the text iconically mirrors what it describes, namely the development from isolated individual in adverse circumstances to the solidarity of the community that the individual, and with her the reader, is meant to identify with for her own good as well as for the strength of the in-group.

Modality

Modality in the extract is purely epistemic, i.e., providing various degrees of certainty, at the total absence of any obligation. Thus, we find the double mitigation of '[s]he may not be fully conscious' (line 8), as well as 'a night that may have been decades long' (line 24–5). Further mitigation of the lesbian's situation in society is present in the adverbs in 'she is in a state of continual war . . . usually with herself' (lines 7–8) and 'learning usually much earlier' (line 16). The same function is met by the verb in '[t]he turmoil . . . tends to induce guilt' (lines 11–12). It should be noted, however, that these adverbs and verbs, while hedging devices, still convey a rather high degree of certainty, compared with, say, 'occasionally' or 'sometimes.' Finally, conditionals and mitigation are also combined with expressions of ability: 'on some level she has not been able to accept' (lines 9–10), 'to the extent that she cannot expel the heavy socialization' (lines 18–19) and 'she can never truly find peace' (line 19). These expressions of ability, or lack thereof, help to reinforce the overall flavour of factuality of the text, most clearly when they come unhedged ('she cannot accept herself,' line 21). Modality therefore ties in with the use of attribution and definition in relational processes as well as with the compression of the complexity of lesbian life into a paradigmatic figure that develops to become part of an allegedly homogeneous community.

Interdiscursivity

The text under investigation combines two formal genres, namely the political manifesto and the *bildungsroman*. Functionally, it therefore represents expository and narrative genres. As for the former, its traces can be found in the definition of the in-group, its features and goals towards the end of the extract. Individuality dissolves in the spirit of a community that the reader, through the figure of 'a lesbian,' is meant to identify with. Identification, and hence recruitment for the cause, is facilitated by making lesbian identity revolve not around desire but around the inability to fully internalize and live out societal stereotypes of women. As criticizing existing gender roles is a hallmark of any feminist agenda, the text works towards conflating feminism and lesbianism, in accordance with the misquoted slogan 'feminism is the theory, lesbianism is the practice' (see earlier discussion).

The development of the paradigmatic heroine in lines 1–23 clearly, if perhaps not consciously, borrows from the genre of the *bildungsroman* (Stein 1997, p. 48). In Example A as well as in the literary genre, 'we see the "national imagination" at work in the movement of a solitary hero through a [fixed] sociological landscape' (Anderson 1983, p. 35). The *bildungsroman* was conceived as the literary reflection of the Enlightenment in the latter half of the eighteenth century. As such, it ultimately goes back to Leibniz' (1646–1716) notion of the human being as a dynamic spirit and an organism striving for individual perfection within a greater order. Accordingly, the *bildungsroman* typically centres on a character that stands for the whole of humankind—or rather, as the times would have it, its male half—in evolving from a state of ignorance and relative brutishness to a state of higher consciousness in which he has realized his full human potential. This development is often initiated and furthered by external influences but finally reaches its climax in the ideal internal state of knowledge, realization and spiritual perfection. This ideal may be a pietist one, as in the development of Christian in Bunyan's *Pilgrim's Progress* (1678), or a more general harmony between the individual and God's creation, as in Goethe's *Wilhelm Meister*

(1795–1829) and, incorporating features of the subsequent Romantic era, in Novalis' *Heinrich von Ofterdingen* (1802). In that the hero usually develops in reaction to outward factors, the *bildungsroman* is closely linked to the quest novel. In this related form, which goes back to the picaresque tale of the early seventeenth century, a literal journey symbolizes the hero's inner one. An example would be Fielding's *Tom Jones* (1749). The two genres have also been combined in lesbian fiction, for instance in Verena Stefan's novel *Häutungen* ('Skinnings,' 1975) and in Rita Mae Brown's *Rubyfruit Jungle* (1973). Brown was a member of the Radicalesbians collective, who authored Example A, so that her novel can be seen as a fictional representation of the notions expressed in that text.

Returning to our example, lines 1–23 can be read as a condensed *bildungsroman*: the paradigmatic lesbian's development is sketched from 'an extremely early age' (lines 2–3) onwards, with the text detailing her alienation from her environment and its negative psychological consequences to her gradual realization of the woman-hating structures of the society she lives in, a raising of consciousness that was facilitated by numerous CR groups at the time. From there, the logical next steps are full epiphany and finally dissolution in the ideal of the loving community. While the struggle and development are typical of the fictional genre the text draws upon, it is important to note that the final, ideal state represents a break away from the notion of individual perfection that is all-pervasive in the *bildungsroman;* although the individual there ultimately lives in enlightened harmony with his surroundings, he very much stays an individual. By contrast, the lesbian in Example A is replaced by the loving and sharing community of women that she becomes part of. The individual coming-out of the paradigmatic lesbian can be equated with the beginnings of a lesbian movement, in fact it becomes its 'representative anecdote' (Nogle 1981, p. 260). The coming-out narrative here also serves as a 'creation myth' (Goldstein 2003, p. 40) and as such it 'reinforce[s] community values and serve[s] to inculcate the proper perspective' (Muniz & O'Guinn 2001, p. 422). This function places the text squarely in the normative realm.

The spiritual, sometimes religious nature of the *bildungsroman* is also reflected in the choice of lexis used for evaluation: words like 'liberation,' 'inner peace' and 'real love' (lines 25–6) not only echo the main buzzwords of the hippie movement, in which many early lesbian feminists had been politicized, but also hark back to Christian religious discourse. The idea of the sharing community thus connects Christian to hippie to lesbian feminist thought (see Shugar 1995, p. 7, for this pedigree). Traces of religious discourse can also be observed in some of the text's main metaphors.

Metaphor

Given the text's proximity to genres such as the quest novel, it is not surprising to find the authors make use of the LIFE IS A JOURNEY metaphor. Pervasive in structuring thought and discourse (Lakoff 1993), this conceptual model is realized in expressions such as 'a tortuous [sic] journey' and '[t]he perspective gained from that journey' (line 24–5). Given the central nature of the Radicalesbians' manifesto as well as the pervasiveness of that metaphor in Western thought (Kövecses 2005), it comes as no surprise to find the COMING OUT AS JOURNEY metaphor in oral accounts as well:

> I was moving on a journey and in 1987 I made the move if you like . . . somebody said to me I was out before I decided to cross the Rubicon as it were.[8] (interview with Laura Donne)

That metaphorical journey conceptualizes the development towards higher consciousness, which is in the present text further metaphorized as a space with an entrance and exit ('on the other side of a tortuous [sic] journey,' lines 23–4). The attribute 'torturous' evaluates the way from one end to the other in negative terms, which is reinforced by the adverbial 'through a night' (line 24). Metaphors of light and darkness, day and night, are a staple of religious imagery (and its adaptations in popular culture genres such as fantasy and western), where they come to represent the forces of good and evil or, in Judeo-Christian terms, God and the devil, as eternal antagonists. Consequently, the individual strife towards perfection involves withstanding evil and breaking through to goodness. The notion of strife and struggle is expressed by means of the WAR metaphor, attenuated as 'painful conflict' (line 6) or intensified as 'a state of continual war' (line 7). War is here 'with everything around her, and usually with herself' (lines 7–8). In the example at hand, this negative condition is ended and the breakthrough to light and goodness achieved once the individual disengages inwardly (and, as separatist thought would have it, outwardly) from values and beliefs that are harmful to her spiritual well-being and instead identifies with the greater good of the lesbian community. The religiously coloured JOURNEY and LIGHT metaphors have proved to be consistent across time: coming-out narratives from the 1990s echo the same set of conceptualizations, realized in metaphoric expressions that indicate an enhanced consciousness and perception, such as 'awakening,' 'seeing the light' or 'seeing everything in colour' (Kitzinger & Wilkinson 1995, pp. 100–1). Interestingly, 'awakening' has also been identified as 'classic nationalist rhetoric' (Reicher & Hopkins 2001, p. 66), showing how texts construct collective identities by using similar metaphors across discourses.

This metaphorical journey into the light is instigated by an initial moment, a 'big bang' referred to in terms of metaphorical force dynamics (Johnson 1987, pp. 42–8; Talmy 1988): 'A lesbian is the rage of all women condensed to the point of explosion' (lines 1–2).[9] This first ignition gives rise to a chain reaction of forces propelling the individual lesbian forward on her metaphorical journey. In that she owes her very existence to the exploding rage of all the women who lived and suffered under patriarchal rule before her, her personal quest is located within a historical narrative of woman-kind's struggle for freedom. The initial explosion manifests itself in her as an 'inner compulsion' (line 3) to strive towards this ideal. This strive soon enough clashes with her less-than-ideal surroundings, leading to 'turmoil [that] drives her' (line 11–13). Thus, even the negatively evaluated struggle is justified as giving further impetus to her development and as a necessary intermediate stage, the 'somewhere between' (line 20) that has to be crossed on the metaphorical journey through the night. By metaphorically realizing a force schema, the authors naturalize the psychological and spiritual devel-opment of the individual away from an adverse society by making it appear as governed by the laws of physics. This conveys the idea of nature running its course and ties in with the factuality that is brought about by the use of scaled-down social actors, present tense and low-affinity modals. At the same time, conjuring up metaphorical forces endows the described develop-ment with a sense of inevitability that helps bear struggles and conflict as necessary stations on the way to the ultimate higher state of being one with a community of equals.

Image of the Community

The scenario projected in Example A is best described by the motto *per ardua ad astra* ('through adversity to the stars'). Stein (1997, p. 67) puts it in a nutshell:

> Lesbian feminists imagined 'coming out' as a journey that began with a discovery of the lesbian within one's sense of self and proceeded through time, as the individual moved from an oppressive environment to one that permitted freer and bolder self-expression.

It is tempting to see Example A as a coming-out narrative that has been com-pressed into a prototypical scenario. However, this is a valid reading only as long as coming-out is not linked to the experience of same-sex desire; after all, the main move of the present text is to re-define lesbianism as emanci-pated womanhood and decouple it from sexuality. For the latter-day reader, this may require quite a stretch of the imagination, and Ponse's (1978, p. 125) following five-part generic structure for coming-out narratives may chime better with her:

- Experiencing a subjective sense of being different that is identified as same-sex desire.
- Developing an understanding of this desire as lesbian.
- Accepting a lesbian identity.
- Seeking a community of kindred spirits.
- Getting involved in a lesbian relationship.

Example A only elaborates on Steps 1 and 4, and that only if we factor out desire. The observation that '[t]hese needs and actions, over a period of years, bring her into painful conflict with people, situations, the accepted ways of thinking, feeling and behaving' (lines 5–7) seems to relate to the 'subjective sense of being different.' However, the needs and actions are not the experience of desire for another woman; rather, they pertain to the 'compulsion to be a more complete and freer human being' (lines 3–4) than is possible in patriarchal society. Step 2 is not addressed at all, and Step 3 only by way of negation ('she cannot accept herself,' line 21). This lack of self-acceptance is counterbalanced and ultimately overcome by understanding the workings of society. Step 5 is omitted altogether, so that Step 4 becomes the true goal of the journey; the desire for another individual is replaced with 'the real love of self and of all women' (line 26).

The JOURNEY metaphor with its attached evaluations proved to be 'an effective rhetorical strategy, for it placed the "well-adjusted" lesbian as one who had successfully completed a journey to a freely chosen womanhood' (Shugar 1995, p. 32) and was therefore a step closer to fully evolved personhood than heterosexual women. In and through the text, 'progress from heterosexuality to homosexuality is [constructed as] healthy and . . . lesbianism [as] a mature developmental achievement' (Stein 1997, p. 5). The text's scenario thus reverses the homophobic notion of monogamous heterosexuality as an indicator of sexual and personal maturity. By relating to well-anchored models in this way, the authors make their own model more convincing. The basic teleological idea of the text provides a 'definitional closure' (Butler 1990/1999, p. 22) in that the lesbian is once and for all seen as brought about by generations of women before her, as the woman who is driven towards, and reaches, the ultimate ideal of a loving and sharing female community.

Widely received, the text helped displace the homophobic notion of 'lesbian chauvinism,' i.e., lesbians oppressing women by aping heterosexual gender roles, which was held by fractions in the women's movement at the time (Johnston 1973, p. 148). In its stead, it provided an ideology to help socialize the lesbian into her newly found community. The onus was now on heterosexual women to face their unenlightened state and realize that their lifestyle choice was a stumbling block on the road to feminist utopia. As Johnston (1973, p. 85) acknowledges, the 'woman identified woman was an excellent phrase to help define the lesbian in her prime womanhood in distinction to all women who still partake of male privilege.' Gradually evolving throughout the 1970s, this line of thinking found an explicit expression in a text by the Leeds Revolutionary Feminists (1979/1981). As an extreme position, the text is helpful in illustrating some discourse topics in stark terms. As a single example, however, it cannot reflect the diversity of lesbian feminist discourse. Rather, this complexity unfolds in the cluster of texts from the late 1970s and early 1980s that spans Chapters 3 and 4. Taken together, the four texts embody one of the major lines of conflict in second-wave lesbian feminist discourses, which in Europe persisted even into the 1990s. The aim of the subsequent analysis is to show how the image of a lesbian community established in Example A was taken up, reproduced and changed in a British context almost 10 years later.

EXAMPLE B: 'POLITICAL LESBIANISM' (LEEDS REVOLUTIONARY FEMINISTS 1979/1981) (EXTRACTS)

Reproduced with kind permission by the publisher.

1 But it sounds like you are saying that heterosexual women are the enemy!
2 No. Men are the enemy. Heterosexual women are collaborators with the
3 enemy. All the good work that our heterosexual feminist sisters do for
4 women is undermined by the counter-revolutionary activity they engage in
5 with men. Being a heterosexual feminist is like being in the resistance in
6 Nazi-occupied Europe where in the daytime you blow up a bridge, in the
7 evening you rush to repair it. Take Women's Aid for example: women
8 who live with men cannot tell battered women that survival without men
9 is possible since they are not doing it themselves. Every woman who lives
10 with or fucks a man helps to maintain the oppression of her sisters and
11 hinders our struggle.
12 But we don't do penetration, my boyfriend and me.
13 If you engage in any form of sexual activity with a man you are reinforcing
14 his class power. You may escape the most extreme form of ritual
15 himiliation [sic] but because of the emotional accretions to any form of
16 heterosexual behaviour, men gain great advantages and women lose. There
17 is no such thing as 'pure' sexual pleasure. Such 'pleasure' is created by
18 fantasy, memory and experience. Sexual 'pleasure' cannot be separated
19 from emotions that accompany the exercise of power and the experience
20 of powerlessness. (If you don't do penetration, why not take a woman lover?
21 If you strip a man of his unique ability to humiliate, you are left with a creature
22 who is merely worse at every sort of sensual activity than a woman is). . . .
23 No act of penetration takes place in isolation. Each takes place in a system
24 of relationships that is male supremacy. As no individual woman can
25 be 'liberated' under male supremacy, so no act of penetration can escape
26 its function and its symbolic power. . . .
27 It is much easier for you in the lesbian ghetto than for me. I have to live out
28 the contradictions of my politics which is a hard, relentless, day-by-day
29 struggle with the man I live with.
30 That's simply not true. Living without heterosexual privilege is difficult
31 and dangerous. Try going into pubs with groups of women or living in a
32 women's house where youths in the street lay siege with stones and catcalls.
33 Heterosexual privileges are male approval, more safety from physical
34 attack, greater ease in dealing with the authorities, getting repairs done,
35 safety from a besieging obscene phone-caller, being able to refer to a man

36   in the bus queue or at work which brings smiles of approval from women
37   and men, let alone the financial advantages of being attached to a
38   member of the male ruling class who has greater earning power. Because
39   we choose to live without these privileges we resent being used by hetero-
40   sexual feminists as fuelling stations when they are worn down by their
41   struggles with their men. Women's liberation groups and women's households
42   should be a refuge and support for heterosexual sisters in resolving their
43   contradictions by getting out but should not be used to prop up heterosexual
44   relationships and thereby shore up the structure of male supremacy.
45   But lesbian relationships are also fucked up by power struggles.
46   That is sometimes true, but the power of one woman is never backed up
47   by a superior sex-class position. Struggles between women do not directly
48   the oppression of all women or build up the strength of men. Personal
49   perfection in relationships is not a realistic goal under male supremacy.
50   Lesbianism is a necessary political choice, part of the tactics of our struggle,
51   not a passport to paradise.
52   I won't give up what I've got unless what you offer me is better.
53   We never promised you a rose garden. We do not say that all feminists should
54   be lesbians because it is wonderful. The lesbian dream of woman-loving,
55   bare-breasted, guitar-playing softballers, gambolling on sun-soaked hillsides is
56   more suited to California, supposing it bears any resemblance to reality,
57   than to Hackney. But yes, it is better to be a lesbian. The advangages
58   [sic] include the pleasure of knowing that you are not directly servicing
59   men, living without the strain of a glaring contradiction in your personal
60   life, uniting the personal and the political, loving and putting your
61   energies into those you are fighting alongside rather than those you are
62   fighting against, and the possibility of greater trust, honesty and directness
63   in your communication with women.

This example combines extracts from a longer pamphlet written by the Leeds Revolutionary Feminists.[10] Referred to as the 'first major appearance of lesbian-feminism [in Britain]' (Hamer 1996, p. 200), it was first presented as a paper at the Revolutionary/Radical Feminist Conference in Leeds in September 1979. Since the text, as the authors explain in their comment, caused considerable discussion and controversy, it was published in the feminist periodical *Wires* two years later. The ongoing debate in the form of letters to the editor led to a reprint of the text in the same year as a book edited and published by Onlywomen Press. The publishers not only reprinted the paper but also some of the letters to the editors of *Wires* as well as their own collective and individual statements. Moreover, the authors of the text, Leeds Revolutionary Feminists, provided their own view of their text two years after it had first been written. In their comments, they modify some of the statements maintained in the pamphlet and look back on the reactions it provoked. The authors also provide information on the circumstances of text production:

'Political Lesbianism' was written very quickly in a high energy brain-
storming session one evening, for discussion at a Revolutionary and
Radical Feminist Conference. It reflected some discussions our group
had had, but in a very condensed form. This was because we knew
that we would be able to expand and unpack these ideas in workshops
at the conference. . . . Because it appeared in WIRES, it was seen as a
finished product, which was never intended. . . . The paper was written
by a small group of women who really were in no position to impose
anything, except a paper for discussion, upon the Movement. We really thought, when writing the paper, that we were merely expressing
commonly held views which were just not usually written down. (Onlywomen Press 1981, pp. 66–8)

The text itself is divided into two parts, the first of which is titled 'What
heterosexuality is about and why it must be abandoned.' In that section,
as the heading already indicates, the authors lay down their basic political
convictions and objectives, centring on the issues of heterosexuality and
its sexual manifestations as the key to the system of male supremacy. The
second part, from which the preceding extract is taken, comprises 'Questions and Comments.' Out of the total of ten questions, the first, second,
fifth, sixth and seventh, as well as the answers to them, are reproduced in
Example B, plus part of the answer to Question 3. The authors comment on
that section as follows:

The second [part] is arranged in form of questions raised and comments
made to us about the subject of political lesbianism and the way we
think they should be answered. . . . A lot of women presumed we made
[the questions] up. In fact, they were questions we'd either asked ourselves, had been asked by friends, or had come up at conferences and
meetings. (Onlywomen Press 1981, pp. 5, 68)

Although the text is overtly addressed at straight feminists, then, it is the
authors' declared objective to provide other members of the in-group, i.e.,
women who became lesbians for political reasons, with a set of arguments to
use in discussions in order to maintain and defend their politics. We can thus
identify a dual audience and a dual persuasive and argumentative purpose.
Argumentative text types are popular in separatist and quasi-separatist discourse, and more generally any marginal discourse in need of making its case
(see e.g., Worden & Andrews 1981; Marty 1983a/1988, 1983b/1988; Trebilcot 1986; Wilchins 1997a; see van Eemeren et al. 1996; Kopperschmidt 2000
for a theory of argumentative strategies in discourse). The frequent instances
of this text type in separatist discourse show the defensive standpoint of separatists, who, as a radical movement, were the object of much criticism. In the
present text, only one of the ten comments is actually a question, and it is perhaps better to call them counter-arguments. Likewise, the answers often take

the form of slogans, the function of which is 'in providing patterned answers to the (patterned) questions raised by members of the established order who oppose the movement' (Kitzinger 1987, p. 128).

The title, 'Political Lesbianism,' sets the agenda by qualifying what kind of lesbian life is at stake. Like in Example A, the in-group is here headlined again. The in-group model is spelled out in the introductory part of the text (not reproduced here), where the authors define a political lesbian as 'a woman-identified woman who does not [necessarily engage in] compulsory sexual activity with women' (Leeds Revolutionary Feminists 1979/1981, p. 5). This semantic extension of the concept of 'lesbian' latches on to Example A by quoting its title and spelling out its understanding of lesbianism as not primarily sexual. It is further in tune with Adrienne Rich's (1980) notion of a 'lesbian continuum,' which she developed around the same time: a woman-centred life in social, emotional, spiritual and only optionally sexual terms.

Social Actors

Since the text takes the form of a simulated debate, it is clear from the very beginning that the writers establish a dichotomy between the in-group (themselves) and an out-group (heterosexual feminists) that they have encountered previously and that is re-imagined for the sake of the argument. However, members of the in-group are nowhere mentioned explicitly. Instead, we find the personal pronoun 'we' (lines 38, 53). Yet even this is introduced rather late in the text and used only sparsely. Reference to the in-group is indirect and abstract, as in the abstract nouns and noun phrases '[l]esbianism' (line 50), and '[l]iving without heterosexual privilege' (line 30). Thus, the in-group of social actors is depersonalized and expressed as a condition discussed in political terms. Elsewhere, political lesbians are metonymically replaced by the institutions and projects they run. In a similar vein, the text on the whole features many grammatical actors that are not social actors: more often than not, reference is made to concepts and ideas rather than people. Examples include 'counter-revolutionary activity' (line 4), 'fantasy, memory and experience' (line 18) or 'superior sex-class position' (line 47). This is in stark contrast to Example A, where only 'society' was cast as a nebulous collective actor, while 'a lesbian' and 'we' were personalized as paradigmatic heroine and loving community, respectively.

In the example of '[w]omen's liberation groups and women's households' (line 41), it is further noteworthy that, as in Example A, 'lesbian' is conflated with 'woman.' While it is true that many feminist projects were and are indeed mainly run by lesbians, substituting 'woman' for 'lesbian' of course renders the latter once more invisible.[11] The most direct references to the collective social actor 'political lesbians' can be found whenever the text assumes the voice of the imagined other; the counter-arguments tend to be directed at a personal 'you' (lines 1, 27, 52). In line 27, this is polemically embellished as 'you in the lesbian ghetto,' which makes the voice of the imagined other appear belligerent. This impression is further underscored by the tendency of the counter-argument to start with an initial 'but,' indicating adversity (lines 1, 12, 45).

The out-group is explicitly mentioned as 'heterosexual women' (line 1) or 'heterosexual feminists' (lines 39–40), elsewhere as 'women who live with men' (lines 7–8), or, more crudely, as '[e]very woman who lives with or fucks a man' (lines 9–10). A tentative approximation between in- and out-group is achieved by referring to the latter as 'our heterosexual feminist sisters' and 'heterosexual sisters' (lines 3 and 42, respectively); here, the possessive pronoun and the kinship term to some extent soften the antagonistic nature of the text. The authors even acknowledge '[a]ll the good work' (line 3) these social actors do, even if they modify this positive evaluation immediately afterwards ('is undermined,' line 4). The debate format ensures a similar 'us vs. them' dualism: direct address by personal pronoun ('you') and by imperative ('[t]ry going into pubs,' line 31) finds its counterpart in the 'we' and 'I' of the imagined voice of the other.

It is noteworthy that the 'we' of the imagined other extends only to 'my boyfriend and me' (line 12), with this voice otherwise formulating her objections in the first person singular. By contrast, the in-group is either referred to by the plural 'we' or abstracted altogether. The imaginary out-group member is therefore represented as much more exposed and vulnerable than the authors, who are represented by the collective 'we' or, if abstracted to their conditions and institutions, disappear as social actors altogether. Although the authors make a political point about the necessity of collective action (in lines 24–5: 'no individual woman can be "liberated"'), they still construct the imagined other as a single individual speaking up against a group. One could argue that the authors thereby show the futility of individual struggles. However, discursively weakening opponents is also a very effective rhetorical strategy to bolster up one's own position. This is a feature of many political texts in the normative realm and has here been taken up to implement a central strategy of lesbian discourses that seek, through texts, to construct and disseminate an image of community.

The conflict emerging from the foregoing analysis is set against the backdrop of a third group of social actors, namely 'men' (lines 2, 8, 16, 37, 41, 48, 59). This group is individualized as 'a/the man' (lines 10, 13, 21, 29, 35), 'my boyfriend' (line 12) or 'youths' (line 32). The individual man is also politicized as 'a member of the male ruling class' (lines 37–8) or, in even more abstract terms, 'male supremacy' (lines 24, 25, 44). This last expression denotes the collective social actor 'men' from a systemic point of view and is as such a depersonalization device similar to the nominalizations and abstract entities found elsewhere. Depersonalization becomes dehumanization when man is reduced to the status of 'a creature' (line 21).

The piece repeatedly refers to 'man,' 'men' or equivalents. These occur a total of 18 times, which is only slightly fewer than the 22 references to 'woman,' 'women,' 'sisters' and 'feminist(s).' By contrast, 'lesbian' occurs only twice (lines 54 and 57), with 'a woman lover' (line 20) as an implicit third example. This tendency is also reflected in the use of adjectives, with 'male' occurring five times compared to no instances of 'female.' Similarly, the text includes a meagre three instances of 'lesbian' compared to 10 for 'heterosexual.' These findings can partly be explained by heterosexual feminists being one target audience. Nevertheless, contemporaneous readers seem to have been bewildered by this focus on men and heterosexuality, because in their afterword, the authors concede that the subtitle 'the case against heterosexuality' is 'more accurate' than 'political lesbianism' (Onlywomen Press 1981, p. 67).

Evaluation

Given the three groups of social actors, Wolf, writing in the late 1970s, identified a hierarchy of evaluation in which 'the lowest category of people is the sexist male. Next are heterosexual and bisexual women who associate with men . . . politically oriented lesbian-feminists are seen as . . . a vanguard of feminism in its purest form' (Wolf 1979, p. 171). Accordingly, men are evaluated negatively throughout. Thus, they are in no uncertain terms defined as 'the enemy' (lines 2–3). By dint of the analogy in lines 5–7, patriarchy is implicitly compared, if not equated, with fascist regimes.[12] Also, men, when compared to women, are degraded as 'creature[s] who [are] merely worse at every . . . sensual activity' (lines 21–2).

Pejorative attitudes towards straight women—'collaborators with the enemy' (lines 2–3)—can also be couched in the religious terminology witnessed in Example A:

> You felt a bit disappointed when your heterosexual female friends didn't feel that they could identify as being lesbian. I don't mind now but in those days it was like an evangelical zeal. . . . Women who said that they did want relationships with men . . . would be judged quite harshly, how they hadn't seen the light. (interview with Paula Kingsley)

Even in a radical feminist text written in 1979, however, negative judgment of other women was regarded as extreme by many other lesbian feminists. The following letter in response to the text illustrates this: 'Leeds Revolutionary Feminist Group's paper . . . offended and angered me, but I'm glad they wrote it . . . because those ideas . . . have never been stated so baldly before' (Onlywomen Press 1981, p. 11).

Lesbians are elevated by being compared with heterosexual women. Their life is identified as 'difficult and dangerous' (lines 30–1), so choosing it raises its value and reflects positively on the women who are courageous enough to make that choice: 'Only the strongest, most politically committed women were able to resist the allure of familial approval, material benefits, and other privileges that accrue to heterosexuals' (Stein 1997, p. 163). This implicitly positive evaluation of the in-group, the communicated value of its beliefs and actions, is further reinforced by the subsequent list of heterosexual privileges (lines 33–8).

What, then, makes lesbian living worth the trouble? The imagined other explicitly challenges the authors on this point (line 52), but the latter fail to give a fully positive evaluation of their way of living. In fact, positive evaluation is even negated: 'Lesbianism is . . . not a passport to paradise' (lines 50–1). This is further elaborated as '[w]e do not say that all feminists should be lesbians because it is wonderful' (lines 53–4). In lines 54–5, the authors sarcastically paraphrase and refute a perceived cliché of lesbian living, and by quoting it in response to the other's challenge, implicitly accuse her of naivety. It is only afterwards that the implied question of line 52 ('I won't give up what I've got unless what you offer me is better') is answered by the declarative statement 'yes, it is better to be a lesbian' (line 57). The attribute 'better,' repeated from line 52, constitutes an explicit positive evaluation; however, given that it appears after the negated 'wonderful' (line 54), the comparative merely denotes that lesbian living is better than heterosexual existence, not that it has absolute positive value in itself. This muted positive evaluation makes for a stark contrast to the almost enthusiastic description of a lesbian community as a loving and sharing brethren of woman-identified women found in Example A. All that is left of this quasi-religious community is the repeated use of the kinship term 'sisters' (lines 3, 10, 42), which is typical of all sorts of feminist texts from the 1970s. The feature even crossed over into popular culture (witness the 1985 Eurhythmics song 'Sisters are doing it for themselves') and persists into the 2000s (see Example G in Chapter 6). Kinship terms are a feature found in many marginalized communities, e.g., the use of 'sister' and 'brother' in African American and Black British communities. As such it is intended to establish and reinforce the social identity of present and prospective in-group members.

Actions

Similar to the initial attribution in Example A ('What is a lesbian?'), the present text opens with an identifying relational process to give a definition. However, in accordance with the authors' focus on the re-constructed opponent, the group to be defined here is heterosexual women rather than the lesbian in-group. The authors clarify that '[h]eterosexual women are collaborators with the enemy' (lines 2–3), even if in their comment, the writers of the pamphlet remark that

> [w]e now think that 'collaborators' is the wrong word to describe women who sleep with men, since this implies a conscious act of betrayal. Even if applied solely to heterosexual feminists . . . it is inaccurate: most feminists do not see men as the enemy. (Onlywomen Press 1981, p. 66)

Since the imagined and addressed other is a heterosexual woman, the negative connotation of this initial definition and the war imagery it conjures up set the scene for what is to follow: establishing an in-group identity by attacking a discursively constructed opponent, rather than presenting the in-group in a positive light.

Out-group members are further characterized by their behaviour. In line with their identification as 'collaborators,' they are said to 'engage in counter-revolutionary activity' (line 4). This activity is metaphorically described as 'rush to repair [a bridge]' (line 7) and later spelled out literally as 'engage in . . . sexual activity with a man' (line 13). The same behaviour is also interpreted in political terms as 'help[ing] to maintain the oppression' (line 10) and making women 'lose' (line 16). So far, then, heterosexual women have, in relational and behavioural processes, been reduced to their sexual activities, which are presented as their most salient feature in the discursive stand-off between them and lesbian feminists. However, lesbians are not defined along the same lines. Rather, in-group members are said to 'choose to live without these privileges' (line 39). Further, lesbian life is said to mean 'living without the strain of a glaring contradiction' (line 59). Hence, heterosexual women are (negatively) defined in terms of their sexuality whereas lesbians are rather presented in terms of politically motivated lifestyle choices.

Most actions attributed to heterosexual feminists are of the material process type. Thus, it is admitted that they 'do good work' (line 3) and may metaphorically 'blow up a bridge' (line 6). In line with the relational and behavioural processes discussed earlier, however, the defining characteristic of straight women is that they prefer to 'live with [a] man' (lines 9–10). These actions are interpreted as directed against the in-group: the straight woman 'hinders our struggle' (line 11) and abuses truly committed feminists as 'fuelling stations' (line 40). Such accusations are exacerbated by switching to direct address in the second person singular: 'you are reinforcing his class power' (lines 13–14). Heterosexual behaviour is here read as an act of aggression against the in-group, rather than as a result of the desires and wishes of members of the out-group.

Thus we see that the mental agency of heterosexual women is limited. They are not granted much agency in verbal processes either. Only once can they be found as sayers in a verbal process, and that instance is negated: 'Women who live with men cannot tell battered women that survival without men is possible' (lines 7–9). In contrast to that, the text opens with an example of the authors and in-group members as engaged in a verbal process: 'you are saying heterosexual women are the enemy' (line 1). What is negated in the answer (line 2) is not the ability to communicate at all, but the contents of the message. The same applies for '[w]e never promised you a rose garden' (line 53) and '[w]e do not say that all feminists should be lesbians because it is wonderful' (lines 53–4). By contrast, along with verbal actions, in-group members are also presented as engaged in mental processes, e.g., 'we resent being used' (line 39). A covert mental process can also be found in the description of lesbian life as 'loving and putting your energies into those you are fighting alongside' (lines 60–1). In terms of material actions, the abstracted state of being a lesbian allows to live out the slogan of 'uniting the personal and the political' (line 60) as well as 'not directly servicing men' (line 58–9), which implies that heterosexual women do just that.

Although men, as collective or individual social actors, are frequently referred to, they have few actions ascribed to them. Most of these are again relational, with men initially identified as 'the enemy' (line 2) and later devalued as 'worse at every sensual activity than a woman is' (line 22). The authors also point out that a man 'has greater earning power' (line 38). As for their material actions, we only learn that individual 'youths lay siege' (line 32). Apart from such concrete acts of aggression, the dynamics between men and women are again abstracted when it is stated that straight sex sees men 'gain great advantages and women lose' (line 16). Interestingly, men are here actors in a material process whereas women are engaged in a particular behaviour. Rather stereotypically, women thus do not impact on their environment, and their losing is presented as all-encompassing.

In summary, the construction of the two social actor groups through the actions attributed to them shows a tendency to define heterosexual women by their negatively evaluated sexual behaviour, while lesbian life on the other hand is presented as emotionally fulfilling and politically necessary, but not necessarily more attractive sexually. This opposition between heterosexual feminists and political lesbians is constructed against the backdrop of a third group, men, who are referred to repeatedly, but about whose actions, behaviours, thoughts and feelings the authors remain largely silent. Thus, men come to be the ominous enemy in the wings, and women are defined and evaluated in terms of their attitudes and behaviours towards them rather then towards each other.

Modality

One of the main differences between Examples A and B is the fact that the latter conveys obligations in the form of deontic modality whereas the former does not. Example B also contrasts with A in that it features hardly any epistemic modality. Rather, the authors of Example B give clear directives about what should ideally be the case, e.g., 'women's households should be a refuge . . . but should not be used' (lines 41–3). The modal marker 'should' is here repeated in two consecutive phrases and occurs again in the claim that 'all feminists should be lesbians' (lines 53–4). Lesbianism adopted for political reasons is presented as the ultimate feminist commitment. In their afterword, the authors state that they were influenced by 'American feminist writing from the early '70s' (Only women

Press 1981, p. 67). Indeed, Atkinson was regularly misquoted as regarding lesbianism as feminism put into practice (as mentioned previously) while Johnston famously said that 'until all women are lesbians there will be no true political revolution' (1973, p. 166). Interestingly, however, Johnston did not advocate lesbianism for political reasons, rather stating that 'sexual satisfaction of the woman independently of the man is the sine qua non of the feminist revolution' (1973, p. 165). The British reception of her text took over a number of slogans and metaphors but rejected the sexual angle, instead adapting Atkinson's dictum of all sex as the opposite of freedom (1982, p. 91) and adopting the understanding of lesbianism as a primarily social and political choice, as witnessed in Example A. Accordingly, deontic modality is expressed not only through modal verbs such as 'should' but also in referring to lesbian life as the 'necessary political choice' (line 50).

Such an authoritative voice is not only conveyed through deontic modality, though; the repeated use of the modal verb 'can' also helps to construct opinions as facts. Thus, readers learn that 'women who live with men cannot tell battered women that survival without men is possible' (lines 7–9). Further expressions of inability and impossibility are '"pleasure" cannot be separated from emotions' (lines 18–19) and 'no individual woman can be "liberated"' (lines 24–5). The negated form of the modal here works in tandem with the scare quotes to denounce the opinions ascribed to out-group members. The imagined other's opinions are refuted in no uncertain terms ('[t]hat's simply not true,' line 30) and what they denote is presented as impossible. However, what *is* possible is not stated with the same certainty. The most declarative instance is 'survival without men is possible' (lines 8–9), but statements about what lesbian life is about other than that are noticeably hedged. For instance, struggles between women are said to 'not directly strengthen the oppression of all women' (lines 47–8) just as lesbians are 'not directly servicing men' (lines 58–9). Most strikingly, the greatest asset that lesbian life, according to the authors, has to offer, namely 'greater trust, honesty and directness in your communication with women' (lines 62–3), is hedged by stating that this is merely a 'possibility' (line 62). This pales in comparison to the elaborate negative evaluation of heterosexuality.

The authors further betray a tendency to generalize, which is partly achieved by using absolute quantifiers like 'each,' 'every,' 'never' etc. Such features, which have been criticized as 'the totalizing gestures of feminism' (Butler 1990/1999, p. 19), are occasionally combined with high-affinity deontic modality: 'to be a true feminist one must be a lesbian and the only way to avoid oppression by men is to remove all women from contact with men through the creation of self-sufficient communities of lesbians' (Eisenstein 1973, quoted in Wolf 1979, p. 68). This linguistic feature of lesbian feminist/separatist discourse is displayed most blatantly in the following quote from Jill Johnston's programmatic autobiography *Lesbian Nation* (1973, p. 174):

> The woman in relation to man historically has always been defeated. Every woman who remains in sexual relation to man is defeated every time she does it with the man because each single experience for every woman is a reenactment of the primal one in which she was invaded.

This statement is echoed in the claim that '[n]o act of penetration takes place in isolation [but] [e]ach takes place in a system of relationships that is male supremacy' (lines 23–4). The slogan-like quality of these statements is corroborated by their recontextualization in other genres. Kitzinger, for instance, uses varieties of both statements in her questionnaire to determine different brands of lesbian politics: 'Penetration is inevitably an act of domination. . . . Whatever the time in history, wherever the place in the world, in every culture women are exploited by men' (1987, p. 130). In statements such as 'If you engage in any form of sexual activity with a man you are reinforcing his class power' (lines 13–14)—criticized as particularly authoritarian by a reader of the pamphlet (Onlywomen Press 1981, p. 11)—the declarative status and the definite pronoun along with the inclusive identifier 'any' indicate a voice which is typical of expository genres.

Interdiscursivity

The text was originally a workshop paper, drawn up to provide input for a discussion. Its published form re-enacts its oral delivery by first making a political statement in the first part ('What heterosexuality is and why it must be avoided') before dealing with a number of reconstructed questions and comments. However, the recontextualization of those questions and the re-enactment of a spoken and spontaneous discussion in a written text shift the power dynamics between authors and audience in a crucial way: because the interaction is no longer temporally and spatially synchronous, claims and reactions, which very likely took the form of direct adjacency pairs in the workshop, now become asynchronous and influenced by the authors' memory and interpretation of them. For instance, the readers' letters included in the 1981 publication used here constitute reactions to an earlier version of the paper. However, the 1981 version already incorporates this criticism. Because of the ensuing time lag and because theirs is the central text in the publication, the authors clearly have the last word. And because they reconstruct questions as they remember them, and answer to them in their paper, they have absolute power over what reactions are included in the first place, over how the question or objection is phrased, e.g., as personal and concrete rather than collective and abstract, and over lengths of turns: the authors allocate themselves a total of 1,256 words in the whole text (656 in the extract), as opposed to only 118 (82) words for their interlocutor, and the answers' length thus exceeds that of the questions/comments by a factor of roughly 10 to 1. Any objections to this biased account can only be expressed in further letters, which again face a time lag. This ensures that the authors continue to have what marketers call a first-mover advantage.

In terms of lexis, it is mostly revolutionary rhetoric that is drawn upon, as in the collocation 'counter-revolutionary activity' (line 4), in the term 'collaborators' (line 2) and the repeated reference to men as a 'class' (lines 14, 38, 47). These interdiscursive traces of revolutionary rhetoric should come as no surprise, given the fact that lesbian feminists for the better part had their political roots in the New Left (Faderman 1991, p. 218), from which they had broken away, disillusioned by its sexism. It may have been this recontextualization of particular discourse features that made some older women perceive lesbian feminist discourse as 'stilted, or overly rhetorical' (quoted in Stein 1997, p. 102).

The use of pre-formulated rhetoric is here at odds with the genre the authors re-enact, namely oral debate. The authors clearly try to invoke an authentic conversation, shown by colloquial contractions such as 'don't' (line 12 and echoed in line 20), '[t]hat's' (line 30), 'won't' and 'I've got' (both in line 52). Further markers of spontaneous conversation are exclamation marks indicating raised voice (line 1) and four-letter words, used both literally (line 10) and metaphorically (line 45). Noticeably, most of these informality markers are ascribed to the out-group member. If we factor in the use of first person singular in the questions, the authors' tendency for abstract reasoning in their answers and the textual space they occupy, we can see that the text is characterized by an authoritative voice, which rather invokes monologic genres such as lectures. Seen as such, the text finds the authors in the role of lecturers, while the out-group member is relegated to the role of the student. The power asymmetry thus constructed is obvious.

The text is of an overall expository nature, and the authors explicitly refuse to have their text meet a persuasive function: 'We never promised you a rose garden. We do not say that all feminists should be lesbians because it is wonderful' (lines 53–4). Indeed, the only two instances in the text which seem to draw on advertising discourse are regarded as problematic by the authors themselves. The first concerns the rhetorical question 'why not take a woman lover?' (line 20), a typical device of advertising. However, the authors retrospectively comment that 'we found some of our comments flip, offensive and inconsistent, such as "Why not take a woman lover?"' (Onlywomen Press 1981, p. 66). The second instance is triggered by the challenge 'I won't give up what I've got unless what you offer me is better' (line 52). Here, the imagined speaker is positioned as a buyer or consumer of a particular lifestyle, provided that certain conditions (better value of the 'product') are met. This is preceded, and perhaps prompted, by the negative identification '[l]esbianism is . . . not a passport to paradise' (lines 50–1), which makes use of a slogan-like alliteration. The challenge is answered with the scenario conjured up in lines 54–6 ('[t]he lesbian dream of woman-loving, bare-breasted, guitar-playing softballers, gambolling on sun-soaked hillsides'). The images invoked are stereotypically found in commercials and immediately refuted by placing them in a quasi-mythical California, which is then sharply contrasted to Hackney. (The contrast of course relies on shared knowledge about the relatively large lesbian population in that part of London.) By positioning lesbian life in the bleak reality of North London, the overly idealistic image is framed sarcastically. Also, mentioning the stereotype at all assumes that the imagined other might believe in it, which in turn enables the authors to point out her naivety.

Although the authors refuse to make an offer upon request, the list of advantages of lesbianism (lines 57–63) does indeed offer a certain lifestyle to the reader. As such, it is set against the earlier list of heterosexual privileges (lines 33–8). Crucially, however, the later list includes hedges ('not directly servicing men,' 'the possibility of greater trust'), making it much less convincing than the amenities that come with heterosexuality. Likewise, the only clearly positive evaluation, 'yes, it is better to be a lesbian' (line 57) comes only after the sarcastic reference to stereotypes. It seems that the in-group model is relatively vague.

Metaphor

The lesbian feminist cause is portrayed as a metaphorical war right at the opening of the piece, when men are defined as 'the enemy' and heterosexual women as 'collaborators with the enemy' (lines 2–3). In its use of the WAR metaphor, the two definitions came to function as a slogan (literally: 'battle cry'; Ammer 1999, p. 225), even to define the ideology of political lesbianism. Critics have read this slogan as 'a reverse-discourse that uncritically mimics the strategy of the oppressor instead of offering a different set of terms' (Butler 1990/1999, p. 19).

The source domain of the WAR metaphor, a typical feature of any confrontational discourse, is elaborated by a simile that draws on the historical scenario of the French resistance under Nazi occupation. The metaphoric notion of heterosexual women as collaborating with the enemy can be traced back to Johnston, who accuses feminists who have sex with men of 'collusion with the enemy' (1973, p. 181). After this definition, another relational process compares the opponent to someone 'in the resistance in Nazi-occupied Europe [who] in the daytime blow[s] up a bridge, in the evening rush[es] to repair it' (lines 5–7). Again, we can discern a direct intertextual link, here to Ti-Grace Atkinson, who likened heterosexual feminists to 'French[men] serving in the French army from 9 to 5, then trotting "home" to Germany for supper and overnight' (quoted in Johnston 1973, p. 277). Faderman (1991, p. 202) sums up the idea of political lesbianism accordingly: 'some feminists . . . came to believe that banding together could be effective only if a woman did not go home to sleep in the enemy camp.' After this unabashed use of the WAR metaphor in the opening stretches of the text, it is in the following attenuated by means of the word 'struggle(s).' As such, it can be found as a description of political activities in 'our struggle' (lines 11 and

50). Towards the end of the extract, the metaphor again becomes intensified as 'struggle' is replaced by 'fighting' (line 61).

The metaphorical war that is the feminist movement is seen as instigated by literal violence. Thus, aggression is waged against 'battered women' (line 8) and in 'physical attack' (lines 33–4). (Incidentally, the two instances contradict each other; while the authors implicitly identify men as the perpetrators of violence against women, 'safety from physical attack' is listed as one of the advantages of living with a man.) The experience of having to defend oneself against literal violence is also conveyed by mentioning a 'besieging . . . phone-caller' (line 35), a phrase that echoes 'youths in the street lay siege' (line 32). The aggression perpetrated by men is directed against female bodies and buildings inhabited by women ('women's house' and 'women's households' in lines 32 and 41). And just as the literal violence gives rise to metaphorical warfare, the object of aggression, patriarchy, is metaphorized as the bridge that gets blown up by the resistance fighter and rebuilt by the collaborator (lines 6–7).

Image of the Community

Of the three actor groups involved in the text, heterosexual women and, to a lesser extent, men are focused on quantitatively, e.g., in terms of how often they are referred to and how many actions they have ascribed to them. However, the in-group engages in a wider range of different actions, including mental processes. Functionally, the two out-groups are defined with a minimum of hedging early on in the text, while the in-group is defined and evaluated only hesitantly, and mitigated by hedging devices like 'possibility' or 'not directly.' Also, the authors erase factors constituting power asymmetries within the in-group such as ethnicity or financial standing. We are thus left with the in-group model being left relatively unspecified while at the same time the text presents political lesbianism as the only viable lifestyle choice for feminists.

Just as heterosexuality relies on hegemonic persuasion, so does leaving it behind for political reasons. Such reasons may be less compelling than desire, and labelling feminists who do so as 'serious' denotes appreciation and is one of the persuasive devices the authors employ to 'offer [something] better' (line 52). What they offer, i.e., lesbian living, is presented as a purely rational 'political choice' and as 'part of the tactics of our struggle' (line 50). Given the emotional appeal of hegemonic discourses on heterosexual romance, the long-term success of this recruiting strategy is doubtful, and the numbers of women returning to heterosexuality once the first revolutionary ardour had burned off (Stein 1997, p. 156) suggest that rational arguments may be beside the point where identity and desire are at stake.

In its emphasis on collective action and the notion of community, the text relates back to Example A. The construction of the lesbian community as a '"haven in a heartless world"' (Stein 1997, p. 136) is clearly linked to the Radicalesbians' metaphorical notion of coming out as a journey from darkness to the light. Yet, the present text foregrounds communal political action rather than individual happiness and peace, and thereby further politicizes the argument. More importantly, it only briefly and circumspectly describes the advantages of this haven. The bulk of the text rather seeks to demarcate the haven from the outside world, which is described in great detail. The description of this world as hostile betrays a sense of being embattled and cornered that had, when Example B was produced, apparently replaced the quasi-religious ardour for a better world that prevailed in Example A.

Against the backdrop of the menacing male out-group, abstracted as the system of patriarchal oppression, the text pits political lesbians against heterosexual feminists. Indeed, the text is a prime example of how lesbian feminists

> did not fight their hardest battles against men who wanted to invade their territory, but against women who would have invited men in, other feminists and lesbians who did not want to exclude men, or did not want to face the disapproval of men. (Creet 1991, p. 148)

In their focus on the established heterosexuality-lesbianism dichotomy, the authors betray an interest in confrontation rather than consensus. Although the form of the text, i.e., the debate format, indicates a communicative exchange, it seems that the form was chosen to set up an opposition and disadvantage the reconstructed other. Furthermore, the authors reduce the complex socio-political structures determining power asymmetries to a binary opposition of 'sex-class positions,' i.e., convey an '"us versus them" mentality that placed a demonic patriarchy as always "other" [and] impeded women's abilities to perceive the ways they oppressed other women' (Shugar 1995, p. 89). Indeed, men are the out-group against which collective identity is formed, namely by pitting lesbians against hetero- and bisexual women.

Such simplification is reflected in the relatively homogeneous character of the text. Fairclough (1992, p. 213) points out that 'a relatively stable social domain and set of social relations and identities . . . manifests itself in texts which are relatively semantically homogeneous.' Production and distribution of homogeneous texts can thus be seen as the social practices of groups which are unified with regard to beliefs and values, or wish to present themselves as such, especially when they attempt to establish a counter-ideology (Kress 1989, p. 15). Text producers usually strictly demarcate themselves from diverging opinions. While reinforcing group identity through demarcation certainly leads to unification within a group, it also hinders communication and productive exchange. The pamphlet thus confirms Bourdieu's (1991, p. 211) observation that 'the right of reprimanding other people and making them feel guilty is one of the advantages enjoyed by the militant.' Texts in the tradition of Example B alienated not only heterosexual feminists but also other lesbians who could not identify with the ideal of the political lesbian. Chapter 4 features two attempts by these latter groups to impact on lesbian discourse from an internally marginalized position.

The analyses have shown how the early US text clearly had an influence on the later text, written in a British context. Given the time lag, Example A can be seen as following a constructive strategy in promoting a particular socio-cognitive representation, while Example B implements a reproductive strategy, by drawing on the established model and endowing it with additional features such as out-group demarcation. The idea of lesbian life as a political statement and the definition and positive evaluation of this existence carry over, even if the positive evaluation is not as explicit in the 1979 text as it was in the 1970 one. In general, there is a strategic shift away from defining the in-group in positive terms to discursively constructing it in opposition to a negatively evaluated out-group. To use Bucholtz' and Hall's (2005, pp. 599–600) terms, Example A uses adequation as a discursive strategy, downplaying intra-group differences, while Example B relies on distinction, suppressing inter-group similarities. This more oppositional stance is most clearly reflected in the introduction of the WAR metaphor. Interdiscursivity changes accordingly, from traces of religious discourse to revolutionary rhetoric. As for the overall image of the lesbian community, we could see that its conceptualization changes from that of a loving community in which individual troubles dissolve, to an undefined 'necessity' that is mostly constructed as what it is not. Relating concepts of community to those of nations, both Examples A and B can be read as instances of

> [n]ationalism [as] a political principle which maintains that similarity of culture is the basic social bond. [Example B represents] its extreme version, [in which] similarity of culture becomes both the necessary and the sufficient condition of legitimate membership: *only* members of the appropriate culture may join the unit in question, and *all of them* must do so. (Gellner 1997, pp. 3–4)

In either case, the defining power lies with a politicized and influential subgroup of the lesbian community who enjoyed privileged discourse access. Chapter 4 will look at how disenfranchised constituencies of the lesbian community claimed discursive space by challenging the dominant model.

4 Challenging the Community
The 1980s

> One of the issues about lesbian internalized oppression is that there's a blame culture and a huge defensiveness, so . . . networking and recognition of solidarity is juxtaposed with its opposite: conflict.
>
> (interview with Laura Donne)

This chapter will look at two challenges to the image of the lesbian community as it was established in texts like Examples A and B in the preceding chapter. While both sample texts in this chapter were published in 1980/1981, they can be regarded as representative, and in the case of Example D indeed seminal, of a debate that would dominate lesbian discourses throughout the decade and beyond, at least in Britain. The intertextual links that they triggered are illustrated throughout this chapter by quoting from later texts. It will be shown how, towards the end of the 1970s, dissenting voices made themselves heard that drew attention to the fact that the dominant representations that were transported by lesbian feminist discourse excluded particular groups. Such exclusion meant that butches and femmes or S/M advocates were made invisible by not being talked about and were silenced by being denied discourse access. The chapter will trace how older and/or working-class women, who felt that their pre-Stonewall culture and identity was at risk of being forgotten, reclaimed their position in the lesbian community. Likewise, sexual minorities who took issue with some of the central beliefs of lesbian feminism, while still regarding themselves as part of that community, struggled to have diversity acknowledged and to enter into a constructive dialogue with lesbian feminists. Two texts will exemplify these challenges. The first, a 1980 essay titled 'Butch,' is written from a position outside the elite discourse. Rather than attacking the dominant elite, however, author Lorna Gulston provides an ironic account of butch/femme identities which reminisces about pre-Stonewall bar culture while anticipating ideas about fluid gender identities that were propounded by queer theory ten years later. The second text, the introduction to an anthology on lesbian S/M, in many ways develops the arguments of, and uses linguistic strategies similar to those encountered in, Examples A and B. The author describes problems within a social group that finds it hard to face diversity, and attempts to maintain a unified community by calling for a dialogue across ideological boundaries.

SOCIO-POLITICAL BACKGROUND: ISSUES AND ARGUMENTS

Despite its heady beginnings following the Stonewall Riots, lesbian feminism as a movement did not enjoy uniformity and consensus for long. As early as 1973, at the first West Coast Lesbian Feminist conference, angry debates on the definition and limits of who was a lesbian emerged (Stein 1997, p. 197). These were repeated on countless occasions at later gatherings in the US, the UK and elsewhere. Towards the end of the 1970s and at the beginning of the 1980s, the perceived desexualization of lesbian feminist discourse came to be seen as negative, leading to a view on lesbian feminism as 'this really repressive movement' (Hollibaugh & Moraga 1981, p. 61). This criticism took place just shortly before the onset of the AIDS crisis, which was to change views on sexuality profoundly. The seemingly unified and homogeneous community which had been discursively constructed during the 1970s began to be fragmented and diversified.

At a time when magazines for gay women provide their readership with the 'hottest ten stripper tips' (*g3,* August 2005) and include advertising for sex toys and escort services in their pages, it is hard to comprehend the wrath and sense of betrayal that the first self-appointed 'sex radicals' caused among lesbian feminists in the early 1980s. The ensuing arguments can be broadly divided into debates about sexual identities such as butch/femme relations and bisexuality on one hand and sexual practices on the other, with pornography and S/M being the most notorious bones of contention.

To some extent, these conflicts were due to the different identities of different lesbian generations, particularly women who had identified as gay before Stonewall and those who came out in the context of feminism. While some accounts foreground how '"old gays" . . . were delighted to change their identity to lesbian-feminist' and were welcomed by the 'new lesbians' (Faderman 1991, p. 210), other oral accounts hint at the gap between lesbian feminists and other lesbians who were not out and/or not politically active: 'I don't always understand the big words feminists use. . . . I used to sit in the women's group . . . and feel that they were out of touch' (quoted in National Lesbian and Gay Survey 1992, p. 49; see also Stein 1997, p. 104). Some older women's narratives relate the basic misunderstandings between the two groups:

> I have known quite a lot of women who came to lesbianism via feminism saying they actually envied women like me. . . . They seemed to feel that we had the advantage because we had more years of knowing

our sexuality but what they didn't realize was the loneliness and the lack of opportunity to talk to people about our sexuality. . . . I don't feel that they [understood my way of life]. I didn't feel that they did at all. (interview with Pam Taylor)

This lack of understanding is conceded by one of Stein's informants (1997, p. 55): 'We had no understanding of the bar scene, of role playing, of the whole range of experience of an "old gay." I'm sure a lot of this inexperience translated into moralistic arrogance.' Others regarded non-feminist lesbians as lacking political consciousness and analysis. At best, their consciousness was seen as 'less developed' and there was a feeling that they should receive help from feminists. Yet as contact between those two groups was only scarce, the reality of the respective other was often not recognized (see Stein 1997, pp. 97–9 for quotes betraying mutual distrust and alienation). It was not before the beginnings of the 1980s that lesbians diverging from the established ideal self-image gained access to discourse and negotiated the socio-cognitive representation of a lesbian community, adding new values and norms to the model and thus making it more differentiated.

While contacts between older women and lesbian feminists were not always without friction, internal debates in the lesbian feminist movement did address diversity of ethnicity, class and (dis)ability:

> I think black and ethnic minority lesbians were underrepresented in the newsletters and magazines of the time and to some extent working-class lesbians because a lot of the publications . . . were perceived to be very middle-class . . . there was a lot of soul-searching if you want about both those issues. (interview with Gillian Eastham)

> [In 1972, the feminists I knew] were almost entirely middle-class, well-educated, white women, mostly in their mid-twenties with young children. . . . They were all much better off than I was and wore Laura Ashley clothes. (quoted in Hall Carpenter Archives 1989, p. 84)

Many lesbians of colour perceived lesbian feminists as well-meaning and anti-racist but ultimately ignorant. Sometimes, they were not even seen as having good intentions or egalitarian principles:

> All those white women treated the group like it was a big dykes' party. They were into drinking and sleeping around. . . . Anything to do with Black people . . . didn't interest them. . . . I just felt these women were in a privileged position and did not use it to change anything. (quoted in Hall Carpenter Archives 1989, p. 165; see also p. 179)

> Disabled lesbians, like most disabled people, can't get into . . . the clubs so in a sense I think that has sub-strengthened disabled lesbians. . . . I don't

think it was recognized at all in the seventies and eighties. (interview with Lola di Marco; see also Hall Carpenter Archives 1989, pp. 68–9)[1]

Increasingly, however, debates focused on sexual practices as the main dividing line:

> The main problem with [the radical lesbian feminist] view is the exaggerated emphasis that it places on sex acts in explaining women's oppression. For these people economics, culture (apart from the representations of sex), socialization, reproductive issues, have all faded into the background. Race and class barely exist for them at all as analytic categories. . . . They believe that feminists should be focusing their energies primarily on eliminating or purifying sex acts and, by extension, sexual fantasies. (Hunt 1981, p. 85)

An issue in which generational conflicts and conflicts about sexuality meet is that of butch and femme identities. To elaborate on the topic of butch/femme, it is necessary to go back to the 1950s. Sexologists had conflated butch and lesbian in the figure of the 'invert,' rendering lesbian femininity invisible (Halberstam 1998a, p. 7), but working-class and/or young lesbians after World War II organized their identities around masculine ('butch') as well as feminine ('femme') roles. In a fiercely heterosexual world, these roles were unsurprisingly modelled on the habits and behaviour of straight men and women. Although this arrangement granted the femme a more liberated sexuality than heterosexual women enjoyed at the time, butch/femme lifestyle in the 1950s entailed a stark dichotomy which newcomers could not opt out of (Faderman 1991, p. 168; Hall Carpenter Archives 1989, pp. 113, 126; Neild & Pearson 1992, pp. 59–60).[2]

> I recall badgering one of my friends to go with me to the Gateways Club [see Example C in this chapter] and being horrified by the whole business of butch/femme and the fact that women had to choose which they were and dress and behave accordingly. . . . If you went to a lesbian pub, there were very often working-class women maybe playing pool, maybe playing darts. They'd be very much into role playing. . . . I have a friend who even now still can't understand when she sees what she thinks are butch women together, she can't understand it. It is beyond her capabilities of accepting just as lesbianism is beyond the capabilities of heterosexual people. (interview with Pam Taylor)

The material repercussions of this dichotomy not only involved clothing, body posture and (perceived) sexual practices but, at its most extreme, even segregated toilets in the bars (Faderman 1991, p. 169).[3] Linguistically, terms for self- and other-reference would equally be borrowed from heterosexual discourses and their gender stereotypes: 'It was fairly stereotypical language about being a wife. . . . It was about being dainty or chivalrous' (quoted in Hall Carpenter Archives 1989, pp. 126, 128).

On the other hand, the homophobia of the 1950s and the 1960s, which resulted in frequent police raids on the bars, turned butch/femme culture into a virtual *ersatz* family for its members, a safe social space in which butches would help other butches to fill their roles and older femmes would initiate their younger counterparts (Hall Carpenter Archives 1989, p. 129; Faderman 1991, p. 174; Bender & Due 1994, pp. 103–4; Halberstam 1998a, p. 62). Also, it has to be kept in mind that only some lesbians would even wish to become part of the bar culture or display butch/femme appearance and behaviour, a difference that more or less coincided with class membership. Other women chose to have private parties because they perceived the bars, which were infamous for violence, sex workers, petty criminals and police raids, as too risky (Wolf 1979, p. 44, n. 4). The following quote reflects on middle-class teachers who lived in lesbian relationships in the late 1950s and early 1960s:

> All those women couples just kept a very very bland image. You didn't get invited to their homes so that it was a private thing, their lesbianism. I mean I was invited to some homes but I was still not shown the lesbianism and . . . I'm now convinced that must have been more than simply sharing accommodation. But it was all so secret and very private. They had learned you have to have the right image. They were the whole bluestocking generation, they were all highly educated. (interview with Vivienne Pearson)

Certainly, the issue of butch/femme was controversial among lesbians even in the heydays of bar culture in the 1960s (Neild & Pearson 1992, p. 76; Healey 1996, p. 49; Stein 1997, p. 29). Nevertheless, butch/femme culture has, in retrospect, become the dominant narrative about the time between World War II and Stonewall, just as lesbian feminism is now seen as the central paradigm of the 1970s.

As a result of this paradigm shift, the idea of butch/femme was frowned upon by 1970s lesbian feminism as an emulation of oppressive heterosexuality: 'The woman in relation to herself is not a butch or femme but a woman' (Johnston 1973, p. 176; see also Brownworth 1975; Penelope 1983; Jeffreys 1989; Hart 1996 for writings in this tradition).[4] According to this line of thinking, femmeness signified uncritical acceptance of patriarchal stereotypes of femininity, while butches were devalued as male-identified. Consequently, the onset of lesbian feminism in the early 1970s meant that the lesbian bar culture of the 1950s and 1960s was marginalized, and although it never ceased to exist it was restricted to public silence, practically eliminated from the dominant representation of a lesbian community (see Brownworth 1975, quoted in Halberstam 1998b, p. 131; Case 1998). However, oral accounts are unanimous about the parallel world of lesbian bars, with butch/femme culture evident until the late 1970s and even early 1980s in places like London, Belfast and Manchester (Hall Carpenter Archives 1989, pp. 142, 189, 205; see also Wolf 1979, pp. 7, 47, 123):

> I think [role-playing] was there, it was already there so that for instance at [feminist magazine] *Spare Rib* they'd have a Christmas benefit or something and people would dress up. . . . Butch/femme, the whole 'role-play' as it was called was something that the non-feminists were into and this was a no-no. But I'm sure there was an element. . . . Ideologically, you weren't butch/femme but actually people were doing it. (interview with Erica Jones)

> During the 1970s there was a continuation of the bar culture of the 1950s and 1960s [and] this went on underground, overshadowed by lesbian feminism. (interview with Pam Taylor)

> There were already places and bars where lesbians went who were not involved with feminism. I can say very little about this, I can only say they existed. There was a bit of an overlap, you would sometimes go somewhere after a meeting, but basically those were very different spaces in which any concept of the self was certainly formed in a different way. (interview with Vera Vaizek)

If the last quote shows lack of familiarity with, and distance from, lesbian bar culture, feminists were regarded with a similar lack of understanding: 'I knew some of the women who worked behind the bar and they were all taking the piss out of these feminists who were taking their tops off when they were dancing!' (quoted in Hall Carpenter Archives 1989, p. 130). Due to different levels of access to public discourse, however, the latter voices have remained anecdotal.

At the end of the 1970s, women who identified with butch/femme roles—along with bisexual women, transgendered people and sadomasochists—clearly fell outside the conformist paradigm:

> I really feel that over the years the most hurtful and cutting rejections I've had have come from my sisters, primarily in the women's movement and later in the PC lesbian movement. Those are the groups that just cut me dead. . . . The political lesbians were very up on the right way to be a lesbian. Being butch was really bad. . . . There was nothing we were doing the right way. When I would open the car door for somebody, I'd get screamed at. When I lit somebody's cigarette, I'd get my face slapped. (Bender & Due 1994, p. 106)

Under the ruling model of politically defined lesbian identity and community, models of butch and femme identity, which focused on sexual desire and behaviour, were gradually derived of their discursive and, indeed, physical space (Stein 1997, pp. 100–1). It was only with the advent of queer theory in the early 1990s that butch/femme experienced a renaissance. By decoupling sex from gender, these identities could 'return as a viable lesbian practice instead of as a sell-out' (Roof 1998, p. 33). These days, gendered signifiers such as gesture, dress, gait and linguistic style are decoupled from biological sex and recontextualized in oppositional and ironic readings of the gender order. Despite early attempts to counter the essentialist gender notions of lesbian feminism (Laporte 1971/1992), however, this post-modern resurrection of butch/femme identities was still a long way in the future at the end of the 1970s. Political lesbianism, while probably not a majority lifestyle, was the dominant ideology of the day and anything that resembled role, let alone power-play, was generally discarded as 'male-identified' and hence anti-feminist.

The increasing focus on politically correct sexual identities and practices that came to characterize late 1970s lesbian feminist discourse has been criticized as championing little more than a list of 'negative sex recommendations' (Halberstam 1998b, p. 133) and as establishing white middle-class values as the defining paradigm at the expense of other, partly ethnically grounded, sexual cultures (Moraga 1983). The lesbian-feminist sexual code thus saw many women fall by the wayside, butches and femmes among them. Likewise, lesbians in the 1970s, who were still struggling to maintain their newly found social and sexual identity in the face of heterosexist aggression and ridicule, accused bisexual women of 'collaboration with the enemy' (Johnston 1973, p. 180; see Example B in Chapter 3) and denied them an identity in their own right: 'Bisexuality is a transitional stage, a middle ground, through which women pass from oppressive relationships [i.e., heterosexual ones] to those of equality and mutuality [i.e., lesbian ones]' (Johnston 1973, p. 180). This attitude clearly belittles bisexuality as 'immature' (quoted in Stein 1997, p. 176) or 'just a phase,' to use the homophobic cliché. Consequently, bisexual women in the late 1970s felt that 'there was a lot of pressure to be either lesbian or straight, there wasn't a lot of room to be bisexual' (quoted in Seif 1999, p. 41), and certainly there was no social identity as bisexual (Stein 1997, p. 76). Apart from defying binary models of identity, bisexuality may also have been seen as irresponsible because it endangered the survival of a lesbian community (cf. Muniz & O'Guinn 2001, p. 424). Confrontations on the issue could turn violent and continued until well into the 1980s:

> We held a lesbian summer school in '86, '87, which was a fund-raiser for the Lesbian Archive. . . . In the evening we'd be showing films and stuff. And it was that film *She Must Be Seeing Things* and it was very avant-garde in the sense that . . . it was a lesbian couple and she portrayed this woman's fantasies that her girlfriend was having this relationship with a man. . . . I remember sitting in my girlfriend's place and watching this film on video, thinking 'Should we show it at the lesbian summer

school?' The film was new, it was just going to be released, it was going to be a general public release. The couple in the film was a black woman and a white woman. We had two women who were doing the film studies course, a black woman and a white woman, and we said 'Yes, we will do this because women are going to be shocked,' they're going to be shocked by the actions in the film, they're going to be shocked by the fact that lesbians had fantasies with men; we can show it and discuss it. . . . We had almost a physical fight at this conference where [some women] were trying to rip the film off the projector. . . . I remember furious shouting. It got very, very bitter and after that there was this big split. (interview with Erica Jones; see also Smyth 1992, p. 39)

Another description of this and similar guerrilla attacks on cinemas trying to show the film across the UK are provided by Healey (1996, pp. 114–18), while Ashton (1996, p. 170) notes that 'in the mid-1980s the vanilla [i.e., non-S/M] lesbian community buzzed with excited stories of projectors being overturned at . . . seminars.'[5]

If butch/femme and bisexuality did more than raise a few eyebrows in the lesbian feminist community, S/M among women was role-playing carried to its extreme. In fact, gendered power inequality was seen as the root cause of the twin 'evils' of butch/femme and S/M, and the two were thus often conflated in discourse:

Heteropatriarchy eroticizes difference. . . . We have these bipolar pairings of male/female, aggressive/passive . . . femme/butch, master/captive, dominant/submissive. (Hart 1996, pp. 70–1)

Butch/femme role-playing, aping the most exaggerated versions of femininity and masculinity available in heterosexual culture, became . . . popularized . . . as a form of watered-down sadomasochism in which lesbians could experience the delights of eroticized dominance and submission. (Jeffreys 2003, p. 127)

Like male/female or butch/femme roles, the roles of sadist and masochist are based on the division into powerful and powerless people. (Nichols, Pagano & Rossoff 1982, p. 140)

Accordingly, reactions to the lesbian S/M discourse emerging in the latter half of the 1970s were swift and often scathing. Again, the tone was set by Johnston's influential autobiography that triggered a number of intertextual chains: 'Role playing is the elaboration of . . . (dis)advantage into the various passive-aggressive or sado-masochistic dualities' (1973, p. 175). The two sides of the debate are epitomized in two anthologies, namely *Coming to Power* (1981), a collection of texts edited by Samois, a San Francisco-based self-proclaimed 'lesbian/feminist S/M organization' and a response titled *Against*

Sadomasochism (Linden et al. 1982). Initially, opponents of S/M showed a willingness to interact with material elaborating on, and groups practising, S/M (Atkinson 1982; Meredith 1982) and even questioned their own motives for rejecting it (Lorde & Star 1982, p. 69). Throughout the above-mentioned volume (Linden et al. 1982), writers stress time and again that their aim is not to lobby for legal restrictions of particular practices or to control other women's sexuality. The main objection in these early responses was not that women were living their sexual fantasies but that they were calling the practice a lesbian feminist one. The argument was thus also one about naming and self-reference, triggered by some discourse participants trying to integrate aspects into the lesbian feminist model of identity that others saw as outside of, if not in direct contradiction to, that category. The argument that S/M represents free sexual choice and thus a liberated female sexuality was dismissed on the grounds of free choice being impossible in a patriarchal society based on power abuse. In the words of one group of writers, '[t]he concept of "free choice" is often a smoke screen for socially determined behavior' (Nichols, Pagano and Rossoff 1982, p. 137). By re-enacting abusive patterns, thus the line of argument goes, S/M practitioners shore up the basis of patriarchal society. Desire was seen as being reduced to lust and as decontextualized from its socio-economic conditions (Hennessy 2000, pp. 185, 189).

Starting from the notion of lesbian relationships and lesbian sexuality as egalitarian, anti-S/M groups saw eroticized power play and its proponents as subverting their agenda. Dismissing as relativist the argument that difference is not the same as inequality, they saw S/M, like butch/femme, as reflecting the violence and oppression witnessed and experienced in heterosexual relationships:

> To feminists who had been working for years, immersed in the realities of women's pain at the hands of men . . . the cheerful concentration on an unproblematic 'desire' seemed like a brutal callousness and indifference to the real material situation of women's lives. (Jeffreys 1990, pp. 263–4)

As can be seen from the above, S/M became linked to, if not conflated with, physical abuse, an 'equation [which] sounds suspiciously like the right-wing's equation of homosexuality with pedophilia' (Stein 1999, p. 48). By way of analogy, S/M was often likened to negatively connoted behaviour like substance abuse, e.g., alcoholism (Hoagland 1982, p. 154) or smoking (Tiklicorect 1982), as well as to criminal offences such as drug trafficking (Hoagland 1982, p. 158) or theft:

> Because of the universality of dominant/submissive situations in our culture . . . most people have responded to sadomasochism at some time and to some degree. This does not mean that one is a sadomasochist, any more than the temptation to steal something makes someone a thief. (Nicholas, Pagano and Rossoff 1982, pp. 144–5)

Finally, S/M is also metaphorically conceptualized as illness: 'it is ridiculous to assume that any of us has not been infected erotically . . . by the patriarchal ideology of authority, of dominance and submission' (Hoagland 1982, p. 155).

A central claim of anti-S/M argumentation is the practice's perceived reflection of power abuse on a societal level, such as sexism, racism or anti-semitism. At its most extreme, this line of argument highlighted perceived parallels between S/M and the 'erotic cult of fascism' (Jeffreys 1994, pp. 210–34) as the epitome of inequality and oppression. In everyday discursive practice, this translated into 'Nazis' and 'fascists' being employed as terms of abuse for members of the S/M community. While it has been noted that 'lesbians could be fascist for not being SM and lesbians could be fascist for having SM sex' (Healey 1996, p. 110), this particular term of abuse seems to have overwhelmingly been directed at advocates of S/M:

> [At the 1978 Gay Freedom Day Parade members of San Francisco lesbian S/M group Samois] were booed and hissed, there were shouts of 'fascists' and 'Nazis,' and some people threatened us or spit [sic] at us. . . . We had been called fascists so often that it was beginning to be predictable. (Califia 1981, pp. 252, 264)[6]

Like their opponents, pro-S/M activists or, more generally, 'sex radicals,' posited that self-defined female sexuality was one of the cornerstones of feminism. Where the two groups differed was in the radical feminists' belief that only particular, i.e., egalitarian and mutual, sexual practices could be regarded as an authentic expression of female sexuality, whereas others enacted patriarchal models and practices. By contrast, pro-S/M activists saw eroticized power difference and other forms of role-playing as a self-determined sexual expression and claimed that a focus on sex in general would be liberating for women. Accordingly, San Francisco lesbian S/M group Samois called itself lesbian feminist, and its members shared a general interest in sexuality and its expressions: 'Everybody went to the Samois meetings, everybody who was at all interested in sex. The butch-femme couples too, not just leather' (quoted in Cassidy 2004, p. 28). These spaces for discussing and living sexual practices and desires enabled many women to explore their sexuality, if not necessarily within the context of S/M (Faderman 1991, p. 263; Stein 1997, p. 142).

As with other forms of non-conformist sexual behaviour, attacks on S/M could be literal, i.e., cross over from heated debate into physical assaults on buildings and even people (Healey 1996, p. 129). This echoes how 'members of national communities can experience . . . fear and anxiety, as responses to impending loss of . . . self or community . . . and anger and hatred to those who have or will cause harm and humiliation [or are suspected to]' (Longman 2006, p. 75).

Another bone of contention was the sex radicals' emulation of gay male dress codes and sexual practices as a signifier of sexual liberation (Faderman 1991, p. 255). To a community regarding male sexuality as the root cause of women's oppression, hanky codes, tricking and dildos must have been a non-consensual slap in the face rather than the expression of a gender-bending, queer spirit of sexual adventure.[7] As two radical feminists put it:

> What have I got to do with [gay men's] promiscuous cottaging, their measuring up of one another's bodies the whole time, their exploitative, youth-based sordid little escapades. . . . And also gay men are into casual sex and cruising and sadomasochism and pornography and drag and stuff like that. I find that quite sickening. (quoted in Kitzinger 1987, p. 114)

While it is true that the reverse phenomenon, i.e., gay men borrowing the iconography and practices of lesbian sex, cannot be witnessed, the question still remains whether such eclectic imitation is proof of male identification or rather a sign that some lesbians have a broader sexual horizon than most gay men. A similar question can be raised about bisexuality, which is anecdotally more common among women than men: does this mean that some women feel the need to attach themselves to a man to gain prestige, or that women tend to be more flexible in their sexuality?

Whether it is butch/femme, bisexuality or S/M, the abyss that often opened up between lesbian feminists and 'sex radicals' meant that the former would use their dominant discourse position to limit publication of material that contradicted their beliefs and values.

PRODUCTION, DISTRIBUTION AND RECEPTION OF TEXTS

As mentioned earlier in this chapter, the ideal of the political lesbian was in fact a construct and far from being the reality of every lesbian in the 1970s. This fact is often and easily overlooked since discourse was dominated by lesbian feminists, and others were to a large extent deprived of discursive resources. Here, aspects of class and ethnicity come in as the prevailing discourse was implemented and elaborated mostly by white middle-class lesbians, a fact which could hinder women of colour to identify, or indeed be identified, as lesbian feminist (Stein 1997, pp. 58, 83). Other excluded and marginalized groups were those not sharing the lesbian feminist political agenda, especially in relation to sexuality, on which the debates increasingly centred. Thus, members of Samois, the afore-mentioned lesbian S/M group, were refused the floor and generally made to feel uncomfortable at feminist gatherings, but also had their offers of dialogue rejected and their pamphlets sold under the counter, if at all, at feminist bookshops (Califia 1981).

Apart from discrediting butches and femmes by aligning them with the opposed social formation of heterosexuals, they were also excluded as a topic from discourse (Roof 1998, p. 29). Occasionally, territorial conflicts would turn literal, e.g., in the practice, reported by Stein (1997, p. 98), of groups of lesbian feminists disrupting butch-femme couple-dancing in gay bars by engaging in circle dances. Other non-verbal cues such as gesture, body posture and gait became similarly influenced by lesbian feminist ideals of middle-class androgyny (Case 1998, p. 41). Consequently, accounts of other self-images and identities are mainly to be found and elicited in oral texts. Another source for alternative identities was the rediscovered lesbian pulp novels of the 1950s and 1960s with their often authentic descriptions of butch-femme bar culture and lesbian sex. Shunned by lesbian feminists, a number of books were re-published in the early 1980s and, with no official censorship to be taken into account, given a positive ending and less biased titles (Forrest 2005: xiv).[8]

As for other groups challenging the ideal-type model of a lesbian feminist community, physical exclusion of (perceived) S/M proponents and their texts went hand in hand with violence and intimidation through textual means:

> One of the things that went on—certainly in the eighties in Newcastle-upon-Tyne around the lesbian scene—was some very fixed ideas and victimization of people who didn't have those [lesbian feminist] ideas . . . there was a huge conflict about perceived incorrectness of sadomasochism as a sexual practice, to the point of somebody spitting in the street at other women and as they stood at bus stops . . . [There were also] letter writing [and] hate mail. (interview with Laura Donne)

The debate exacerbated when the question of legal restrictions became the focal point of the conflict: on one hand, anti-pornography fractions saw pornography as bearing the illocutionary force of hate speech (Butler 1997, p. 18), i.e., representing a kind of injurious, violent language behaviour in itself, and consequently advocated censorship in order to protect women from violence and further the lesbian feminist cause (Dworkin 1979; MacKinnon 1993). On the other hand, pro-sex groups, such as Feminists Against Censorship in the UK, focused on sexual liberation as one of the key demands of feminism, reprimanded lesbian feminists for their perceived 'sexual purity and moralism' (Halberstam 1998b, p. 136) and demanded freedom of expression. This fundamental conflict was especially central to US feminist politics in the mid-1980s and culminated in the attempts at censoring pornography by law, which were put forth by Andrea Dworkin and Catherine MacKinnon (and duly co-opted by the Christian Right).[9] The argument about pornography was also at the heart of what came to be known as the 'sex wars' of the 1980s in both the US and the UK. It was in many ways a struggle not only about material practices and political strategy but also over discursive practices: who in the lesbian community had access to the means of public discourse production such as workshop and meeting space? Who had access to means of distribution such as newsletters and magazines, and who could persuade bookstores to display and sell their texts? Who was given the chance to receive instances of controversial discourse? Ultimately, this struggle over discursive practices boils down the issues of censorship and free speech. On one hand, there are

> social practices beyond media uses of language, according to which a community disallows certain acts, including speech acts of various kinds, because they are in some way offensive to views and beliefs widely held and respected in the community.

Such acts can be censured in a number of ways, such as withholding opportunities to participate fully in community life. (Anthonissen 2008, p. 405). If discourse access was restricted for proponents of lesbian S/M, it was often done out of a feeling that those women had positioned themselves outside the acceptable framework of feminist values:

> Lesbian-feminist publications do not exist to print anything and everything anyone might wish to publish. Our publications do not print speeches and papers by Nazis. We do not print essays advocating a return to slavery, or essays justifying white or male supremacy. . . . The simple fact that we have set up Lesbian-feminist newspapers, journals, magazines, research newsletters, presses, publishing houses and bookstores in and of itself is a declaration that there are limits, that we have a set of values, and that we want to explore ideas within these values. (Hoagland 1982, p. 154)

As one instance of the effects that this line of thinking had on discourse access, feminist publisher Amazon Press stopped printing the Manchester magazine *Mancunian Gay* in 1982, as it insisted on carrying adverts for porn videos.

On the other hand, 'there is the argument from citizen participation in a democracy, which . . . asserts the crucial role of freedom of expression in the formulation of public opinion' (Anthonissen 2008, p. 406). In lesbian discourse, the battle lines in this fundamental conflict were drawn in the late 1970s and would remain firmly in place for at least the next decade. The original editor of the lesbian porn magazine *on our backs* summarized the situation regarding censorship vs. free speech, remarking that 'the politically correct dykes were controlling the lesbian media' (quoted in Cassidy 2004, p. 28). For Britain, this situation was particularly ironic, because it mirrored the state censorship enforced by Clause 28, which was introduced by Margaret Thatcher in 1988 and prohibited the 'promotion' of homosexuality by local authorities. As a way to counter attempts at silencing on the part of other lesbians, producers of internally censored material communicated to their readers that '[i]f your lesbian and gay or women's book shop doesn't have us, ask them why not and keep asking until you're happy with the answer' (Quim 1991, n.pag.).

Censorship involves a paradox in that 'the censor is compelled to repeat the speech that the censor would prohibit' (Butler 1997, p. 37), and any attempts at denying access to particular subjects therefore only establishes them as subjects in the first place, just as trying to curb modes of expression will ultimately lead to their dissipation in discourse. Also, a view of lesbian feminism as oppressive may give rise to a desire to 'transgress' the norms it is perceived to postulate. Thus, any restrictive norms, whether imagined or actually propounded, will destabilize themselves (Richardson 1996, p. 150). Perhaps this is why, throughout the 1980s, an attenuated S/M iconography became more and more central to lesbian discourse, and 'by 1989, a full 95 percent of all the feminist and gay bookstores [in the US] carried [*on our backs* porn] magazine' (Cassidy 2004, p. 29). Indeed, it seems that 'the wheel has gone completely full circle because S and M practice is now supposedly a liberating thing and magazines like *Diva* advertise it' (interview with Laura Donne). This development parallels the increasing pornographization of heterosexual images that can currently be observed in fashion shows, advertising and TV programming. At a time when (genital) plastic surgery for women is a virtual industry and retail chains market and sell make-up, high heels, g-strings and padded bras for pre-adolescent girls, marketing to lesbians has followed suit: 'in an era where teens are wearing stripper gear . . . erotic accessories are getting sweet, street-friendly makeovers,' notes a feature on girly 'sex toy art' for lesbians (Anderson-Minshall 2005, p. 25), while another lesbian magazine reports on one woman's plastic surgery make-over (Jeffs 2005). There is clearly an inhumane regulation of the female body at work here, and the fact that in 'Western' countries this development relies on hegemonic persuasion rather than physical coercion makes it no less disturbing. However, the diffusion of S/M representations in lesbian discourses seems to have had some positive effects in that it broke the silence surrounding sex in lesbian feminism. Anecdotal evidence (Faderman 1991, p. 263; Stein 1997, p. 142) also suggests that it has led to an enlarged sexual repertoire and more guilt-free pleasure for some women. (Whether this is also the case for straight women would be the topic of another investigation.)

Of course, these later developments were unforeseeable in the late 1970s, when S/M lesbians and women who lived butch/femme lifestyles first struggled for discursive space. In doing so, they reacted to what they perceived as the increasing sexual prescriptivism that had come to dominate lesbian feminist discourse and which they sought to replace with sex-positive attitudes and values as well as different models of identity. Example C dates back to 1980, about 10 years before the queer revival of butch/femme and at a point when prestige for role-playing was at its lowest in the lesbian feminist community. It is for this reason that the text is rather isolated, with hardly any other texts of the same period related to it. Still, it can be seen as implicitly quoting earlier, fictional accounts of butch/femme communities (e.g., 1950s and 1960s lesbian pulp novels) and as anticipating later texts that signal a revival of butch/femme as lesbian gender identities (e.g., the anthologies edited by Burana, Roxxie & Due 1994; Newman 1995; Kuhnen 1997). The text's location between these historical periods and against the background of a dominant lesbian feminist image of community makes Example C particularly interesting. The analysis will investigate how established models of lesbian collective identity are challenged by an author who seeks to preserve quite a different identity. In that sense, the text is also transformative because it requests that another facet be added to the image of lesbian community. As the analysis will show, the author employs irony, paradox and parody to make for an entertaining text that also communicates her model of a lesbian community. These stylistic devices, together with its detailed examples, locate Example C in the operative realm.

EXAMPLE C: 'BUTCH' (GULSTON 1980) (EXTRACTS)

Reproduced with kind permission by the author.

1 Once upon a time before the Well of Loneliness became a Whirlpool of
2 Propinquity we were a force to be reckoned with, we oldfashioned butches.
3 Even as recently as 15 years ago there were reported sightings of us at the
4 Gateways, hair short-back-and-sides, trousers impeccably pressed, shirts
5 crying scorn at Brand X, blazers smartly draped over square and capable
6 shoulders, ties knotted to a millimetre, wafting our distinctive scent of
7 aftershave lotion to entice a shy yet eager mate. Now, from the current trend
8 of lesbian literature it seems that our endangered species is wellnigh extinct
9 as boundaries blur, unisex-unisex takes over, and 'role-playing' is strictly for
10 thespians. So before we quite sink without a trace, for those who think the
11 only butch in the world is the Sundance Kid's buddy, let me try to analyse the
12 *other* kind. . . .
13 We dress *like* men (not *as* men) and smoke pipes and cigars because it feels
14 absolutely natural and right, though we would be at a loss to explain why, or
15 why as tiny children far too young to have been moulded by those
16 'environmental influences' invented by psychiatrists we instinctively loathed
17 dolls and their dreadful mini-teasets, prams and other nasty appurtenances,
18 and avidly collected soldiers, dinky cars, guns and cricket bats; why in
19 adolescence we shunned frocks, frills, makeup, jewellery, flimsy shoes and
20 all the other standard symbols of femininity which our classmates couldn't
21 wait to rip off their gymslips to get into; why many of us have a rapport with
22 fuse-boxes and wood and nails and electric drills and the entrails of vehicles;
23 why we recoil in horror from chintzy ornamental tweeness and knicky-
24 knacky clutter. Somewhere along the butch's assembly line the kind of built-
25 in domesticity which womanly women displayed as they lay gurgling in their
26 infant cots mentally redecorating their nurseries has been omitted. The sight
27 of a holey sock or a detached button is not to the butch a stirring challenge for

28   invisible repair but an urgent signal that it's time she found a skilful
29   needlewoman to share her life, especially if the lady can also cook. . . .
30   When it comes to choice of a career a butch gravitates towards the Forces
31   where her penchant for uniforms and qualities of decisiveness and leadership
32   can have full rein for, like or lump it, the butch is the type of woman to whom
33   less forceful women instinctively turn in crises. . . . She is, however, unlikely
34   to swell the ranks of hairdressing, cosmetic or lingerie saleswomanship,
35   modelling, domestic or culinary work, air hostessing, dressmaking or
36   nannying. She stoically endures the brick and concrete prisons wherein the
37   majority of livings are earned, for the typical butch's natural habitat is The
38   Great Outdoors, preferably accompanied by a bevy of pet animals towards
39   whom she is besottedly adoring and who in consequence exploit her
40   shamefully.
41   At this stage I must make it clear that I don't presume to speak for the entire
42   spectrum of butchness since that, like every other manifestation of human
43   behaviour, is in the mind of the individual. Indeed, there may be butches who
44   can lounge happily in high-rise flats, display a propensity for sheer nylon and
45   stunning frocks, whip up a souffle which would turn a cordon bleu into a
46   cordon blanche, collect Dresden Shepherdesses (in porcelain!), read those
47   astounding cryptograms whimsically called knitting patterns with one eye and
48   watch 'Coronation Street' with the other or run a hairdressing-salon-cum-
49   beauty parlour while clutching a brace of babies to their bosoms. True, I have
50   never *met* such a butch—but perhaps I just didn't recognise her. At the
51   opposite extreme was the hulking stomping beerswelling Superbutch in
52   donkey jacket and cowboy boots whom I encountered at a meeting
53   Somewhere in Ulster. Growling 'C'mere, baby, I wancha' she grabbed and
54   mauled every femme in sight, only to spoil the effect a trifle by leaving early,
55   announcing as she lumbered out that her husband and four kids were awful
56   good at lettin' her go to the meetings but she gotta get their supper now. . . .
57   Well, there you have us for what we're worth. We are rare now, collector's
58   items, perhaps indeed museum pieces. Treat us with due deference for we are
59   the sad survivors of a once proud tribe and it would be a Dodo-like tragedy
60   if the only record of us left for posterity was that monstrous celluloid libel 'The
61   Killing of Sister George.' . . . [Gentlemanly Fundamental Butches] also make
62   enchanting household novelties and desirable Christmas Gifts for the Lesbian
63   who has Almost Everything.
64   Ladies, *is* there a Conservationist in the house?

The magazine *Sequel,* in which the this text was published, was in the definition of the editors' collective a 'non-profit, bi-monthly magazine for isolated
lesbians' and was published between 1978 and 1983. Like other magazines,
such as *Arena Three* and *Sappho, Sequel* also organized meetings to help
women overcome their isolation (Neild & Pearson 1992, p. 126). It advocated issues of the women's liberation movement, the peace movement, of

animal liberation and environmental campaigns.[10] The *Sequel* collective encouraged and printed contributions (poems, stories, letters) by readers and tried to include as many aspects of lesbian life as possible. The publication lacked a general layout, so that the variety of topics was reflected in a rather haphazard appearance. The magazine was a low-budget project in which everybody worked on an unpaid basis and was distributed mainly via subscription. In 1983, the last issue was published and the collective stated that they saw themselves unable to continue due to 'lack of womanpower and lack of funds' (Sacha-Savannah 1983, p. 3). Lorna Gulston had already contributed to *Arena Three*, the 1960s UK magazine for lesbians, and her essay in *Sequel* clearly harks back to that time.

Social Actors

Example C was triggered by lesbian feminists' privileged access to discourse resources. The author clearly fears that butchness as a model of lesbian gender identity is in danger of being degraded and subsequently forgotten, and her text defines what it means to be butch, so as to strengthen that particular identity position. As such, the text follows an overall preservative strategy, although the community that the author seeks to preserve is quite different from the models propagated in Examples A and B. Unsurprisingly then, the one actor group to feature most prominently is 'butches' (line 43); a prototypical representative of that social group is given salience by being headlined. The in-group is mostly referred to by the inclusive 'we,' and this personal pronoun also features in 'we oldfashioned butches' (line 2), the metaphoric elaboration 'our endangered species' (line 8) and the quantifier 'many of us' (line 21). A stylistic variation consists of referring to the prototypical singular butch (lines 27, 30, 32; note also the ironic label 'Superbutch' in line 51). This is very similar to 'the lesbian' who featured in Example A; by scaling down the complexity of a whole group to an imagined prototypical individual, the author facilitates comprehension and identification on behalf of the reader.

Butchness as an identity is contrasted with femmeness, whose representatives are referred to as 'womanly women' (line 25) and 'less forceful women' (line 33). In accordance with the title, references to butches far outnumber those to femmes, at 34 to 7 in the actor role. There is also a slight tendency to present femmes rather than butches as the objects of others' actions (e.g., 'entice a shy yet eager mate,' line 7). Throughout the text the author constructs an environment for these two social actor groups which is characterized by behaviours, appearances and artefacts carrying culturally masculine and feminine connotations. The text opens with a descriptive listing of the characteristics of butch appearance (lines 4–7). This enumeration serves to construct a stereotypically masculine image. One half of the butch-femme dyad is thus set up. Further lists can be found when reference is made to preferred toys (line 18) and special skills (lines 21–2). Masculinity is also prevalent in a butch's professional life and her particular penchant for the armed forces (line 30). This choice of profession has been corroborated by a number of biographical accounts:

> You see, a lot of women my age, quite a lot in fact joined the Forces. . . . They went into the army. Air force maybe, mostly army and air force. And in that way, they got a group of lesbian friends. (interview with Pam Taylor; see also Kenyon 1968, quoted in Hamer 1996, p. 187; Neild & Pearson 1992, p. 52)[11]

Another figure of hegemonic masculinity (Connell 1995; Connell & Messerschmidt 2005), the cowboy or ranger, is alluded to by describing 'The Great Outdoors' as 'the typical butch's natural habitat' (line 37).[12] Irony is at work when, in contrast to her role model, she does not tame wild beasts but is seen in the company of 'pet animals' (line 38) for whom she has a soft spot. The author also draws on external, homophobic stereotypes of female masculinity which she satirizes in the description of the 'Superbutch' (line 51). This figure displays all the negative features usually ascribed to working-class men in that she lacks good manners, especially towards women ('grabbed and mauled every femme in sight,' lines 53–4), behaves without grace or elegance ('hulking stomping' in line 51, 'lumbered out' in line 55), and is generally uncouth ('beerswilling,' line 51). Her language use also marks her as stereotypically masculine and working-class (with that class marker carrying connotations of heterosexual masculinity itself; Livia 2002b, p. 91), in that she is inarticulate ('[g]rowling,' line 53) and uses nonstandard speech features like phonetic variants of the –ing suffix ('lettin','' line 56), contractions ('c'mere,' 'wancha,' 'gotta' in lines 53 and 56), substitution of adjectives for adverbs in attributive position ('awful good,' lines 55–6) and informal lexis ('kids,' line 55; see Queen 1997, p. 240). The irony here of course resides in this homophobic caricature of a butch turning out to be a heterosexual wife and mother.

In the dichotomy of femmeness and butchness, the 'femme is flamboyant, spectacular, showy, highly ornamented in dress [and] mannerisms' (Livia 1995, p. 252) while the butch betrays typically masculine interests and qualities (e.g., firmness). The two parts to the dyad are entangled in the text, which is syntactically realized through the conjunctions 'but' and 'however' as well as the adverbial '[a]t the opposite extreme' (lines 28, 33, 50–1). The author therefore not only constructs particular identity representations in opposition to each other but furthermore presents these identities as brought into being through interaction between butch and femme. Textually, such 'tactics of intersubjectivity' (Bucholtz & Hall 2004, pp. 493–4) are at work whenever one of the two social actors acts with reference to the other, as in 'the butch is the type of women to whom less forceful women instinctively turn in crises' (lines 32–3) and 'entice a shy yet eager mate' (line 7).

The author's view of a lesbian community brought into being by the mutually constitutive identities of butch and femme of course stands in stark contrast to both the utopian vision of a lesbian life that we found in Example A, as well as Example B's construction of a cohesive lesbian in-group under attack from both the patriarchy and its willing executioners, i.e., heterosexual feminists. These images of a lesbian community are hinted at when the author describes how 'boundaries blur [and] unisex-unisex takes over' (line 9). The complexity of butch-femme identities and relations was disparagingly referred to as 'role-play' in lesbian feminist writing, and the present author intertextually quotes this label by putting inverted commas around '"role-playing"' (line 9) and referring to 'the current trend of lesbian literature' (lines 7–8) as its source. On the whole, however, lesbian feminists are not granted the status of social actor, neither as a genericized group nor as specific individuals.

The distribution of social actors is quite complex as a whole; although the text focuses on butch as an identity, it also makes the point that this position is only brought into being through its counterpart, the femme. We are therefore dealing with a representation of identity that incorporates particular interactive scripts. Further, there are lesbian feminists in the background tarnishing the butch's reputation, which has the author materialize in the first person (lines 41, 49, 50, 52) to enlighten the reader about the nature of butch-femme identities. The only group not to play a role at all is men; the text largely stays true to the author's dictum (omitted in Example C) that '[m]en . . . simply do not exist for [the butch].' Given this relative importance of butches and femmes as social actors, it is not surprising that they are evaluated in detail.

Evaluation

In stark contrast to Example B (in Chapter 3), Gulston's piece does not construct an out-group to further in-group cohesion. This is all the more remarkable given that lesbian feminism had ascribed a very low prestige to butch and femme identities at the time the text was published, and lesbian feminists would therefore have been the obvious Other to protest against.

Rather, the focus is on evaluating expressions of butch and femme identities. Butches are introduced with the attribute 'oldfashioned' (line 2), which not only sets the scene for a nostalgic look back on the past, but also ironically reclaims an evaluation by others. The attribute 'old-fashioned' carries positive connotations in the text by being linked to valuable old things such as 'collector's items' and 'museum pieces' (lines 57–8). Linguistically, being old-fashioned is illustrated by instances of formal speech, which can be found throughout the text. For instance, the syntax is generally hypotactic, showing a high degree of complexity. (At the most extreme, we find a sentence that spreads over lines 13–24 and contains no fewer than 13 clauses at seven different levels.) The agentless passive in 'the majority of livings are earned' (lines 36–7) is another such instance, as is the use of Latin in 'flores omnia vincit' (omitted from Example C).

Other positive character traits are being good-natured (lines 39–40), polite as well as physically ('square and capable shoulders,' lines 5–6) and mentally strong. That 'fortitude is one of the cardinal virtues [of butches]' (Livia 1995, p. 252) is demonstrated by the possessive pronoun in 'her . . . qualities of decisiveness and leadership' (line 31). Finally, the paradigmatic butch is positively evaluated in terms of her outer appearance as well (lines 4–7). Positive evaluation is coupled with ironic self-commodification when the author closes by advertising butches as 'enchanting household novelties and desirable Christmas Gifts' (line 62). (Note that the attributes here also parody perceived feminine speech styles; see Queen 2004, p. 292).

Signs of femmeness, by contrast, are couched in negative terms. This is partly done through mental processes experienced by butches when faced with feminine signifiers ('we . . . loathed,' 'we shunned,' 'we recoil in horror' in lines 16, 19, 23) and partly through evaluative attributes like 'dreadful' and 'nasty' (line 17). It is important to note, however, that this negative evaluation does not extend to femmes themselves. Signs of femininity are rejected by the butch for herself, but often admired when shown by femmes. Accordingly, the butch's counterparts are described in neutral terms ('our classmates,' 'womanly woman' in lines 20 and 25) or with admiration for their skills ('a skilful needlewoman,' lines 28–9).

In sum, lesbian feminists hardly feature in the piece and are not evaluated at all, while femmes are described in neutral or positive terms, although their semiotics are rejected for butches. Given that butches feature predominantly as social actors and have the most uniformly positive values ascribed to them, it is no surprise to find that they are also portrayed as engaging in most, and the most varied, actions.

Actions

The author stays true to her endeavour to 'analyse the *other* kind [of butch]' (lines 11–12) in that social actors like 'we' 'she' and 'I' are seen as engaging in most actions overall (36), compared to a mere 16 for 'womanly women' (line 25) and their synonyms. As we could already see in Example B, the focal social actor is also depicted as being involved in a wider variety of actions. Most notably, butches alone can be found in attributive relational processes. These are rather numerous and help to define the actor in question (e.g., 'we were a force,' 'our . . . species is wellnigh extinct'—another expression marked as archaic—or 'many of us have a rapport,' in lines 2, 8, 21). Behavioural processes include the metaphorical 'sink without a trace' (line 10), '[w]e dress *like* . . . men' (line 13) or 'a butch gravitates towards the Forces' (line 30). In total, behavioural processes are the second most frequent type of action that the butch is seen as engaged in. Material processes such as '[w]e . . . smoke pipes' (line 13) dominate, although some can be classified as covert relational ('[butches] make enchanting household novelties,' lines 61–2), verbal ('I must make it clear,' line 41) or mental processes ('we . . . loathed dolls,' 'we shunned frocks,' lines 16–17 and 19). There are no overt mental processes, but a case for yet another covert one could be made for '[s]he stoically endures' (line 36), which is moreover an example of how the fictional butch 'exhibits moral strength and stoicism' (Livia 1995, p. 252). Occasionally, the butch is cast in the role of acted-upon entity. Although the author denies that she could 'have been moulded' (line 15) by psychiatrists and their notions, her two objects of love and admiration are indeed given power over her. Thus, a butch's pets can 'exploit her shamefully' (lines 39–40), while femmes are asked to '[t]reat us with due deference' (line 58). This closing imperative, which has the illocutionary force of a plea much rather than a command, illustrates the complex power dynamics between butches and femmes.

As for their actions, femmes are described in much less detail. Their description includes the list of actions in lines 44–9, since the author ironically infers that by no stretch of the imagination could a woman engaging in them be regarded as butch. Over two thirds of the relevant processes are material (e.g., 'redecorating the nursery' or 'whip up a souffle' in lines 26 and 45), with the rest falling into the behavioural category (e.g., 'the lady can also cook,' line 29). Given the focus of the text, no attempt is made to define femmes in relational terms or inform the reader about their thoughts and feelings in the form of mental processes. The allocation of different actions to the two social actor groups, as well as the actions themselves, is underscored by modality markers.

Modality

In line with the author's aim to give an account of butch as an identity, her actions tend to be reinforced through intensifiers. Thus, 'absolutely' stresses the following 'natural and right' (line 14), just as 'instinctively' (line 16) emphasizes the loathing experienced by the butch when faced with feminine accoutrements. A central point of the argument, namely that 'butchness . . . is in the mind of the individual' (lines 42–3) is given extra weight by the deontic 'I must make it clear' (line 41). The opposite of intensification, i.e., attenuation, can be observed whenever the bleak future of butchness under lesbian feminism is the topic. The threat of ceasing to exist altogether is mitigated by a number of hedging devices ('wellnigh extinct,' 'before we quite sink,' 'perhaps indeed museum pieces' in lines 8, 10, 58). Conditional clauses such as 'it would be a . . . tragedy' (line 59) further help to rhetorically lessen the danger. Finally, epistemic modality is used to talk about actions that are perceived as atypical of butches: 'She is . . . unlikely to swell the ranks of hairdressing' (lines 33–4) and 'there may be butches who can lounge' etc. (lines 43–4). This conveys the defining features of the author's mental model of the prototypical butch, and modality thus serves to further define butchness and give it a voice.

Interdiscursivity

There are some traces of genres and discourses from other domains, such as the fairy tale genre ('Once upon a time,' line 1) and the discourse of advertising; the author closes by praising butches as 'enchanting household novelties and desirable Christmas Gifts' (line 62) in an attempt to persuade the prospective 'buyer,' i.e., the 'Lesbian who has Almost Everything' (lines 62–3), of their value. These two are not the most prominent examples of interdiscursivity, however, since the central irony of the text relies on adapting an essentialist discourse on gender.

The stereotypical notions of gender that are often found in such discourses are mocked by the seemingly endless lists of feminine versus masculine toys, interests and skills. The gender binary thus established is naturalized through intensified attributes. The fact that the processes in lines 15–24 have a temporal sequence—illustrating the stages from early childhood to adolescence to the present—implies persistence of an allegedly pre-discursive identity. The idea that the butch's gender identity is 'natural' is also supported by lexis from the domain of biology, as in 'there were reported sightings of us' (line 3), which constructs the in-group as some natural phenomenon or species. Parallels to the animal world are further drawn by the expression 'a shy yet eager mate' (line 7), while reference to the in-group as 'proud tribe' (line 59) invokes the Euro-centric image of the 'noble savage' and once more associates butchness with naturalness. Of course, the subject position of the writer alone makes this interdiscursive strategy a prime example of queer irony: it is one of the hallmarks of essentialist discourses on gender that its proponents assume direct causal links between biological sex, gender identity and desire. Being written by a masculine woman, Example C ironically appropriates this particular discourse in order to prove it wrong, while pretending to subscribe to it.

In doing so, the author delivers a rare example of what could be called 'butch camp.' Starting with Susan Sontag's seminal essay (1964/1994), camp has usually been regarded as an attitude and behaviour mostly found in gay men. Its typical characteristics are exaggeration, flamboyance, aestheticism and (self-)irony, which often combine into a parody of stereotypical femininity. Harvey (2000, p. 243) also links camp to gay male culture and provides the following list of camp strategies and their surface features in (fictional) language:

- Paradox: incongruent registers, explicitness and covertness, 'high' culture and 'low' experience.
- Inversion: gendered proper nouns and grammatical gender markers, flouting expected rhetorical routines and established value systems.
- Ludicrism: heightened language awareness through motivated naming practices and puns, pragmatic force through sexual double entendre.

- Parody: of aristocratic mannerisms through the use of French, of femininity through innuendo, hyperbole, exclamation and vocatives.

Rather than being limited to gay men, elements of camp can occasionally also be found in the linguistic style of femmes. Consider the following typical passage from *The Femme's Guide to the Universe* (Rednour 2000, p. 124):

> Remember, *you* are the Queen, and shoes are the throne upon which you are perched, so choose that throne wisely; you wouldn't want any trash in the palace. Or, if you prefer, you are the goddess, and your shoes are the altar and are therefore to be approached only on bended knee. If your gal doesn't do religion, she will, because honey, it's worship time.

In the preceding quote there is incongruity of registers in that religious lexis is combined with colloquial expressions ('gal'); it further flouts the established system that grants higher values to all things male and masculine, there is possible double entendre ('on bended knee'), parodic reference to the aristocracy as well as hyperbole, exclamation (as shown in the stress on '*you*') and a vocative ('honey').

While engaging in a camp parody of femininity as a female is a hard enough thing to do, the 'essence of Camp, [namely] artifice and exaggeration' (Sontag 1964/1994, p. 275) seems to downright contradict the stereotype of the butch as stoic and taciturn. Indeed, it has been argued that butch performance cannot be camp, since masculinity as the unmarked and more powerful gender position is both less noticeable and, to a certain degree, more acceptable in women than femininity in men (Kennedy & Davis 1993, p. 77; but see Core 1984/1999, p. 84 on the campness of male impersonators). Nevertheless, Example C manages to do the impossible and perform butch camp. The text is paradoxical at the macro-level in that it destabilizes essentialist discourses of gender by adapting them, thus illustrating that the 'whole point of Camp is to dethrone the serious' (Sontag 1964/1994, p. 288). Linguistically, paradox is realized through the high-culture term 'thespians' (line 10)—both a pun and another instance of old-fashioned terminology—being used in the context of 1960s lesbian bar culture, indicated by the mention of 'Gateways' (line 4). While there is no gender inversion in pronouns or grammatical gender markers,[13] the text does invert established value systems: not only are the power dynamics between butch and femme portrayed as more complex than the simple dominance-submission pattern that critics accused them of; far from being 'a fake or bad copy' of heterosexual men (Butler 1991, p. 17), butches are implicitly seen as superior to them, in that they are considerate, chivalrous and good-natured.

To continue, ludicrism is perhaps the strategy least employed in the text, although there is some word play ('thespians,' line 10) as well as motivated naming ('Gentlemanly Fundamental Butches' or GFB as a label in line 61). In terms of parody, French is used less to hint at aristocratic mannerism but rather to characterize stereotypical femininity ('whip up a souffle which would turn a cordon bleu into a cordon blanche,' lines 45–6); in the butch's language use, frivolous French is replaced by the sterner Latin ('flores omnia vincit,' omitted) and Latinate lexis (e.g., '[p]ropinquity,' 'spectrum,' 'posterity' in lines 2, 42, 60). This replacement ties in with the last point: obviously, it is not femininity so much as masculinity that is being parodied. The author engages in parody when she assumes a macho pose ('especially if the lady can also cook,' line 29) or provides an exaggerated account of butch chivalry (omitted from Example C). Another form of masculinity is depicted in the caricature of the 'Superbutch' (line 51), who embodies every stereotype of working-class loutishness in her linguistic and other behaviour, but turns out to be straight.

There is a final twist to the argument in that the author, once she has claimed masculinity as the defining characteristic for the in-group, deconstructs it again, rendering any gendered subject position shifting and preliminary. The traits of hegemonic masculinity that she claims for herself (e.g., the cowboy image) are contradicted by elements that do not fit ('a bevy of pet animals,' line 38). Linguistically, there are the classical camp markers of exaggerated femininity as well, from vocatives ('[l]adies,' line 64) and exclamations (note the frequent indication of stress, as in lines 12, 13, 50, 64) to innuendo and hyperbole. Innuendo is present whenever the author merely hints at the dominant lesbian feminist discourse ('current trend of lesbian literature,' lines 7–8). The most dominant feature however is hyperbole, as in the absurd exaggeration of 'they lay gurgling in their infant cots mentally redecorating their nurseries' (lines 25–6) or the three-part attribution 'hulking stomping beerswilling' (line 51). The exaggeration in meaning is mirrored by an exaggeration in semantic complexity and overly long lists of gendered traits. At the macro-level, hyperbole is present in the exaggerated dichotomous gender stereotypes. However, the author is quick to deconstruct this binary opposition again, by admitting that butchness is in the eye of the beholder, by introducing examples that contradict the dichotomy, and by including femininity markers in her own linguistic style.

The whole text is thus camp in its 'parodic repetition of the original [that] reveals the original to be nothing other than the parody of the *idea* of the natural and original' (Butler 1990/1999, p. 41). As an example of camp, the text appropriates features associated with gay male language use and transforms them into linguistic devices used to represent reality from a specifically lesbian perspective. It is also highly interdiscursive, mixing discourses, genres and styles in what can be described as a piece of queer writing *avant la lettre* (see Chapter 5).

Metaphor

Metaphor supports interdiscursivity in the text in that it reinforces the idea of a natural, innate gender identity. In the opening paragraph, butches are

referred to as 'our endangered species' (line 8), which uses biological terminology to metaphorically conceptualize a group of social actors. The
metaphoric expressions 'mate' (line 7), 'natural habitat' (line 37) and 'Conservationist' (line 64) further corroborate Rothbart's and Taylor's (1992)
observation that there is a tendency to conceptualize social categories as
natural kinds, even if the present author does so consciously for stylistic
and argumentative purposes. Moreover, the quoted metaphoric expressions
stress the ostensible naturalness of a masculine identity. Masculinity itself
is suggested by the MACHINE metaphor realized in 'the butch's assembly
line' (line 24) and 'built-in domesticity' (lines 24–5). The author here once
more appropriates and subverts hegemonic models to implement strategies
of lesbian discourse.

Image of the Community

Example C attempts to define a particular identity position rather than foster in-group cohesiveness and therefore transports no explicit image of a
lesbian community. However, the author draws heavily on shared cultural
knowledge and therefore assumes that her piece will be read by members
of the same community as hers. Thus, the mythical past that the text conjures up is indicated by a reference (line 1) to Radclyffe Hall's classic novel
The Well of Loneliness (1928). Other hints at cultural knowledge are the
mentions of the Gateways club (line 4) and of the film *The Killing of Sister
George* (lines 60–1). The Gateways has been described in many accounts
of lesbian lives in the 1950s and 1960s (Johnston 1973, pp. 159–61; Hall
Carpenter Archives 1989, pp. 38, 55; Neild & Pearson 1992, pp. 39, 58–9,
73, 76; Groocock 1996; Hamer 1996, p. 185; Gardiner 2002), and parts of
The Killing of Sister George were filmed there.[14]

The author's statement that 'butchness . . . is in the mind of the individual' (lines 42–3) claims that gender roles are mental representations, being
'performed by the selection of particular semiotic items encoding gender
information' (Livia 1995, p. 253), such as clothing ('trousers impeccably
pressed . . . ties knotted to a millimetre,' lines 4–6), accessories ('[we] . . .
smoke pipes and cigars,' line 13) or language ('[g]rowling "C'mere, baby"',
line 53). Such semiotic markers are decoded by their recipients who, for the
sake of processing the information and creating meaning, rely on a matching socio-cultural and cognitive background. By describing butch semiotics
in great detail then, the author assumes that her readers will be able to draw
on the same prototypes and other background knowledge.

The fact that the last phrase in the text is a question provides an open ending, requiring an answer or action on part of the reader. Here, reading the
text as an instance of camp is again helpful; camp, in contrast to kitsch, relies
on an identification of the reader with the author as well as on the reader
realizing that they are indeed the intended audience (Sedgwick 1990, p. 156).
So while basically the author of Example C seems to address all lesbians, she

may in particular aim to draw in those readers who will recognize the camp nature of the text, seeking their understanding and help in the face of lesbian feminist criticism of butch/femme lifestyles. Although this criticism is only hinted at, the final question could still be read as a plea for solidarity against the silence surrounding such lifestyles in the heyday of lesbian feminism.

By implication, the lesbian community itself is seen as split into a dominant lesbian feminist group that to a large extent dictates (life-)styles, and the remnants of an earlier butch/femme culture, which the author hopes to revive/preserve. In her queer construction of lesbian genders as fluid and negotiable, she is not so much behind as ahead of her time. The advent of queer theory in the 1990s would ultimately lead to a revival of a playful version of butch/femme. In 1980, however, the largely lesbian feminist-defined community was only just beginning to be challenged. Example C was one of the earliest examples—to be followed by historical accounts such as Nestle (1981) and Kennedy and Davis (1993)—and it was unique in combining memories of the pre-Stonewall past with the vision of a queer future.

Where Example C challenges lesbian feminism from the outside, Example D does so from within. Like Examples A and B it draws on linguistic and cognitive resources that are typical of political texts and adapts them for the specific purpose of negotiating models of a lesbian community. It is therefore a prime example of a discursive event pursuing a transformative strategy. The text had a considerable impact, triggering intertextual chains that spanned more than a decade. The stand-off it engendered became paradigmatic for debates in many local lesbian communities throughout the 1980s and beyond.

EXAMPLE D: 'INTRODUCTION: WHAT WE FEAR WE TRY TO KEEP CONTAINED' (DAVIS 1981) (EXTRACT)

1   Few of us have been able to admit to anyone our interest in S/M or have been
2   able to talk about the content of our fantasies. Some of us could not even
3   admit those fantasies to ourselves. Social and political costs run very high. In
4   the public arena of the lesbian, feminist, and gay press, positive feelings about
5   S/M experiences have been met for the most part with swift negative reaction
6   and authoritative reprimands. In this context, trashing has been renamed
7   'feminist criticism,' honest dialogue has been submerged by wave after wave
8   of ideological censure calling itself 'debate,' and those of us who continue to
9   resist this treatment are accused of being contaminated by the patriarchy.
10   What we fear we try to keep contained. The intense political battle over S/M
11   is increasingly polarizing members of the lesbian-feminist community. Is S/M
12   good or evil? Is it 'feminist'? Anti-feminist? Or should we even be bothering
13   to discuss it at all?
14   This turbulence is symbolic of a much deeper, more invisible and less-than-
15   direct ideological power struggle. S/M lesbians have been accused repeatedly
16   of being a threat to lesbian-feminism as it is currently defined. In certain ways

17   this may be true. But what is the fear which lies behind the virulent attacks
18   and the apparent building of an anti-S/M mini-movement? Why the concerted
19   attempts to invalidate, to politically neutralize us? . . .
20   The wall of resistance is strong. Lesbian-feminist politics have lost flexibility.
21   Our own presence cannot be resolved by the currently accepted politics,
22   therefore some of us are being caught in the odd situation where we must,
23   politically, disown ourselves. Those of us who have been working actively in
24   the movement for many years are being labelled anti-feminist, mentally ill, or
25   worse. Lines are drawn and we find ourselves, quite unexpectedly, on the
26   'other' side. We are being cast out, denied. We become heretics.
27   It doesn't have to be this way—but the alternative is a much longer, more
28   difficult road. We must re-examine our politics of sex and power. The
29   challenge of talking personally and explicitly about all the ways we are
30   sexual, and about how our sexuality differs, is not so much destructive as it is
31   corrective, and necessary. The logical place to begin is to talk about our
32   sexuality as it is. We must talk about what we do as much as who we do it
33   with. We will find many differences among and between us, but it is better to
34   do this work than to continually hide from our fears and insecurities. We must
35   put the rhetorical weaponry aside and willingly engage each other, without
36   simply jumping ahead into a new sexual conformity. We must have precisely
37   the same dialogues about the texture of our sexuality as we have been having
38   about classism, racism, cultural identity, physical appearance and ability.
39   How do all these differences converge, to make us who we are? We must all
40   ask and answer these questions.

This extract is taken from the introduction to Samois' anthology *Coming to Power* (1981). The book represents the extended version of a 1979 pamphlet of 44 pages which was itself a reproduction of several magazine articles (Califia 1981, p. 269). The book in turn saw an updated second edition in 1987 and is therefore a good example of how texts from emerging discourses are distributed through an increasing number of outlets with ever wider circulation as the discourse gains momentum. Preceded by the 'sex issue' of US lesbian magazine *Heresies* earlier in 1981, both the booklet and the anthology faced censorship issues within the lesbian community, since most women's bookstores refused to stock and/or display them, at least not without disclaimers. Most women's bookstores were run as collectives at the time, and members who argued in favour of Samois publications apparently ran the risk of being ostracized (Califia 1981, p. 265).[15] At their most extreme, opponents did not shrink from burning copies of the book, as done publicly in London in 1983 (Chenier 2004). More moderate reactions included counter-anthologies such as *Against Sadomasochism* (Linden et al. 1982). Whatever form reactions took, declaring oneself in favour of or against the Samois position became a defining line in lesbian discourse of the 1980s. The following analysis will investigate how this position was formulated and what image of the lesbian community it reveals.

Social Actors

The first thing to note about the text is its lavish use of the first person plural pronoun 'we,' which occurs 18 times in the preceding extract alone. It is moreover the only pronoun to be found, signalling a strong focus on the community rather than on individuals or even representative prototypes (as in Examples A and C). However, the use of 'we' needs to be differentiated into an inclusive and a specific form. The extract starts by differentiating the community, introducing sub-groups like '[f]ew of us,' '[s]ome of us' and 'those of us' (lines 1, 2, 8). These sub-groups share the topical 'interest in S/M' (line 1) with which the extract begins. The next instance of 'we' in line 10, repeated from the title, is a generic one, making the general statement 'What we fear we try to keep contained.' The inclusive 'we' that comprises the whole lesbian community is repeated in line 12, but then abandoned in favour of a more specific 'we' referring to 'S/M lesbians' (line 15). Thus, the author uses both inclusion as well as differentiation and labelling her in-group. She thereby illustrates that identity can simultaneously include membership in a macro-level demographic category (lesbian), a specific cultural position (lesbian feminist, S/M lesbian) and interactional stances (someone seeking dialogue; Bucholtz & Hall 2005, p. 592).

In the extract, the Other is only ever referred to in the abstract, as 'anti-S/M mini-movement' (line 18) and '[l]esbian-feminist politics' (line 20), with the latter being rephrased as 'the currently accepted politics' (line 21). Such a tendency to abstract from actual people is strongly reminiscent of Example B and shows that both advocates and critics of S/M were members of the same discourse community. This shared community membership is expressed by the inclusive 'we,' which is taken up again in lines 28–39. Community members are said to operate in 'the public arena of the lesbian, feminist, and gay press' (line 4), with S/M critics forming 'an anti-S/M mini-movement' (line 18). The text ends on a very inclusive note, reinforcing the notion of joint community membership by talking about '[w]e . . . all' (line 39).

Evaluation

The negative evaluation of S/M by others is achieved through collocation and connotation, as when the author states that '[f]ew of us have been able to admit . . . our interest in S/M' (line 1), which is intensified in '[s]ome of us could not even admit those fantasies to ourselves' (lines 2–3). Since 'admit' collocates with negatively evaluated things,[16] S/M becomes connoted as something negative. Much of this negative evaluation, however, is quoted as something critics have said. Thus, the reader learns about 'negative reaction and authoritative reprimands' (lines 5–6) and, less explicitly, that S/M advocates have been 'accused of being contaminated' (line 9, see also line 15). 'Accused,' having equally negatively connoted collocates as 'admit,'[17] works in tandem with the ILLNESS metaphor to convey the critics' verdict.

We have seen that the middle part of the text distinguishes between different groups in the lesbian community by labelling the two sub-groups explicitly as 'S/M lesbians' (line 15) and, in abstract terms, '[l]esbian-feminist politics' (line 20). Unsurprisingly, these two groups are evaluated in opposite ways; while the in-group is said to engage in 'honest dialogue' (line 7), the out-group is presented as engaging in 'trashing' (line 6), 'ideological censure' (line 8) and 'virulent attacks' (line 17). The allegedly unfair behaviour of the Other is referred to more often, reinforcing the impression of the in-group as the well-meaning but helpless target of aggression. The split of the lesbian feminist community that Example D illustrates is almost reminiscent of George Orwell's famous parable of a revolution gone wrong, *Animal Farm*. After witnessing the brutal show trial and public executions of regime critics, the loyal horse Clover muses about how things went wrong:

> If she herself had had any picture of the future, it had been of a society of animals set free from hunger . . . all equal, each working according to his capacity, the strong protecting the weak. . . . Instead—she did not know why—they had come to a time when no one dared speak his mind, when fierce, growling dogs roamed everywhere, and when you had to watch your comrades torn to pieces after confessing to shocking crimes. (Orwell 1945/1987, p. 58)

While it is hard to believe that the aggressor and victim roles should have been so unambiguously allocated in the debates on lesbian S/M, it is clear that the lesbian community had moved away from the utopian vision presented in Example A and towards a climate of distrust, aggression and internal strife. The Samois author traces this negative development to a breakdown in communication, and indeed verbal exchange is another recurrent theme in the text. The respective lexical and semantic field comprises words such as 'discuss' (line 13), 'dialogue(s)' (lines 7 and 37), 'debate' (line 8), 'talk(ing)' (lines 2, 29, 31, 32) and 'rhetorical' (line 35). The scare quotes around '"feminist criticism"' (line 7) and '"debate"' (line 8) suggest that the Other only claims to be engaging in positively evaluated dialogue, when what they really do is engage in much more negative verbal activities such as 'trashing' (line 6). The author portrays the in-group as already attempting an 'honest dialogue' (line 7), which is recommended for the community as a whole. Despite the negative evaluation of the out-group, the piece ends on a conciliatory note, returning as it does to the inclusive 'we' and explicitly asking for everyone to re-enter the discussion to solve the community's problems: 'it is better to do this work' (lines 33–4).

The focus on verbal activity and discussion, together with the propensity to abstract from social actors, shows that neither the authors of Example B nor the present one can claim to represent the lesbian community as such. Rather, they represent a privileged elite that has the financial and intellectual means to publish, debate and generally define the topics and arguments in lesbian discourse. Voices like the one in Example C seem to be on the outside, trying to enter the discursive space set up by others.

Actions

The emphasis on verbal activity is most obvious when we look at the kinds of action found in the text. Admittedly, there is only a small number of overtly verbal processes: '[f]ew of us have been able to admit,' '[w]e must talk' and '[w]e must . . . ask and answer these questions' in lines 1, 32, 39–40. Covert verbal actions, however, are present in a number of other processes. For instance, the relational '[w]e must have precisely the same dialogues' (lines 36–7) can be classified as a covert verbal process. There are also a number of verbal processes taking the overt form of material actions, such as the instances of 'admit' and 'accuse' (lines 1, 3, 9, 15).

Like the previous texts, Example D seeks to define social actors and also argues, in metaphoric terms, for a particular future direction of the community they form. Consequently, there are a rather high number of attributive relational process types, especially for the in-group (as in 'being a threat' or 'we become heretics,' lines 16 and 26). The inclusive 'we' also features in relational actions ('we are sexual,' lines 29–30, and 'who we are,' line 39). This social actor is moreover the only one to engage in a mental process, and very prominently so, both in the title as in the 'we fear' of line 10. Both the inclusive and the specific 'we' feature in a range of material processes, too, including '[w]e must re-examine our politics' (line 28), 'we must . . . disown ourselves' (lines 22–3) and 'we find ourselves' (line 25).

The two reflexive, i.e., self-directed, processes just mentioned point to a tendency in the text to portray the in-group as either acting upon itself rather than others or indeed as the affected entity of other people's actions. Examples of the latter include '[w]e are being caught' (line 22), 'attempts to invalidate, to politically neutralize us' (line 19) and '[w]e are being cast out, denied' (line 26). By contrast, the inclusive 'we' is never acted upon. This self-imposed passivity of the in-group reinforces the image of them as the victims of aggression.

More often than not, this aggression is dealt out by abstract actors (e.g., 'the concerted attempts to invalidate . . . us' lines 18–19), if the actor is not backgrounded altogether. Indeed, agentless passives abound in the text whenever there is no inclusive 'we.' Thus, we get '[we] are accused' (line 9), 'lesbian-feminism as it is currently defined' (line 16) or '[we] are being labelled' (line 24). The fact that the out-group is only mentioned in abstract terms may not only reflect the typical style of the discourse community, but may also have been intended as a de-escalation strategy, so as to avoid direct accusations. However, negative evaluation is rather prominent at the same time.

Modality

In her attempt to describe, and find a solution to, the problems ailing her community, the author uses a number of modality markers. The problem to be solved is the discursive dominance of a particular elite and their beliefs, which makes it difficult for dissenters to articulate their contradicting beliefs and interests. The concomitant silence on parts of the community is realized by expressions of (in)ability: 'Few of us have been able to admit to anyone our interest in S/M or have been able to talk about the content of our fantasies. Some of us could not even admit those fantasies to ourselves' (lines 1–3). Epistemic use of 'can' is at work when solutions to this problem are discussed: 'Our own presence cannot be resolved by the currently accepted politics' (line 21; note how the agentless passive that backgrounds the out-group contrasts with the possessive pronoun used for the in-group). The solution deemed viable by the author is expressed by a lavish use of high-affinity deontic modals. These appear first in a question ('should we even be bothering to discuss it at all?,' lines 12–13), which is answered in the affirmative in lines 27–40. Here, the deontic modality is intensified, shifting from a mere 'should' in question form to the repeated use of a 'must' in declaratives ('We must re-examine,' 'We must talk,' 'We must put the rhetorical weaponry aside,' 'We must have precisely the same dialogues' and 'We must all ask and answer these questions'; lines 28, 32, 34–5, 36–7, 39–40). The rhetorical figure of repeating the same sentence structure ('We must [verb]') various times in a row is varied with another high-affinity, albeit epistemic, modal ('We will find many differences,' line 33) and the attribution '[t]he challenge [is] necessary' (lines 28–31). Together, these devices make for a categorical macro-proposition informing the meaning of the whole paragraph, if not text (van Dijk & Kintsch 1983); discussion is presented as the only promising solution and even as obligation, placing the text within the normative realm. Example D not only ideationally presents a worldview but also enacts a likely persuasive purpose, hoping to engage the out-group in a dialogue. It thereby acts as a vehicle for the author's values.

Ironically, the text's closing call for discussion of sexual issues across ideological lines is almost echoed by the critics of Samois. In the introduction to *Against Sadomasochism,* an anthology responding explicitly to Samois' *Coming to Power,* for instance, co-editor Robin R. Linden states: 'We desperately need to learn how to disagree and debate—vociferously, respectfully and passionately—but with a new sense of compassion and purpose' (Linden 1982, p. 11). Later on in the volume, separatist writer Sarah Hoagland puts a similar obligation on the lesbian community, claiming that 'we need to explore and develop a new language for naming and describing our sexual feelings and experiences' (Hoagland 1982, p. 155). With obligation placed so prominently on the in-group on either side of the debate, an approximation, or at least an agreement to disagree, did not seem out of reach.

Interdiscursivity

The text is not so much interdiscursive in the sense of drawing on discourses and genres not normally associated with the community, but rather intertextual, in that it ascribes evaluation and metaphors (see the next subsection) and loosely quotes others. In this sense, the author already opens up the debate she calls for.

The speech acts of others are represented by the writer by hinting at their perlocutionary effect, as in 'swift negative reaction and authoritative reprimands' (lines 5–6) and 'the virulent attacks' (line 17). Indirect speech combines with ascribed negative evaluation in the passive constructions '[we] are accused of being contaminated' (line 9), 'S/M lesbians have been accused repeatedly of being a threat' (lines 15–16) and '[we] are being labelled antifeminist' (line 24).

For parts of the text, a parallel can be drawn to Example B. In both cases, a debate is re-enacted, although the present example does so less explicitly. It is similar, however, in turning around evaluations and discrediting the Other. Where Example D differs markedly though is in that it goes beyond argument and strife by suggesting a solution to the predicament. Rather than defining the groups and drawing the lines, the author thereby tries to develop a vision for the future.

Metaphor

This future vision is in turn reminiscent of Example A. In both texts, we find the JOURNEY metaphor, realized in the present text as 'the alternative is a much longer, more difficult road' (lines 27–8). The crucial difference lies in the fact that, 11 years earlier, the authors of Example A had presented the establishment of a lesbian community as the goal of that journey. The 'journey through a night' (Example A, line 24) ends with the troubled individual being absorbed into a loving community of like-minded women. From Example D, however, it seems that the teleological vision of the Radicalesbians' earlier text is not the endpoint after all. Communities have a habit of not being as homogeneous as their most vocal members often wish them to be, so sooner or later, once the first revolutionary enthusiasm has worn off, differences in beliefs, goals and models of the self and the group are bound to surface and cause conflict.

In the present text, such conflict is realized in the form of the WAR metaphor ('[t]he intense political battle,' 'the virulent attacks' and 'the rhetorical weaponry' in lines 10, 17, 35). Given the text's focus on verbal interaction, the examples represent a version of the pervasive metaphor ARGUMENT IS WAR (Lakoff & Johnson 1980). Again, the WAR metaphor could already be found in Examples A and B. Crucially, however, the opponents in that metaphorical war have changed. It is no longer the paradigmatic lesbian who is at war with her straight environment, nor do we see lesbians engaged in conflict with heterosexual feminists or men. By the early 1980s, the battle lines run right through the lesbian community itself, with the same effects of internal silencing and subsequent feelings of guilt; compare 'she is [at] war . . . with herself' (Example A, lines 7–8) to 'Some of us could not even admit those fantasies to ourselves' (lines 2–3).

The WAR metaphor is later attenuated to a 'struggle' (line 15), and is also replaced by a metaphor of natural disaster ('wave after wave of ideological censure' in lines 7–8 and '[t]his turbulence,' line 14), which excludes human agency and hence any assignation of blame. After all, it is the author's aim to overcome the present strife; she even explicitly and in no uncertain terms demands that '[w]e must put the rhetorical weaponry aside' (lines 34–5). The destructive image of (civil) war is supplemented by the non-violent but equally uncooperative one encapsulated by the BUILDING metaphor: out-group members are represented as withdrawing into an uncommunicative fortress by 'building . . . an anti-S/M mini-movement' (line 18), whose 'wall of resistance is strong' (line 20).

It was noted previously that the text contains a number of indirectly quoted evaluations that are ascribed to the out-group in their judgement of the in-group. Metaphor aides in this process, by intertextually representing two widespread categorizations, i.e., that of S/M advocates as bearers of an illness ('[we] are accused of being contaminated by the patriarchy' in line 9, literalized as '[we] are being labelled . . . mentally ill,' line 24) and as apostates ('We become heretics,' line 26). As for the former, the metaphorical illness relates to internalized misogyny and the subsequent re-enactment of dominance and submission, a power dynamic many lesbian feminist theorists have labelled as typical of heterosexual relationships (e.g., Jeffreys 1990). The ILLNESS metaphor can be found in texts by S/M critics, while the present author extends the religious metaphor found in Example A to describe the status of S/M advocates as dissenters from the perceived lesbian feminist belief system. Similarly, Rubin claims that 'S/M has come to symbolize the feminist equivalent of the Anti-Christ' (1981, p. 216), and that '[m]inority sexual communities are like religious heretics' (1981, p. 225). This self-description elaborates the parallels between religious zealotry and revolutionary movements of all descriptions, e.g., lesbian separatism (see Chapter 5 for a discussion). Thus, Hunt (1981, pp. 88–9) likens anti-S/M lesbian feminism to Calvinism:

> There is no free will, no free choice. Nothing you can do will save you. Everyone around you except the tiny group of the elect is irrevocably depraved and destined to burn in hell. You can know who the elect are

by their certainty that they are the chosen of God and by the resolute purity of their lives. And I thought about Calvinist Geneva, policing the sex-lives of its citizens . . . and justifying these authoritarian policies with the argument that since people had no free choice in the great and hopeless struggle with sin (read 'patriarchy'), they needed to be saved from themselves.

Interestingly, the metaphors in Example D describe a problematic state of the lesbian community, with only the JOURNEY metaphor hinting at a possible solution. There is, however, no metaphor to conceptualize a better future, so that in this respect, the image of the community is mostly of its present state.

Image of the Community

We can read the text as an attempt to save the lesbian feminist community from internal strife and self-destruction. The aim seems to be to preserve its larger unity while also acknowledging difference within. The focus is exclusively on the community itself; external factors no longer play a role. It seems that other endeavours, such as building a counter-culture (as reflected in Example A) or convincing non-members of the inherent value of the community (Example B), have been backgrounded in the face of internal difficulties. Although the author tries to be conciliatory and appeal for dialogue to end the current affliction, she cannot refrain from negative evaluation of the out-group either. While rejecting unconditional unity, she still seems to believe that a unified, if heterogeneous, community is possible once sub-groups have settled their disputes, and that this larger community is a goal worth striving for. The overall discursive strategy is transformative rather than destructive or, in the words of the author, 'talking . . . about all the ways we are sexual . . . is not so much destructive as it is corrective' (lines 29–31).

Despite calls for dialogue from both sub-groups, what began with the Samois publication turned into an increasingly bitter battle during the 1980s, epitomized by central events such as the 1982 conference on the politics of sexuality at Barnard College (New York State) in the US (Faderman 1991, p. 251) and the debate about which groups would be allowed to meet at the London Lesbian and Gay Centre, which was staged in 1985 (Healy 1996, pp. 98–100). By the end of the 1980s, however, battle fatigue, increasing external pressure in the form of enforced free market economics on both sides of the Atlantic and the subsequent lack of public funds, as well as the AIDS crisis[18] brought about a renewed focus on lobbying for lesbian and gay rights in the face of a homophobic backlash. In addition, the lesbian community saw a new generation coming out, whose impact will be investigated in the following chapter.

The notion of a homogeneous lesbian community could not be maintained for more than a couple of years. The 'erasure' (Bucholtz & Hall

2004, p. 495) of intra-group differences negated the identity of many lesbians with less discourse access. Starting in the late 1970s, women whose sexual identities and/or practices differed from those purported by lesbian feminists increasingly tried to enter a discourse space set up and defined by that elite. In this context, Example C is very much written from the outside, and rather than engage in debate with her critics, the author constructs butch as an identity position by ironically drawing on essentialist discourses of gender. Lesbian feminism is merely hinted at, with the focus on butches and femmes as social actors constituting each other. Example D, by contrast, very much seeks, and already anticipates, a dialogue with lesbian feminists by quoting some of their criticisms of the author's in-group. Although the author does engage in negative evaluation of the Other, e.g., by ascribing a particular metaphor usage to them, the text closes with an appeal to enter into constructive talks which conveys a strong sense of obligation and necessity. The community is constructed as being in danger of self-destruction, and the author seeks to preserve it as a unified whole, while demanding that it be transformed to acknowledge the diversity of all its members. If we see lesbian communities as quasi-nations, the voices raised in the early 1980s unwillingly led intra-group relations to deteriorate into sectarian violence that would last well over a decade.

For the new generation entering the lesbian community in the 1990s, however, many controversial issues were more or less unproblematic. While earlier ideas still lingered, giving rise to hybrid discourses, the image of the lesbian community changed with new members attempting to set themselves apart from an earlier generation. Chapter 5 will spell out these processes, and their textual reflection, in greater detail.

5 Contradicting Voices within the Community
The 1990s

> My current lesbian friends [are] all of them younger than me, all could
> be my daughters. (interview with Vivienne Pearson)

The previous chapter outlined the challenges that were mounted to the
model of a homogeneous lesbian community that had been constructed and
reproduced in the 1970s. As a result of those challenges, models of a lesbian
community became increasingly diverse, with the 1990s showing inherent
fragmentation of, and contradiction within, lesbian communities and their
discourses. This chapter will demonstrate how 'the increasingly complex,
fragmented but also dynamic nature of collective identities' (Triandafyllidou
& Wodak 2003, p. 209) mapped out in two specific texts. The first of these
is an interview conducted with Sheila Jeffreys (see Example B in Chapter 3)
for one of the first lesbian lifestyles magazines to be published in Britain. The
community is there shown as marked by a quasi-generational conflict, even
though the interview partners are actually of the same age. Reversely, the then
twenty-year-old author of Example F, a text from a personal homepage, advocates lesbian separatism, a political strategy that dates back to the 1970s and
will be discussed in some detail in the present chapter. However, both texts
reflect the ongoing commercialization and individualization of lesbian communities in the UK and the US and are therefore paradigmatic of the decade.

SOCIO-POLITICAL BACKGROUND: ISSUES AND ARGUMENTS

As outlined in the previous chapter, the late 1970s and beginnings of the
1980s saw an emerging discourse on the sexual aspects of lesbian identity as
a reaction to what was perceived as the desexualizing tendencies of 1970s
lesbian feminist discourse. During the 1980s, these two discourses became
intertwined in a heated debate sometimes referred to as the 'sex wars' (Ashton 1996, p. 164; Healey 1996) or, less belligerently, as the 'sex debates'
(Stein 1992, p. 48). As in any war, both literal and metaphorical, there were
no winners. Rather, a number of historical factors led to the struggle being

backgrounded, if not resolved. Whether it was the AIDS crisis and the subsequent renewed collaboration and closeness between lesbians and gay men in the face of a pandemic (Stone 1988), or the external threat of increasingly conservative politics in the Reagan/Thatcher era, or sheer exhaustion after a decade of in-fighting, the fact remains that the debates on lesbian sexuality began to abate towards the end of the 1980s. (In Europe, they lingered on for some more years.) By then, the quasi-nationalist utopia of a homogeneous lesbian community had been profoundly shattered.

The controversies over sexuality experienced a revival of sorts with the emergence of transgender activism. Where in the 1980s, the issue had been whether to allow boy children and S/M lesbians into women's spaces such as the Michigan Womyn's Music Festival, the conflict in the 1990s centred on access for transgendered women and, sometime later, butch lesbians-cum-transmen. Some lesbian feminists defined transsexuals as individuals who suffered from such deep-rooted internalized homophobia as to undergo self-mutilation (Raymond 1979; Jeffreys 1996). While many lesbian feminists were appalled by the stereotypical images of femininity and masculinity often presented by transgendered persons (be they drag queens and kings, transvestites or transsexuals), transgender activists were injured and routinely infuriated by the others' refusal to acknowledge the complexity of their gender identity. Both sides accused each other of ascribing to an essentialist notion of gender that led to gender-adaptive surgery on the one hand and disclaimers at women's events ('for biological women only,' 'for women-born women only' etc.) on the other. Such reproaches were flung at the respective Other despite the fact that lesbian feminists criticized the very idea of gender as expressing heteropatriarchal relations of dominance and submission, and quite a few transgender persons took a social constructionist view of gender (Bornstein 1994; Wilchins 1997b; Gloria G. 2001).

The new decade started with the publication of Judith Butler's *Gender Trouble* (1990/1999), which heralded the advent of queer theory (see also Chapter 2). Conceived and first disseminated in academia, queer theory set out to 'deconstruct . . . normative categories of gender and sexuality, exposing their fundamental unnaturalness' (Kitzinger & Wilkinson 1994, p. 452). Both gender and sexual identity are seen as located on a continuum instead of forming binary oppositions. Gender becomes a series of reiterable performative acts, which are characterized by 'parody, pastiche, and . . . carnivalesque reversals' (Kitzinger & Wilkinson 1994, p. 454). In queer theory and queer politics, gender and sexuality are seen as self-fulfilling prophecies in that they quote previous gender performances—language use, body posture, leisure time and consumption practices etc.—and by the same token reproduce a model that has no original instance. According to this line of thinking, 'identity is performatively constituted by the very "expressions" that are said to be its results,' and attributes of gender and sexuality 'effectively constitute the identity they are said to express or reveal' (Butler

1990/1999, pp. 33, 180). Such a discursive construction of gender and sexuality can be endlessly repeated, but recontextualization or 'displacement' will change the meaning of the gendered signifiers, affording potential subversive readings.

Although not denying materiality, the notion of performativity and the role discourse plays in constructing and reinscribing identities extends to biological sex, arguing that meanings and connotations of sexed bodies are only constructed and disseminated in discourse, as instantiated in text and talk. The notion of gender, and even sex, as a reiterable system of signs and therefore performative and fluid was met with feminist concerns that women in general (Richardson 1996, p. 146) and lesbians in particular (Vance 1987, p. 30) were made invisible, even obliterated, through deconstruction. Recognizing this problem inherent in constructionism, Butler herself acknowledges 'the sign's strategic provisionality,' i.e., 'the political necessity to use some sign [e.g., the identity 'lesbian'] . . . in . . . a way that its futural significations are not foreclosed' (Butler 1991, p. 19). This yields the notion of 'post-modern' lesbians, i.e., 'people occupying provisional subject positions in heterosexual society' (Phelan 1993, p. 779).

Another often-voiced criticism is queer theory's academic and, as some critics claim, elitist nature that ignores the material factors impacting on people's lives. As such, queer theory is accused of becoming self-centred and detached: 'queer strategy . . . replaces resistance to dominant cultural meanings of "sex" with carnivalesque reversals and transgressions of traditional gender roles and sexualities, which revel in their own artificiality' (Wilkinson & Kitzinger 1996, p. 377). Indeed, queer theory finds its most obvious expression in the practice of camp (see Example C in Chapter 4).[1] As the notions of irony and parody are hallmarks of queer theory, it is worthwhile quoting an early word of caution: taking Nazism as an (admittedly extreme) example, Hoagland (1982, p. 159) rightly states that 'the parody still validates Nazism by perpetuating the language game, the conceptual framework, and thereby allows those who work with deadly earnest toward fascism . . . to live in an ideological framework necessary for their growth and development.' Seen as such, parody and irony are similar to negation in that they are frame-preserving (Lakoff 2002), i.e., they still activate the mental models they seek to subvert.

Outside academia, a trickled-down version of queer theory meant, first and foremost, sexual transgression and, more generally, a resexualized notion of 'lesbian.' This resexualization of lesbianism as witnessed in the 1980s debates on pornography, butch-femme roles, sadomasochism and bisexuality (see Chapter 4) were sanctioned by queer theory and resulted (in some local communities at least) in a decidedly hedonistic lifestyle. Among a new generation of lesbians who had come out only in the late 1980s, some saw 1970s-style lesbian feminism as an old-fashioned, essentialist and restricting movement, and positioning oneself in opposition to it became a performative act defining a new in-group. Younger lesbians set themselves up in opposition to the codes and values of older feminist lesbians and aligned themselves more closely with urban youth culture, formulating new lesbian styles (Luzzato & Gvion 2007). In this metaphorical mother–daughter conflict, the balance between symbiosis and separation was definitely tipped towards the latter, with the queer daughters 'opposing their own values to the model presented by the [lesbian feminist] mother, rebelling against her hold on them, creating a new model in reaction to hers' (Wodak & Schulz 1986, p. 90). The opposing models are sketched, albeit indirectly, by Norah Vincent (who we will meet again in Chapter 6) in an early text titled 'Beyond lesbian' (1996):

> The bimbo character [in a lesbian screenplay] was a caricature of lesbian youth as seen through the eyes of the ossified gerontocracy. The writer's message was clear: Don't be young, don't accept beauty, don't trespass, don't be yourself; instead, be disgruntled and carping, self-deprecating in your dress and demeanor, avoid anything that passes for accomplishment or assimilation in the mainstream, be a real lesbian and sing along.

As Healey puts it: 'It is "Nanny" . . . who we are criticising when we write off lesbian feminist opinion' (1996, p. 204; but see Carraher et al. 1996 for young women aligning themselves with lesbian feminism).

This breaking away from the morally superior, repressive and sexually prohibitive symbolic mother that feminism came to represent (Creet 1991, pp. 138, 143) was often met with politicized expressions of hurt and anger (or emotionally charged political criticism): sexual liberalism is seen by its critics as a 'marginalization and demonization of . . . lesbian-feminism' (Walters 1996, p. 836) and as being co-opted by patriarchy. Despite Butler's extensive discussions of theorists like Simone de Beauvoir, Luce Irigaray, Julia Kristeva or Monique Wittig, queer theory as the intellectual underpinning of queer activism is accused of relying on the work of male theorists such as Derrida, Lacan and Foucault and of centring, in its activist form, on 'gay maleness [for the] reconstruction of queer as radical practice' (Walters 1996, p. 846). At worst, younger lesbians were regarded as denouncing the goals the older generation had fought for and as traitors acting 'in the interest of the male ruling class' (Jeffreys 1990, p. 314). Sexuality and politics still seemed irreconcilable, at least in the conceptual framework of a 1970s-style discourse accusing queer theory of de-politicizing notions of lesbian identity and community (Raymond 1989). However, proponents of a 'liberal' lesbian discourse claimed to redefine, rather than abandon, politics, thus acknowledging lesbian feminist ends, if not its means.

Since the 1990s, communities have increasingly been regarded as 'based on the ways in which individuals imagine them rather than [as] identifiable entities' (Queen 1997, p. 235). If there are no longer any transhistorical, essential qualities and characteristics which constitute identity and membership in a particular community, communities are but imagined and discursively constructed. As a result, the concept of a pre-discursive, unified identity is abandoned in favour of multiple identities cutting across each other in their permanent alteration. In its view of gender and sexual identity as fluid concepts that are continuously constructed and performed in discourse and material practices, queer theory is radically anti-essentialist. According to queer theorists, 1970s discourse naturalized lesbian identity as an inherent, fixed and ahistorical component in the individual and as a basis for the formation of a collective group identity.

> [Consciousness-raising was about] the whole essentialist stuff which is absolutely taboo now. But we all come from that and that [we went through that process] was certainly a prerequisite for abolishing it now . . . and the feminine that was supposed to come out of it had a lot to do with tender and soft and being close to nature. Yes, that's true. Flowing and kind and peaceful. This image was potentially contradictory because we were also fighting and . . . learning self-defence. (interview with Vera Vaizek)

Ironically, lesbian feminism and queer theory start out from the same anti-essentialist premise, in that they both regard gender as a social construct. Lesbian feminism conceives of gender as a heteropatriarchal invention propagated to maintain the dominance–submission relations between men and women. This is not too far away from Butler's notion of 'the heterosexual axis along which gender subordination is secured' (Butler 1997, p. 121). As a consequence, queer theory's thrust to de-essentialize the links between sex and gender does hold some appeal for lesbian feminism (Wilkinson & Kitzinger 1996, pp. 378–9). However, for lesbian feminists, gender, understood as patriarchal notions of masculinity and femininity, is an eroticized binary difference, which becomes conflated with harmful inequality (Jeffreys 2003, p. 44). In effect, every erotic desire and/or sexual practice that centres on dominance and submission becomes defined as 'heterosexual,' and it is this kind of sexuality that reproduces gender as defined by lesbian feminists (Jeffreys 1996). Queer theory, on the other hand, allows for a range of genders and subsequent queerness in heterosexual relations. While not 'homosexual' in the lesbian feminist sense of eroticizing sameness, 'queer heterosexuality' captures a fluid understanding of difference where unstable gender identities and flexible practices allow for breaking the patriarchal mode that ails the majority of relationships between people of different biological sexes.[2]

Apart from queer theory and its street versions, the second major factor in the socio-political context of 1990s lesbian discourses is the changing economic climate and conservative backlash that had persisted throughout the Reagan/Thatcher decade. Lower taxes and less public funding, privatization and a focus on individual wealth creation through investment had profound effects on a lesbian community that had, for the better part, not only espoused a collectivist ethos, but also crucially relied on public funding for projects and space. The general paradigm shift away from collectivity and towards individualism that began in the 1980s led to a relative decentring of the lesbian community and had many women redirect their focus (Stein 1997, p. 131). Under the impression of the individualistic ideology of the day, it must have seemed tempting to replace the downwardly mobile life in the lesbian feminist 'subsistence community' (Wolf 1979, p. 101) with the prospect of a more comfortable existence, even if that ultimately came at the cost of less solidarity. Cox (1993, p. 63) describes such effects of hegemony in a very vivid simile: 'Hegemony is like a pillow: it absorbs blows and sooner or later the would-be assailant will find it comfortable to rest upon.' On a material level, withdrawing into the private sphere was, in Britain, facilitated by Thatcher's policy of promoting private home ownership and enabling women to buy property in their own name without the signature of a male guarantor. In 1980s Britain, local friendship communities evolved around refurbishing newly bought houses, showing that housing as a social practice is a crucial element in community-building. Yet its significance for lesbian communities has changed dramatically, from enabling collective living, where local communities are instantiations of imagined communities, to sparking practices within local communities without necessarily activating models of wider imagined ones, to an expression of wealth, individualism and coupledom (see Chapter 6).

As noted previously, many queer theorists identify essentialist notions of gender as the basis of lesbian identity in 1970s discourse. Furthermore, some consider it, and particularly separatist discourse, as an expression of nationalism, especially with regard to the idea of the 'lesbian nation,' which was sometimes mystified by the invocation of prehistoric matriarchal cultures (Valeska 1975/1981, p. 25; Duggan 1992, p. 16; Kappeler 1992, p. 11). At their heyday in the 1970s, separatists attempted to live in all-women communities as much as possible to gain complete financial, sexual, social and cultural independence from men. However, the new paradigm and politics ushered in during the 1980s initiated a shift from socialist-inspired collectivism to consumerist individualism. As a consequence, lesbian separatism had been reduced to a fringe phenomenon by the end of the decade. Apart from the wider socio-economic framework and internal erosion, a number of external factors contributed to the decline of separatism: the AIDS crisis led to renewed collaboration with gay men, and many separatists who were active in the environmentalist and peace movements saw some of their causes evaporate with the changing face of world politics in the late 1980s. For instance, Healey (1996, p. 78) outlines how the feminist protests at UK cruise missile base Greenham Common, which had begun in 1983, gave rise to separatist camps that dissolved when the missiles were destroyed at the end of the Cold War in 1989.

Separatism is practised to a degree whenever women seek to gain 'a room of one's own' to further political causes. In the highly politicized lesbian discourse of the 1970s, separatism was seen by many as the logical extension of feminism. Considering the patriarchal conditions women continue to be subjected to and the consequent suffering inflicted on them, it seemed logical to the advocates of separatism that all women would have to be lesbians and all lesbians separatists (Lettice 1987, p. 109). Women who maintained relations of any kind with men were seen by separatists as unable to dissociate themselves from a society structured in terms of heterosexuality and masculinity. The final goal was to overthrow patriarchy, and the way by which this goal would be reached was through a total withdrawal of female energy from men. Based on the notion of 'parasitism of males on females' (Frye 1978, p. 33), the dominant male system was thought to collapse when it was denied the energy it lived on. Any form of co-operation with men, as proposed by socialist feminism and women bonding with gay men, or even superficial contact with men runs counter to the idea of separatism because '[w]hen we engage in a system . . . we contribute by consensus to its underlying structure even when also challenging it' (Hoagland 1987, p. 25).

However, separatism was not meant to stop at withdrawal and exclusion (Geraldine T. 1988, p. 4). The separatist movement was to go further and create a veritable female/lesbian counter-reality, re-defining such broad concepts as 'ethics, language, sexuality, culture' (Geraldine T. 1988, p. 5). This counter-society was meant to entail a counter-discourse empowering the women who participated in it. Separatist communities can be likened to dissident national groups; although establishing new nation states does not usually aim at destroying the former host state, the move is similar to separatist withdrawal because

> [i]f [marginalized groups] can distinguish themselves culturally from their exploiters and oppressors, it is very much to their advantage to hive off politically [into] their own sovereign territory. Here they can protect their development . . . and here their own dialect is spoken with pride. (Gellner 1997, p. 35)

Separatism in its ideal form was meant to be woman-centred, prioritizing women's needs and concerns in terms of the allocation of energy. In short, 'it was not so important to be anti-men as it was to be pro-women' (Doyle 1996, p. 184). This woman-centred approach had one major drawback, however, in that it saw women's lives as the 'subject of revolution' (Lorde & Star 1982, p. 67), thus shifting the onus of effecting societal change onto women.

The feminist aim to abolish patriarchy and the focus on women were taken literally by separatists, entailing concrete steps to change everyday life. Before outlining these changes, however, it should be mentioned that many lesbians found their social, sexual and working lives to revolve around women, not as a conscious choice but as a logical result of their interests. These women did not, in spite of the separatist tendencies in their lives, necessarily identify as separatists:

I think that separatism was regarded as something positive by many, many women in the late 1970s. By older as well as by younger women. That was certainly seen as something which enabled women to experience themselves completely independent of everything. . . . Among my friends there were a lot who had very separatist tendencies. But in my immediate circle of friends there was nobody who really pulled it off. (interview with Ina Feder)

I remember at that time that I ended up—I worked with women, I did political work with women, I socialized with women and not because I hate men but just because of what my interests were. My relationships were with women . . . it was an ideal, I suppose . . . you have to have space to write things, you have to generate discourse and language. I think separatism was about trying to find out. So many women thought it was the solution when separatist and women only communities were just as fraudulent as every other community ever is. (interview with Erica Jones)

Every manifestation of patriarchal discourse—including not only spoken and written texts but also music, paintings etc.—is to be removed from the life of a lesbian separatist. This seclusion led to self-reliance and the emergence of women's housing and work co-operatives in the 1970s. While women in urban areas formed task-oriented collectives (e.g., a publishing collective), residential separatist communities were often geographically located in the countryside as contact with men could be more easily avoided there (Faderman 1991, p. 238; Shugar 1995, p. 57; but see the Urban Amazons collective in 1980s London):

I knew and still know women who really withdrew to the country, because you can't [live as a separatist] in the city. In Mendocino in California, which I visit often, there is still a women's community, they live on their fenced-off piece of land with guns. I'm not sure if they ever went that far in Europe. (interview with Ina Feder)

Additionally, 'women's land' seemed to promise a closer relation with nature, which was perceived as the paradigmatic female raped by male power and technology and therefore became an important topic in separatist discourse. However, the hard physical work involved and lack of skills and experience of previously urban separatists meant that most separatist country communities lasted less than 10 years (Faderman 1991, p. 239). For a certain period of time, however, separatism or at least a woman-centred life was the ideal for many women.

I used to have a friend who lived in a women's house and they definitely didn't invite men into their house, and any work that they had done on the house was either done by themselves or by women. . . . I thought it was very admirable. It was a nice ideal I thought. (interview with Paula Kingsley)

Many texts from the period can be said to advocate a form of quasi-separatism as the 'purest' form of lesbian feminism (e.g., Example B). The notion of purity has religious overtones and indeed, it has been noted that '[s]eparatism is to feminism what fundamentalism is to Christianity' (Dixon 1988, p. 69). This analogy hints at the intersection of religious and separatist lesbian discourse, which is corroborated by the use of religious terminology in a radical feminist and separatist context, e.g., '[m]any of us make an annual pilgrimage to Michigan [Womyn's Music Festival]' (Brunet & Turcotte 1986, p. 42) and '[radical lesbian feminism is] a "thou shalt not" litany of inverted sexual repression' (Ashton 1996, p. 169). These and other examples make it possible to infer a metaphoric concept of separatism that finds its expression in a word field comprising, amongst others, the terms 'conversion,' 'faith,' 'heresy,' 'pilgrimage,' 'saint,' and 'zeal.' While it is noteworthy that the religious metaphor is especially drawn upon by opponents of separatism, negatively connoted use still points to the concept's relevance in the context of separatism. The reasons for this conceptual alignment of separatism with religion are for the better part historical: many activists in the women's movement of the 1970s had been politicized in the civil rights movements of the previous decade, which in the US saw a substantial in-pour of white Christian women from the South of the country (Shugar 1995, p. 7). Many of these women became frustrated with the chauvinism of the male civil rights activists and broke away to form a more women-centred movement. Although the links are certainly indirect, aspects of a religious worldview are likely to have influenced radical feminist and separatist discourse. On a wider scale, the legacy of the Pilgrim Fathers' puritanism, which cannot be disregarded in any discussion of US politics, also impacted on separatism. What then are the shared concepts between the political separatist and a religious movement?

The Puritan 'wish to establish a holy community' (Swaim 1993, p. 8) in which 'a genuinely ethical and spiritual life could be lived' (Bellah et al. 1985, p. 29) is directly reflected in the desire to establish lesbian-separatist communities as spaces where women could be creative and regain energy unhampered by patriarchy. The religious element first comes in the form of 'deified womanhood,' with separatist 'lifestyle [being one] of attempted purity . . . an exhausting act of faith' (Dixon 1988, p. 69). The newly converted member of either community may experience 'almost daily visions of a cathartic kind, with the . . . religious intensity of those experienced by Paul on the road to Damascus' (Dixon 1988, p. 78).[3] This corroborates Spender's (1980, p. 130) point that the term 'conversion' originally belongs to the religious domain and is metaphorically mapped onto the feminist domain.

Internal consciousness-raising and the outwardly directed aim of separatist communities to overthrow patriarchy by their very existence find their equivalent in Puritan ideology as 'inwardly, a radical analysis of the self, and outwardly, a radical critique of the social order' (Damrosch 1985, p. 21, quoted in Swaim 1993, p. 296). Such a dual nature entails a blurring of the boundaries between the private and the public. Indeed, it is one of the basic beliefs of lesbian feminism that the 'private is political' and therefore public.[4]

> That [the private is political] was *the* revolutionary thought of feminism in the 1970s. How the private was political then, that was . . . a very difficult process of learning and finding out. (interview with Vera Vaizek)

To secure political effectiveness, the community in either case had to be stable and coherent, consisting of 'separatist, congregational, independent saints' (Swaim 1993, p. 132). Thus, Puritan or separatist values came to form a 'fixed, limited, and unalterable universe' (Miller 1961, pp. 365–6, quoted in Swaim 1993, p. 5), with its respective inhabitants being characterized by ardent faith and inner bonding.

Since adopting a separatist way of life represented a difficult break in many women's lives and 'people's adherence to an institution is directly proportional to the severity and painfulness of the rites of initiation' (Bourdieu 1991, p. 123), loyalty to the movement was secured to some extent. Yet social control was exerted to guarantee uniformity, up to the point of separatists being regarded by dissidents as 'social policemen' [sic] (Doyle 1996, p. 184). This again has a parallel in what Moscovici (1988/1993) has observed for Puritanism, stating that 'Puritan movements . . . had to inculcate in their devotees an ever-present discipline, with all that this implied: an often difficult initiation, a strict control by coreligionists, asceticism in everyday life, yet also reciprocity in the matter of duties' (p. 187). Such a stance can lead to the self-righteousness that Weber (1920/1930, p. 166) has observed for ascetic religious groups: 'thankfulness for one's own perfection by the grace of God penetrated the attitude toward life of the Puritan middle class, and played its part in developing [its] formalistic, hard, correct character.'

Such an attitude usually renders the community a target of criticism and ridicule to the outside world. Thus, Puritans 'earned their neighbors' enmity for divisive scrupulosity and hypocritical self-righteous zeal' (Cohen 1986, p. 4, quoted in Swaim 1993, p. 1). Similarly, separatist communities were accused by other lesbians of dividing the women's movement as well as being elitist, escapist, racist and, at worst, fascist. The last epithet represents an intertextual link to debates around sadomasochism (see Chapter 4).

> I know of endless discussions at women's conferences at what age boys would be allowed in the crèche, a bit of that stuff at women's music festivals—terrible, terrible things which would find you saying 'Hang on, this is what the Nazis did to the Jews in the Second World War, they treat boys in the same way,' coralling them off and out. (interview with Erica Jones)

Constant 'hostility, disparagement, insult and confrontation' (Frye 1978, p. 32) led to further withdrawal, the subsequent development of a quasi-religious notion of martyrdom and, since 'a segregated community thrives on persecution' (Bainton 1970, p. 109, quoted in Swaim 1993, p. 303), to an even stronger bonding within the community.

Yet over the years isolation became stifling and with the changing image of separatism from utopia to counter-productive extremism, the outward pressure proved too strong. The separatist movement found itself cornered and gradually began to turn its energy and aggression inside, i.e., against its own members. Oppressive behaviour, explained as 'false consciousness' by separatist theory, reared its ugly head in the form of racism or class bias (Shugar 1995, pp. 94–9). This was a cruel reality for separatists, many of whom 'felt they were free of the behaviours that oppressed them' (Shugar 1995, p. 95). On another level, splits were effected by the debate over the question whether boy children should be allowed in separatist communities, a debate which hurt and estranged many women (Shugar 1995, p. 101; Stein 1997, p. 119):

People had a horrible time because they had a boy child. Other lesbians in Todmorden gave them a horrible time.[5] (interview with Lola di Marco)

There were really wild discussions, like at the Michigan Womyn's Music Festival, whether little boys should be admitted. . . . Many separatists or women with separatist tendencies who had artificial insemination or artificially inseminated themselves—they would not have themselves inseminated—I think 70 or 80 percent of them had boys and not girls [see also Stein 1997, p. 132] . . . and what's so strange about that is that they have their boys and as long as they were infants that fact could be disregarded. [But] when they grew older and when [the mothers] were the ones who went to the music festivals where there were restrictions for boys over seven not being admitted, those women then started to undermine those laws because suddenly they themselves were in the situation of what do to with their children. (interview with Ina Feder)

I remember very clearly a lesbian [who] lived in a house with a gay man. He was a friend of mine [and] he'd been one of their pool of donors so she got pregnant. . . . It was always agreed that if it was a boy [the sperm donor] would bring up that child, because she wouldn't want to bring up a male child. . . . I remember I had to go round to [their house] that night when the kid was born and it was like [the mother's partner] came in, slammed the door and said 'It's a bloody wanker!' (interview with Erica Jones)

This debate paradoxically inverts hegemonic discourse with its higher value placed on all things male and masculine. It has been argued that separatist discourse 'shifted the emphasis of blame . . . from a social ill (sexism) to its perceived sole agent (men) . . . [making] the leap from social institution to biology' (Shugar 1995, pp. 41–2). Indeed, separatist discourse was perceived by some of its participants as being centred on men, with 'time and energy [being] spent in endless discussions on the evils of men' (Dixon 1988, p. 81). We can here draw another parallel to (anti-)religious movements in that atheism is not a renunciation of faith or even independence from faith-based ideologies; it is inverted faith. As such, 'atheist' prioritizing of men in the form of anti-men feeling or even violent men-hating contradicts the separatist ideal of always putting women first.[6] If 'the reference of separatism is patriarchy' (Geraldine T. 1988, p. 5), then 'men manage to exhaust us even in their absence' (Dixon 1988, p. 82). Given this focus on men, it is perhaps not surprising that many separatists later, and despite their earlier condemnation of men and living with them, went back to heterosexual lives (Stein 1997, pp. 161–2):

> Turning straight, that was certainly absolutely yucky back then and how terrible, although of course it happened then as it does now. Only I think that a woman who had lived in a lesbian context for a while and then decided to get involved with men again after all, that she would have been excluded much more vehemently from her lesbian networks than this would perhaps be the case now. (interview with Ina Feder)[7]

Blurring the boundaries between the public and the private could take the form of rigidly prescribing political convictions as well as social and even sexual behaviour. Due to external and internal pressure as well as the development of rigid dogmas, the separatist community and its discourse, just like its Puritan counterpart, became 'a system for social and personal control, homogenizing its members' (Swaim 1993, p. 304). The extremism that separatism was prone to is even acknowledged by separatists themselves; Hoagland (1982, p. 153) concedes that 'political correctness has been used coercively among Lesbian-feminists, deeply and inexcusably hurting many wimmin.'

As a result, a growing number of women in the late 1980s were of the opinion that separatism had 'stopped being a crazy, wonderful experiment and [had become] a dogma' (Doyle 1996, p. 185). Separatism had started to implode, and although small communities still existed in the 1990s, their members deplored the hedonistic and apolitical nature of contemporary lesbian communities, the want of a separatist network and the overall isolation and censorship separatists saw themselves as suffering from (*Bev Jo, Strega & Ruston 1990; *Ziggy n.d.). Separatism may have survived into the 1990s and even beyond, but it has diminished to a marginal phenomenon. Full-time separatism as a political strategy seems to have failed. As radical feminist Valerie Solanas would have it:

Dropping out gives control to those few who don't drop out; dropping out . . . plays into the hands of the enemy; it strengthens the system instead of undermining it, since it is based entirely on the non-participation, passivity, apathy and non-involvement of . . . women. (quoted in Johnston 1973, p. 20)

Nevertheless, separatism was still propagated in the 1990s. The analysis of Example F will show how features of 1970s discourse are combined with devices more typically found in contemporary consumerist discourses. The fact that those later, hybrid texts on separatism were distributed through emerging electronic media points toward the changing practices of text production, distribution and reception in lesbian communities.

PRODUCTION, DISTRIBUTION AND RECEPTION OF TEXTS

In the 1990s, lesbian discourse communities took two routes to textually construct and mediate their group and individual identities: while some sought to harness commercial publishing for lesbian interests, other went the opposite way and expanded independent publishing, with the latter strategy greatly helped by the emergence of new electronic media. As far as magazines are concerned, commercial lesbian publishing began in the early 1990s, when the US nationwide magazine *Curve* (then *Deneuve*) was founded in 1991. This was followed by its competitor *Girlfriends* magazine in 1994 (defunct since March 2006) and, in 1993, its UK counterpart *Diva,* which is published by the same company that had launched *Gay Times* ten years earlier. Their predecessors were short-lived magazines such as *Lip* (see Example E) and *Shebang* in the UK. While the former relied on word-of-mouth advertising and distribution by the writers themselves, *Shebang* was a free magazine distributed with the *Pink Paper* (Simmons 1997, p. 24).

While the first nationwide glossy magazines seem far removed from the low-budget self-publishing of the 1970s and 1980s, it is worth noting that more politically oriented alternative publications persisted at a local level until well into the 1990s. One example is *Gutter Girls* magazine, which was published between 1993 and 1997 in Lancaster/UK. Founded by a group of students and academics from the local university's women's studies department, its four issues a year were sold at a low price at an organic food cooperative. The pages were photocopied and partly hand-written, featuring drawings, poems, and articles and interviews on political, cultural and spiritual topics, but no advertisements. It is this kind of alternative, independent publishing that was taken up by women who did not wish to go down the commercial route. Lesbian separatists obviously fell into this category. Ever since the 1970s, separatists had had few media outlets to disseminate their ideas, either because their ideas were perceived as too radical to find an audience or because separatists themselves preferred to keep a splendid isolation:

> A few feminist presses . . . had been established and did publish separatist material; for the most part, however, separatists passed copies of their works among friends and published their own journals . . . even when access to mainstream publishers or the media was available, separatists often refused these routes because of their inability to control the makeup of the audience or an unwillingness to provide profits for what were perceived to be male-dominated organizations. (Shugar 1995, p. 38)

Indeed, many sources used in this book that relate to separatism are newsletters and pamphlets hidden away in archives and reserved explicitly 'for female readers only' (these sources are marked by an asterisk). Within the lesbian community, however, separatists achieved almost paradigmatic status for a time. As long as their model of a homogeneous in-group could be maintained, separatists were highly organized and the fact that many separatist women were university-educated meant that they were also a vocal minority, often setting topics in lesbian discussion and ensuring that their views were heard (Stein 1997, p. 119).

Besides education, another factor that contributes to the central importance of publishing in separatist communities is the links between ascetic religious and separatist groups in terms of genres. Thus, the 'intense introspection' (Swaim 1993, p. 137) typical of Puritan communities was also recognized by separatists who felt 'insistent pressure . . . to repent' (Dixon 1988, p. 69). Constant reflection and meditation on either religious or political topics manifests itself in the importance of writing as a spiritually, politically and socially relevant process. Such Foucauldian *écriture de soi* and its pre-occupation with one's own past brought about the genre of the (spiritual) autobiography, the purposes of which are 'catharsis, devotion, and propaganda' (Swaim 1993, p. 147). The autobiography which develops in a Christian context, such as the pietist diary (Maasen 1998, p. 44) can be seen as a pattern for recording quasi-religious experiences. Indeed, lesbian literature in the 1970s was dominated by autobiographical narratives establishing the tradition of the coming-out story. Stein points out the interdiscursive links with religious genres when referring to the coming-out narrative as 'a kind of collective confessional' and 'the gay community's development myth' (1997, pp. 68, 70; see also Chapter 3). The most paradigmatic and influential of those autobiographies is probably Johnston's vision of a 'lesbian nation' (1973). Under the separatist paradigm, self-examination was in turn intended to cleanse the mind of either wrong religious dogma or 'false beliefs . . . implanted by patriarchy' (Geraldine T. 1988, p. 3).[8]

Converts could rely on the support of the group in this process. The supportive function was, in the feminist context, often performed by consciousness-raising groups. Here, another parallel to religion shows in the common reference to relating experiences as 'giving testimony' (*Aspen 1979). Moreover, 'the telling of the narrative may serve to demonstrate how the addressee herself should behave in similar circumstances' (Liang 1997, p. 289). Conversion narratives thus also take on an instructional function. Such retrospective narratives can moreover be regarded as confessions which, as Foucault has claimed (1976/1977), may seem liberating but in fact lead to submission to the authority or institution one confesses to.

Although separatism has to be understood as a reaction to oppressive patriarchal structures and therefore never existed in a vacuum, its theoretical foundations require that separatists insulate themselves from other discourses in order to break the influence of these discourses on women's lives. In terms of text production and dissemination, this means that separatist discourse is mostly instantiated in independent, low-budget media, such as zines. 'A zine is . . . a mini-magazine, made and distributed on a small scale through informal non-corporate networks' (Dawson 2007, p. 14), such as mail order, stalls at festivals and independent bookshops. While the medium has proliferated into the virtual sphere in the form of blogs, podcasts and webzines, paper-based zines are still going strong. While any zine can address whatever its producer wants to write about, many zines are produced to disseminate left-of-centre politics and express the views of emancipatory movements. They are thus 'a living example of intellectual and creative expression beyond the bounds of capitalism' (Dawson 2007, p. 14).

Non-commercial media have been discussed as the communication channel of choice for other non-mainstream groups as well; thus, Grech (1998) sees paper-based zines as giving teenage girls a voice and building communities through a focus on experience and creativity. Further, Gregory (1991) expands from zines to other forms of community publishing, which are seen as a move 'away from passive consumption of meanings made and imposed by others' (p. 113) and towards production, from (mis)representation by others to self-representation, from invisible private talk to public recognition. In view of the changing models of lesbian identity, we can here establish a tentative link between a view of lesbian identity as a political project and zines as a medium of publication on the hand, and a view of lesbianism as lifestyle and magazines on the other.

The competing models of 'lesbianism as a political movement [vs.] lesbianism as a lifestyle' (Raymond 1989, p. 149) seem to be the hallmark of heterogeneous 1990s discourse. These discourses find their reflection in different forms of media and publishing, but also in hybrid texts that show a combination of radical political discourses with those of consumerism. Example E is taken from an early lesbian lifestyle magazine published in the UK and in many ways typifies a conflict along those lines. (Please refer to Chapter 2 and to the glossary for technical terms.)

EXAMPLE E: 'THE LESBIAN HERESY'
(USZKURAT 1994) (EXTRACT)

Reproduced with kind permission by the author.

 1   Sheila Jeffreys has her own version of Back to Basics. Lesbians shouldn't be
 2   parents at all. Carol Ann Uszkurat caught up with the controversial author of
 3   The Lesbian Heresy.
 4   Sheila Jeffreys' latest book harks back to 70's feminist radicalism. Maybe
 5   this was why her minders felt the need to screen me when I phoned for an
 6   interview. Them: What do you think of Sheila's work? Me: Er, I think she
 7   makes a valuable contribution to the debates. I made it through that hurdle.
 8   The next one was clothes. Jeffreys thinks lesbians should be anti-feminine,
 9   anti-butch, and anti S/M. So the frock was out, as were the leather jacket and
10   black trousers. I settled for jeans, sneakers and sweatshirt. When we meet
11   Sheila's dressed almost identically. Phew.
12   Jeffreys is a champion of what she calls 'simple, straightforward politics.' For
13   instance she has little hesitation in condemning lesbian parents. 'They have
14   socially and politically constructed desires. We don't need to be following
15   down the track of heterosexuality.' She doesn't condemn single mothers: she
16   condemns parenthood itself.
17   It wasn't until Jeffreys became active in feminist campaigns against
18   pornography that she realised the incompatibility of her lifestyle and her
19   politics. Can you be a heterosexual revolutionary feminist?' [sic] She became
20   an apprentice political lesbian until she did the emotionally correct thing and
21   fell in love with a woman.
22   Not that it was hard. 'When you're in meetings every evening and making
23   posters together and going to women's events, you have this tremendous
24   excitement which inevitably leads to a loving expression between women.' I
25   asked whether the door of desire might be another way into lesbianism, but
26   Jeffreys was adamant there was only one way. Those who don't travel the
27   political route come out negatively. 'They come to lesbianism,' she told me,
28   'through the experience of stigma and oppression so it's difficult for them to
29   have positive feelings about their sexuality.'
30   She believes that for all lesbians men are central, even if it's only to knock them
31   out of the picture. 'Even for lesbians who aren't consciously making
32   feminist decisions, the rejection of men is somewhere on their agenda.' It's
33   not all politics, although Jeffreys finds it difficult to explain why being with
34   women is so much better. From the Jeffreys perspective any attempt at role
35   play, including butch and femme roles, 'is a very hostile, controlling and
36   negative way of looking at lesbian and gay identity.' . . .
37   Jeffreys rightly states in her book that lesbians should feel comfortable with
38   what they do sexually. 'What,' I asked, 'about the lesbian who feels
39   comfortable using a dildo?' Her reply was typically uncompromising. 'It
40   seems extraordinary that anybody who loves herself as a woman would feel

41   deficient enough to think that something like a penis could be necessary.'
42   The sexologists popped up when I asked for her views on queer politics. 'It's
43   Victorian values again. Queer includes in its manifestos transsexuals,
44   sadomasochists, paedophiles, lesbians and gay men: it's all the categories
45   stated by the sexologists.' I argued that a constructive view of queer politics
46   was that it freed us to play with our desires whereas the sexologists have seen
47   us as fixed in our sexuality. Jeffreys [sic] response was immediate: 'there is
48   nothing free about transsexualism. It's a terrible abuse of human beings by
49   male supremacy and the medical system that wants to make a profit.'
50   But complications are not the name of the game with Sheila Jeffreys.
51   Basically we all have the wrong consciousness and need to build a new one
52   along with a new sexuality. Being a lesbian will give you the new sexuality.
53   Reading the book will give you the new consciousness.

That article was taken from the lesbian magazine *Lip* (an acronym for
Lesbians in Print), a few issues of which were published in the first half
of the 1990s. A nationwide British publication, it was among the first
periodicals which was printed rather than duplicated and provided less
overtly political, more lifestyle-centred information and entertainment for
lesbians, following the short-lived *Artemis and Gay Girl* (1986–7) and
Shebang (1992–4; Simmons 1997). The editors of the magazine were well
aware that their product represented a departure from the way lesbian
periodicals had been produced before and that *Lip* was thus a novelty
in both style and content which might not be given a warm welcome by
everybody. This awareness shows in the editorial from December 1993:

> The things [an older generation of lesbians] fought so hard for are being
> taken for granted by younger dykes. . . . A scene which enables younger
> women to come out with such ease, is a compliment to those who strug-
> gled so hard to create it. . . . You mean we're pandering to the superfi-
> cialities of consumer culture? Our answer is yes, Yes and YES. . . . We
> want fun by the bucketful. And when it runs out we want more. (*Lip*
> editors 1993, p. 4)

The stance of the editors shows traces of conflict and ambivalence towards
an older generation, with no more than a grudging nod of admiration
towards the achievements of lesbian feminism (see Wodak & Schulz
1986, p. 83). Clearly, this quasi mother–daughter conflict sees lesbian
feminists cast in the role of 'the repressive mother who stands in the way
of sexual pleasure and imposes uniformity on the diversity of desires,
identities, and practices' (Stein 1997, p. 2). The editors are both defensive
with regard to the anticipated reproaches and aggressive in the way the
new lifestyle is not only defended but actively, and defiantly, demanded.
A generational conflict between radical feminist lesbians from the 1970s

and 'younger dykes' seems inevitable: 'it was time for some . . . good old-fashioned teenage rebellion. And who better to rebel against than [the] lesbian feminist foremothers?' (Healey 1996, p. 155). Just as early lesbian feminism sought to overcome pre-Stonewall lesbian lifestyles, twenty years later it had come to be seen as 'the stodgy, moralistic parent that queers must rebel against, often replacing hegemonic culture as the primary opponent' (Phelan 1998, p. 197).

This conflict finds its most noticeable expression in the interview Uszkurat conducted with lesbian feminist Sheila Jeffreys. The text was chosen for analysis because it epitomizes one of the internal contradictions of 1990s lesbian discourse in the UK and the US, namely ideological struggle over the representations of lesbian identity and community. Interestingly, and despite the young image that *Lip* gave itself, the interviewer was actually of the same generation as her interviewee, showing that opposing political stances do not always neatly map onto generations. Further proof of this complexity is the fact that the author of Example F (see later in this chapter), a passionate advocate for lesbian separatism, was twenty years old when she wrote her text. The analysis of Example E will spell out what respective discursive strategies the interview partners pursue and how they use language—and ascribe forms of language use—in order to implement their model of what a lesbian community is or should be about.

Social Actors

The genre of the interview determines the interviewee as the central social actor, with the interviewer playing a secondary role. Indeed, there are 23 references to Sheila Jeffreys, but only 12 references to the interviewer. Outside this dyad, the most important social actors to feature in the interviewer are other lesbians with another 12 references, either in general or in specific sub-categories. Other social actors ('men,' 'the sexologists') play a comparatively negligible role with four and three instances, respectively. This is in contrast to Example B, where men were a prominent social actor group. Personal pronouns feature fives times for both the first person plural ('we') and the second person ('you'), with the referential range of these pronouns varying throughout the text.

Apart from deictic pronouns ('she'), the interviewee is mostly referred to by her last name only. It is only in the lead-in to the article, its opening and closing paragraphs (lines 1, 4, 50) as well as underneath the pull quote that her full name is given. Even rarer is personal reference by first name only. This predominantly formal nomination (van Leeuwen 1996, p. 53) distances the interviewee from the reader. The two instances of informal nomination by first name both occur in the opening paragraph (lines 6–11), where the author sketches her uneasiness in approaching her interview partner. This is achieved by bringing in another, collectivized social actor, namely Sheila Jeffreys' 'minders' who 'felt the need to screen me' (line 5). The interaction between the author and the anonymous 'minders' is represented in direct speech, as an exchange between 'them' and 'me' (line 6). During the screening process, metaphorically described as a 'hurdle' (line 7), the author uses the hesitation marker '[e]r' (line 6) to allude to her doubts and uneasiness. The episode closes with a paralinguistic sigh of relief ('[p]hew,' line 11). The 'minders,' being close to the interviewee, are quoted as using her first name only ('Sheila's work,' line 6). This kind of reference is echoed by the author, when the fact that 'Sheila's dressed almost identically' (line 11) brings relief for the author and even makes her refer to Jeffreys by her first name. The amount of space that is spent on clothing (lines 8–11) proves the point that the 'formation of a lesbian identity is at least partly a matter of developing proficiency in manipulating codes and symbols' (Stein 1997, p. 89). Such a skill is all the more important in times when the identity thus signalled is undergoing change, as was the case in the early 1990s. Clashing signifiers could become a cause for conflict ill at ease with the collaborative genre of the interview.

The short narrative about the screening process preceding the interview sets up a conflict through a 'me vs. them' distinction. Interestingly, the author does not establish an 'us vs. them' dichotomy but presents herself as being alone in the face of out-group members. This echoes the stand-off between individual and group that was constructed in Example B. She thereby implicitly asks for the reader's sympathy and constructs herself and the reader as being part of the same victimized in-group. The interviewer further distances herself from Jeffreys' perceived viewpoint by referring to it as 'the Jeffreys perspective' (line 34). Here, the theorist's name is used attributively and her perspective presented as a kind of school. This representation falls in line with the 'me vs. them' dualism established in lines 5–7.

This dualism is organized largely across temporal lines; the opening paragraph describes Jeffreys' book as 'hark[ing] back to 70's feminist radicalism' (line 4), and the author speculates that this makes herself suspicious as a representative of 1990s feminism. The two versions of feminism and lesbian existence are comprised in the words 'lifestyle' and 'politics' (lines 18–19). By bringing these two buzzwords of the debate into the text, the author establishes a dichotomy which constitutes the conflict that is at the centre of the text. This opposition is also hinted at with Jeffreys' proclaimed sympathy for 'simple, straightforward politics' (line 12). This direct quote can be seen as an implicit critique on the part of Jeffreys of queer theorists and their sometimes arcane linguistic style, as well as of queer politics and activism that builds on irony, subversion and parody, all of which are less than straightforward strategies.

Throughout the interview, both Uszkurat and Jeffreys refer to the out-group as a social actor. It is noteworthy in this regard that the interviewer's representations of Jeffreys' perceived opinions include much less differentiated social actor groups than do the direct quotes by Jeffreys. Thus, the interviewer claims that according to Jeffreys, '[l]esbians shouldn't be parents at all' (lines 1–2), that 'lesbians should be anti-feminine' (line 8) and that 'for all lesbians men are central' (line 30). By contrast, Jeffreys is directly quoted as referring to '[t]hose who don't travel the political route' (lines 26–7), to 'lesbians who aren't consciously making feminist decisions' (lines 31–2) and to 'anybody who loves herself as a woman' (line 40). These modifications allow for a more differentiated picture of the out-group. It seems that the interviewer simplifies Jeffreys' argument to set her up as an out-group member.

In-group reference on part of the author is largely effected through the first person singular ('I'), which reinforces the idea of her alone as a specific person in the face of genericized out-group members. This alleged helplessness not only asks for sympathy from the reader, as mentioned before, but also constructs the interviewer as relatively powerless. Only once do we find a 'we' that refers to her and her interviewee; in line 10, this use of pronoun reinforces the momentary closeness between the two that is brought about by matching sartorial styles and represented by use of the interviewee's first name. Elsewhere, 'we' and 'us' refer to lesbians as a group (lines 14 and 47), albeit from two different perspectives. It is only at the end of the piece (lines 51) that there is an inclusive first person plural ('we all') that refers to the author's in-group. This is replaced immediately afterwards by direct address of the reader ('[r]eading the book will give you the new consciousness,' line 53), showing that the reader is considered part of the in-group. If we further regard 'the book' as a metonymic way of referring to Sheila Jeffreys, it becomes clear that the basic conflict is merited end weight, but not solved, in the article.

Evaluation

While there is not much explicit evaluation in the text, the respective attributes and modifiers judge the actors and actions they refer to unambiguously. The lead-in already sets up the conflict between different actors by calling Sheila Jeffreys a 'controversial author' (line 2). The possible causes of controversy are elaborated by attributes such as 'typically uncompromising,' 'adamant,' and 'immediate' (lines 26, 39, 47) to describe and evaluate Jeffreys and her perceived style of discussion. These attributions are reinforced through 'has little hesitation' and 'condemning' (line 13).

In Jeffreys' own words, the same qualities take on a more positive evaluation, as embodying 'simple, straightforward politics' (line 12). The fact that the author uses a direct quote introduced by 'what she calls' (line 12) serves to mark off Jeffreys' politics from those of the interviewer. The final statement that 'complications are not the name of the game with Sheila Jeffreys' (line 50) refers back to a political stance that allegedly translates into a particular linguistic style. Incidentally, this evaluation is both echoed and modified in a more recent interview with Jeffreys (Bindel 2005), in which the interviewer observes that 'she refuses to couch her arguments in inaccessible, academic language . . . [f]or Jeffreys, the word "complicated" does not exist' (p. 41).

Evaluation of the interviewee is not uniformly negative, however. Thus, the author concedes that 'Jeffreys rightly states in her book' (line 37), even if what she states ('lesbians should feel comfortable with what they do sexually,' lines 37–8) is a peg for further disagreement. The honesty of the only other positive evaluation ('she makes a valuable contribution to the debates,' lines 6–7) is compromised by the hesitant 'er' at the beginning of the statement and the interviewer's perceived need to say something positive about Jeffreys in order to be granted an interview in the first place. The strongest negative evaluation is done indirectly; the interviewer implicitly attacks her interview partner by describing her own view of queer politics as 'constructive' (line 45), contrasting it with Jeffreys' stance on the issue.

Jeffreys also engages in negative evaluation. While she is not seen as directly criticizing her interviewer, the attributes she is presented as using for practices she disapproves of are more starkly negative than the interviewer's. Thus, she is said to judge role play as 'very hostile, controlling and negative' (lines 35–6) and gender-adaptive surgery as 'a terrible abuse' (line 48). As a consequence, anyone engaging in such practices sets themselves up in opposition to Jeffreys, potentially including the author and the readers. It is probably in reaction to this perceived criticism of herself and others in her in-group that the author ironically concludes that, according to Jeffreys, 'we all have the wrong consciousness' (line 51).

This final irony throws into relief the differences in discursive style between the interview partners. Where the interviewee is presented as direct and unmitigated in her evaluations, the interviewer uses accumulative attribution to describe Jeffreys' style, and irony to evaluate her ascribed beliefs. The interviewer's strategy is one often employed by discourse participants in relatively powerless positions and therefore underscores the self-victimization that can be observed elsewhere in the interview.

Actions

The three main social actors–Sheila Jeffreys, the interviewer and other lesbians–feature mostly as actors rather than the goals of other's actions. Unsurprisingly, the majority of actions (19) are carried out by Jeffreys, who is also never seen at the receiving end of someone else's action. By contrast, the author engages in an action 10 times and is the goal/target of someone else's twice. In both instances, she is seen as being acted upon by out-group members: 'her minders felt the need to screen me' (line 5) and 'she told me' (line 27). Although otherwise an unmarked term, 'she told me' here implies a perceived condescending stance on Jeffreys' part; since her statement here is explanatory and declarative ('They come to lesbianism . . . through the experience of stigma,' lines 27–8), the phrase acquires overtones of talking down to the addressee. This is again modified by the later interview (Bindel 2005), in which the interviewer states that '[a]lthough a funny and charismatic speaker, [Jeffreys] can irritate those who feel they are being dictated to' (p. 38). Even more starkly, Jeffreys is, in the present text, represented as having 'little hesitation in condemning lesbian parents' (line 13). Condemning is a performative speech act that has a strong impact, so the relational process 'she has little hesitation' underscores Jeffreys' perceived radicalism. The same process recurs twice (lines 15 and 16), with the reflexive pronoun in 'she condemns parenthood itself' (lines 15–16) constructing an undifferentiated radicalism on Jeffreys' part.

All three of the main social actors engage in a range of process types. Given the interview genre, Jeffreys and Uszkurat feature as sayers in a number of verbal processes; in fact, this is the most frequent kind of action for the author. Examples are 'she told me' or 'I asked' (lines 27 and 42). The structure of question-answer adjacency pairs is once abandoned when the interviewer argues with Jeffreys (line 45). A covert verbal process type is 'she makes a valuable contribution to the debates' (lines 6–7). Jeffreys is additionally shown as a senser in mental processes; for example 'she realised' and '[s]he believes' (lines 18 and 30), or 'Jeffreys finds it difficult' as a covert mental process (line 33). Whether or not Jeffreys really 'finds it difficult to explain why being with women is so much better' (lines 33–4) in the context of the interview is impossible to tell. As an interpretation on part of the interviewer, the statement is reminiscent of the relative short, mitigated description of the lesbian community as a better world for women that could be observed in Example B.

Attributive and identifying relational processes are most prominently associated with Jeffreys. Examples include 'has her own version,' 'became active' and 'was adamant' (lines 1, 17, 26). Here, the intention of earlier texts, such as Example A, to define lesbians as a group has given way to representing a concrete, individual woman in an interview. While this choice of genre may represent the shift from collective to individual identity that began in the 1980s, in the quotations lesbians as a group still feature prominently in mental and relational processes such as 'should be anti-feminine,' '[t]hey have socially and politically constructed desires' and 'anybody who loves herself as a woman' (lines 8, 13–14, 40). Neither the author nor her in-group are defined through relational process types, with the exception of the ironic 'we all have the wrong consciousness' (line 51), an opinion ascribed to Jeffreys. While the *Lip* editorial quoted earlier defines the in-group to some extent, the present interview portrays the out-group member in detail, but shows few traces of an emerging in-group identity.

Modality

Modality is equally divided between deontic forms conveying obligation and epistemic ones encoding likelihood. The respective modal verbs and adverbs also incorporate a range from relatively low to high-affinity modality. Starting with deontic modality, this is mostly ascribed to Jeffreys, in free indirect speech such as '[l]esbians shouldn't be parents' (lines 1–2) and 'we all . . . need to build a new [consciousness]' (line 51). In direct quotes, Jeffreys engages in little deontic modality, and the one instance where she does is rather low in affinity ('[w]e don't need to be following down the track of heterosexuality,' lines 14–15). This mismatch echoes the interviewee's differentiated reference to lesbians as a social actor group in contrast to the undifferentiated treatment of that group that the interviewer ascribes to her.

The use of epistemic modality is more complex. Crucially, it features in a debate on lesbian identity, in which Jeffreys is directly quoted as saying that feminist political activity 'inevitably leads to a loving expression between women' (line 24). This high-affinity epistemic modal is contrasted with the interviewer's question whether 'the door of desire might be another way into lesbianism' (line 25). The interviewer's turn is a question, which appears less certain than Jeffreys' statement. The interrogative status and the modal verb 'might' render the content negotiable. The interviewer indeed sees herself as being promptly opposed ('but Jeffreys was adamant that there was only one way,' lines 25–6). The conjunction 'but' together with the attribute 'adamant,' the declarative status and absolute quantifier ('there was only one way') make Jeffreys' reproduced answer much higher in affinity than the interviewer's question. Note, however, that the statement takes the form of reported speech, with no such high-affinity epistemic modality featuring in direct quotes. The same ascribed modality can be observed in the free indirect speech that closes the article ('[r]eading the book will give you the new consciousness,' line 53). The only direct quote to feature epistemic modality includes two rather low-affinity modal verbs, i.e., 'would feel deficient' and 'could be necessary' (lines 40–1). This shows how ascribed high-affinity deontic modality serves to discredit the other's argument.

Interdiscursivity

The conflict between the two views on lesbian identity and politics, represented by Jeffreys and Uszkurat, can also be witnessed in the text incorporating markers of other discourses and genres. In line with the opposition between 'lifestyle' and 'politics' (lines 18–19), we find traces of informal conversational genres on one hand and of the discourse of political lesbianism on the other.

It is not only Jeffreys' book which 'harks back to 70's feminist radicalism' (line 4), but the linguistic devices she is seen to employ also show parallels to Example B. That earlier text is almost quoted verbatim in the phrase 'heterosexual revolutionary feminist' (line 19) as well as in the abstractions 'transsexualism' and 'male supremacy and the medical system' (lines 48 and 49). By abstracting transsexual people to an '-ism' and assigning them the role of a goal acted on by 'the medical system,' transsexual people are here denied agency and self-determination. Jeffreys' quote on 'transsexualism' also includes an absolute quantifier, namely 'there is nothing free' (lines 47–8), another hallmark of 1970s lesbian feminist discourse (see Examples A and B). On the whole, though, absolute quantifiers are rather ascribed to her by the interviewer, e.g., in '[l]esbians shouldn't be parents at all,' 'she condemns parenthood itself,' 'Jeffreys was adamant there was only one way' and 'for all lesbians men are central' (lines 1–2, 15–16, 26, 30). The most notable of these ascribed quantifiers occurs toward the end of the text, where Jeffreys is ironically, and indirectly, ascribed the belief that 'we all have the wrong consciousness' (line 51). Echoed in 'the new consciousness' (line 53), this is an ironic reference to the consciousness-raising groups of the 1970s. The irony becomes even more obvious in the expression 'apprentice political lesbian' (line 20), which metaphorically conceptualizes lesbianism as a profession rather than a form of desire.[9] Apprenticeship further includes supervision, and the term thus also invokes social control. Irony is also used as a device in the coinage 'the emotionally correct thing' (line 20). By changing the collocation 'politically correct,' the dualism of politics and desire is further elaborated. The ultimate question is which model of lesbianism is more genuine, the one constituted by politics or by desire.

The use of irony is not only typical of queer politics, but also serves to ascribe features of 1970s lesbian feminist discourse, such as relevant key words and absolute quantifiers, to a representative of the out-group. This is even more prominent in *Lip* magazine's December 1993 editorial, which caricatures lesbian feminists as 'feel[ing]the need to justify their sexuality in terms of world revolution or saving the whale' and as 'hav[ing] the impulse to knit Tampax into the wire at Greenham Common.' The same strategy of ascribing features of 1970s discourse to the out-group could be observed for devices such as undifferentiated reference to social actors and high-affinity deontic modality.

What Jeffreys does do, however, is to use predominantly declarative statements and abstract nominalizations. Both strategies are combined in 'the rejection of men is somewhere on their agenda' (line 32). Despite this statement, men as a social actor group are marginal, and the fact that the quote is used as a pull quote shows that it is given undue prominence. The quote is paraphrased as 'for all lesbians men are central, even if it's only to knock them out of the picture' (lines 30–1), which differs considerably with regard to the level of formality. By using an informal expression the author of the article separates herself from the linguistic style of her interview partner. The same strategy is to be found in '[t]he sexologists popped up' (line 42), as well as in the magazine issue's table of contents, which closes by stating 'and thats [sic] is all girls.' Such informal language use sets the lifestyle and fun-centred in-group apart from an out-group perceived as dogmatic and humourless. Interdiscursivity, including traces of ascribed discourses, is therefore another device of constructing an 'us vs. them' dyad, and again, the out-group and its discourse are given much more prominence than the in-group.

Metaphor

Apart from the ironic reference to the 'apprentice political lesbian' (line 20) discussed previously, metaphoric expressions relating to lesbian identity and relations among different lesbian communities mostly realize the JOURNEY metaphor that was prominent in Example A. For example, one exchange between Jeffreys and her interviewer employs the metaphor of coming-out (itself a metaphoric expression) as a journey, elaborated by 'way into lesbianism' as well as 'one way' (lines 25 and 26), and extended as 'the door of desire' and 'travel the political route' (lines 25 and 26–7). The metaphor is also deployed in the expression 'the track of heterosexuality' (line 15). Thus, it serves the ideational metafunction of conceptualizing lesbian identity, the interpersonal metafunction of negotiating, by being elaborated, the different views held by members of different lesbian communities, and also meets the textual metafunction of creating coherence. Extensions of the JOURNEY metaphor at the conceptual level are the event-structure metaphor (Lakoff 1993) PURPOSES ARE DESTINATIONS and HINDRANCES TO ACHIEVING A PURPOSE ARE OBSTACLES. In the text at hand, this extended metaphor is realized as 'I made it through that hurdle' (line 7), used to describe the difficult interaction between in-group and out-group members.

It was noted before that, although the two interview partners are actually of the same age, the two groups they come to represent are constituted along generational lines, enacting a metaphorical mother–daughter conflict. This metaphor is realized as an analogy in the aforementioned December 1993 editorial of *Lip*, the magazine that Example E is taken from:

> Apparently here at LIP we're having too much fun. My Mother used to say something similar about young people. Apparently we didn't understand how lucky we were to have fridges. Now an older generation of lesbians have the same problem, not with kitchen appliances but with political progress. (*Lip* editors 1993, p. 4)

This metaphoric conceptualization of inter-group relations at the linguistic level translates into a rejection of the lesbian feminist out-group, mostly through indirectly negative evaluation, irony and ascribed linguistic style.[10] Ironically, the text resembles earlier examples analyzed in this book in that it has little to say about the in-group other than the basic dualism of identity-through-desire versus identity-through-politics. In their struggle over lesbian identity, both Uszkurat and Jeffreys constitute identity through demarcation as can be observed in the numerous shifts in the 'us vs. them' dyad. Their struggle is exemplified in the ambiguous title: although it is mentioned that 'The Lesbian Heresy' is a book by Jeffreys, it is not clear who the heretic actually is (cf. Example D, line 26 for this metaphoric expression). The ambiguity of the title shows that the conflict, while displayed, remains unsolved.

IMAGE OF THE COMMUNITY

The author constructs an image of a lesbian community in which 'young Turks' struggle to disseminate their models of lesbian identity against those propagated by lesbian feminists. The models in question differ mainly in what constitutes sexual identity, i.e., a political agenda or desire. The author of Example E constructs herself and her in-group as relatively powerless, whereas the out-group is ascribed attitudes and linguistic behaviours that are opposed to those of the in-group, even though these are mostly not corroborated by the language use found in direct quotes. In general, the out-group's beliefs and practices are represented in a simplified and radicalized way. By offering a counter-model, the author follows a transformative strategy, while her interview partner is seen to pursue a reproductive strategy.

Arguing with the interviewee and challenging their beliefs and values is the typical way in which interviews are conducted in the British media.[11] In the present example, this culture-specific feature is adopted to negotiate models of lesbian community and identity. The fact that the text takes the form of an interview is indicative of a focus on representative individuals rather than collective social actors. As an example and illustration of a wider conflict, the text is located in the operative realm and is fraught with tension and hybridity.[12]

Hybridity is also a defining feature of the next example. Rather than setting up an opposition between group representatives, however, different discourses are used by one and the same author, who tries to adapt a political programme of the 1970s to the socio-political context of the 1990s.

EXAMPLE F: 'FINDING YOUR INNER LESBIAN SEPARATIST' (HANSON 1998) (EXTRACT)

1   Finding Your Inner Lesbian Separatist
2   Deep inside each woman is a little voice crying out. It is our own, inner
3   lesbian separatist. That's right, you too can be a lesbian who, in profound
4   enlightenment, can live independently of males. With a dedications [sic] and
5   the few simple tips provided in this self-help essay, you will emerge into your
6   new, enlightened, dyke identity.
7   You may be asking yourself, 'why would I want to be a lesbian separatist?'
8   perhaps you've notice [sic] that women make less money than men, to this
9   very day, even when a woman is compared to a man in the same job with the
10   same amount of education. Or perhaps you have become aware that every few
11   minutes, a woman is sexually assaulted. Perhaps you've noticed that nine out
12   of ten people who suffer from debilitating eating disorders are female. You

13   may be tired by now of the portrayal of women as helpless creatures, always
14   mutilating and torturing themselves to look good for men. Or you may be
15   tired of seeing real women do those things. Are you sickened by the fact
16   that women get breast enlargements to look good for men despite the risks
17   involved? Are you sickened knowing that women all over the world are being
18   raped and beaten by men as you read this? Are you tired of the rude stares or
19   comments about your looks from complete strangers? Are you horrified by
20   the fact that your friend is in a physically and emotionally abusive
21   relationship with a man but won't get out of it because society has made it
22   impossible for her to imagine living without a man? Then you can benefit
23   from being a lesbian separatist. You can take yourself out of the patriarchal,
24   cruel world and surround yourself with your sisters.
25   This is not a step by step process. Your lesbian separatist identity is
26   discovered through enlightenment and a series of epiphanies or revelations. It
27   starts with you being sick and tired of the sexist, racist, classist, and
28   homophobic society you live in; a society created by males, with laws made
29   by males, a government and education system run by white males. Starting to
30   get the picture? If you don't like this society, if you think it's sick and wrong,
31   then you can't like the males who are the leaders of it. . . . . Every man is
32   responsible for the oppression against women. And how many of them do
33   you see fessing up? Sure some men may say 'I think it's awful that women
34   are oppressed,' but what do they do about it? . . .
35   Are you thoroughly disgusted by men? Good, now, to discover your lesbian
36   separatist you must educate yourself. Evidence of enlightenment leading to
37   lesbianism abounds in our history. . . . . It has been found in contemporary
38   studies that lesbians tend to complete a higher level of education. Lesbians
39   are enlightened, therefore your route to lesbianism is to become enlightened. .
40   . .
41   Read books—lots of books—on judaism, buddhimsm [sic], taoism. Books
42   on thje [sic] history of Native Americans, Blacks in America and the
43   women's movements. Books by lesbians, natives, Chicanos and anyone else
44   who isn't white, male, Christian, rich, straight or temporarily able.
45   Turn off the TV. TV is a major source of sexist, homophobic, and oppressive
46   propaganda. At most you can watch one or two hours of TV a week (I still
47   watch x-files and Startrek a couple of times a month. I guess I'm addicted).
48   Also, when you read papers and magazines—don't believe everything you
49   read. Be critical. Try to pick out untruths or stereotypes. Analyze articles and
50   pictures: do they reflect the oppressive ideas of our dominant culture? . . .
51   Involve yourself in the arts, whatever arts you can afford. A pen and paper is
52   all you need to draw. You can join a choir, learn to paint, crate [sic] fimo
53   beads, or anything. Art is a part of enlightenment. And write. Write poetry or
54   prose. Write a diary or journal. Write anything, write about yourself and the
55   world. Write about the pizza you had for lunch. Write about the meaning of
56   life. Don't try to write the way you're 'supposed' to, just write. That's part of
57   discovering yourself. . . .

58   All of the elements described above will help you to discover yourself and
59   your world. Ultimately, chances are that you will find your inner lesbian
60   separatist.

Reproduced from the homepage of its author, the preceding text is one of the
very few separatist links that can be found on the internet. While there is a vast
number of lesbian links in general, it seems that separatists have not found
their way into the medium. Although some initially saw a chance that 'during
the 1990's, computer bulletin boards and the Internet will become part of [the
lesbian separatist] network' (Brown 1995) and started using the medium to
spread their ideas and contact others, most separatists seem to have remained
critical of the medium itself. Such a stance shows either in absence from the
medium altogether or in a suspicious and defensive attitude conveyed on the
internet, a sort of criticism from within. Separatists on the internet are intent
on keeping their independence from 'men with $5,000 computer systems[13]
who advocate child pornography as the ultimate example of free expression'
and emphasize their politics by warning their readers/visitors that should they
be 'looking for heteropatriarchal thrills, [they] might be happier if [they] just
go home' (Brown 1997). It is obvious that free access to information, the cor-
nerstone of the internet, is anathema to lesbian separatism since restriction of
access is, in the political concept of separatism, seen as a way of deriving the
dominant culture of the energy it thrives on. Privacy, albeit not necessarily
for political reasons, also seems behind the relative popularity among lesbians of email discussion lists rather than any other form of computer-mediated
communication, which Wakeford (2000, p. 406) has reported for the 1990s.
Since most texts on separatism are published in non-digital form (pamphlets,
articles, anthologies), the text of this example represented a rare exception at
the time of its writing.

Yet it is precisely the exceptional form of the text, as well as the fact that
it adapts 1970s concepts to the 1990s, which renders it particularly interesting for linguistic analysis. The analysis will show that the author combines
features from three different discourses, namely the lesbian separatist/radical
lesbian feminist discourse of the 1970s, religious discourse and, as a new influence, advertising discourse. Such hybridity indicates the changing images of a
community that a younger generation of lesbians brought about in the 1990s.

Social Actors

By far the most prominent social actor incorporated into the text is the reader,
referred to in the second person ('you'). She is foregrounded right from the start,
with the title employing a possessive pronoun ('your inner lesbian separatist')
that directly addresses the reader. The second person pronoun is used throughout the text, 27 times in total. Direct address is to be found in statements
('you too can be a lesbian,' line 3) and even more so in rhetorical questions

('[a]re you thoroughly disgusted by men?,' line 35) and imperatives ('[t]urn off the TV,' line 45). Another way of involving the reader in the text is anticipating and answering her questions while reading. This is done elliptically in the emphatic '[t]hat's right, you too can be a lesbian' (line 3) and spelled out in '[y]ou may be asking yourself, "why would I want to be a lesbian separatist?"' (line 7). Taken together, these devices help include the reader and make her identify with the text.

The reader is envisaged as female, and women as a group are indeed the second most prominent actor, being referred to 11 times throughout the extract. There is wide variation however, ranging from indefinite plurals ('women') and singulars ('a woman,' 'each woman') to paradigmatic women such as 'your friend' (line 20). General references ('women . . . are being raped,' lines 17–18) alternate with specific ones ('your looks,' 'your friend,' lines 19 and 20). Specific examples are supposed to be the reader's, who is moreover included by means of the circumstantial 'as you read this' (line 18). By drawing together the reader, her friends and women in general, the author juxtaposes the personal and the political, indicating that individual suffering is a consequence of structural violence. This intended identification of the reader with women as a group is also reflected in the opening lines of the text; here, the generalization 'each woman' (line 2) is turned into the first person plural ('our own,' line 2), which includes the author, the reader and all other women in a collective identity not unlike that constructed in Example A ('we are all women,' line 27).

Lesbians as a sub-group of women are mentioned just as often, mostly in the collocation 'lesbian separatist' or simply 'lesbian.' As a group, lesbians are defined by demarcation, as 'anyone . . . who isn't white, male, Christian, rich, straight or temporarily able' (lines 43–4). This list embodies the covert prestige of oppression that can be observed as a value in separatist discourse in general. Positive definitions of who or what a lesbian separatist actually is occur in the opening stretches of the text ('a lesbian who, in profound enlightenment, can live independently of males,' lines 3–4). This initial definition is reminiscent of Example A's opening question, 'What is a lesbian?' It is noteworthy that attraction to other women is not mentioned as part of lesbian (separatist) identity at all; rather, the defining moment seems to be a woman-centred life which is open to 'each woman' (line 2). This disregard for desire and the equation of lesbians with women is, as we have seen, typical of 1970s lesbian feminist discourse.

Given the separatist agenda of living without men, it is noteworthy that 'men' as a social actor group actually feature 18 times, referred to generically as 'males,' 'men' or 'a man,' in absolute terms as '[e]very man' (line 31) and more specifically as 'some men' (line 33). Reference is therefore very similar to that for women as a group, pointing towards an understanding of either group as homogeneous, with each representative typical of the group as a whole. The higher number of references to men reflects a similar phenomenon in Example B and shows once more the paradoxical separatist occupation with this group of social actors.

Men are identified as 'the leaders of [society]' (line 31) and throughout, the abstract actor 'society' is closely linked to males. Thus, society is said to have 'made it impossible for [a woman] to imagine living without a man' (lines 21–2), it is referred to as 'the patriarchal, cruel world' (lines 23–4) and said to have been 'created by males' (line 28). Male disagreement with patriarchal structures is refuted by the author (lines 33–4), who thereby anticipates and counters assumed objections to her viewpoint of all men as responsible for a system she perceives as 'sick and wrong' (line 30). She thus secures the basis of lesbian separatism: in order to develop a group identity, women must leave male-defined society.

Next to the prominent second person, the text also includes a few instances of the first person singular pronoun ('I'). Two of the five uses are to be found in ascribed direct quotes by the reader ('why would I want to be a lesbian separatist?,' line 7) and by 'some men' ('I think it's awful that women are oppressed,' lines 33–4). The same device was used in Example B, where the imaginary interlocutor of the authors was likewise represented in ascribed direct speech. The other three instances of the first person singular constitute the only reference the author makes to herself. Set in parentheses, the pronoun occurs at a sensitive moment in the text (lines 46–7), where it is used as a politeness device to repair a previous potential offence to the reader (see later subsection on "Modality"). On the whole, however, it is the reader who is very much in the foreground, accompanied by genericized references to women and men as social actor groups. While the latter two devices echo the treatment of social actors in Examples A and B, the direct involvement of the reader—other than to refute her standpoint, as in Example B—is an original strategy that ties in with the text's overall persuasive purpose. The same function is met by evaluation of the different social actors.

Evaluation

The most explicit evaluation is that of society, which is characterized as 'patriarchal' and 'cruel' (lines 23–4), 'sexist, racist, classist, and homophobic' (lines 27–8) and 'sick and wrong' (line 30). Mainstream media like TV and magazines are likewise branded as channels for 'sexist, homophobic, and oppressive propaganda' (lines 45–6), communicating the 'oppressive ideas of our dominant culture' (line 50). Living in such as society has 'debilitating' (line 12) effects on women, who are presented as 'mutilating and torturing themselves' (line 14) and living in 'abusive' (line 20) relationships. Expected reactions on part of the reader are scaled from noticing, and becoming aware of, such negative effects (lines 8, 10, 11) to being 'tired' of them (lines 13, 15, 18), being 'sickened' (lines 15 and 17), and, most strongly, being 'horrified' (line 19). This kind of evaluation through connotation is repeated in the reader's expected reaction to the proponents of society, men: being 'thoroughly disgusted' (line 35).

While intensified, this negative evaluation stops short of the dehumanization found in other quotes from separatists, who, e.g., refer to men as 'parasitic male mutants' (quoted in Faderman 1991, p. 237) and to heterosexual couples as 'the pussy cats and their toms' (quoted in Faderman 1991, p. 238).

The alternative to being damaged by living in patriarchal society, i.e., becoming a lesbian separatist, is evaluated in uniformly positive, albeit fewer and less varied terms. Positive evaluation is mostly effected through the metaphoric attribute 'enlightened,' used to characterize lesbians (lines 6 and 39). This evaluation is bolstered up by reference to unspecified 'contemporary studies' (lines 37–8) showing that lesbians have higher overall educational levels. Along with the agentless passive ('[i]t has been found,' line 37), this is a typical hedging device suggesting scientific research to support the author's claims.[14] Other forms of positive evaluation are once more verb connotations, as in 'you can benefit from being a lesbian separatist' (lines 22–3). There is one instance where the negative and positive are contrasted at sentence level, namely in '[y]ou can take yourself out of the patriarchal, cruel world and surround yourself with your sisters' (lines 23–4). The kinship term harks back to Examples A and B, and is here set in opposition to 'patriarchal' and 'cruel,' idealizing all-female communities as egalitarian and loving.

Notably, positive evaluation of the propagated way of life is sketchier and less varied than the negative evaluation of mainstream society. On the whole, we can see a gradual erosion of the mental model of a lesbian community: while the Radicalesbians' manifesto (Example A, 1970) made strong affirmative statements about coming-out as the light at the end of the tunnel, Example B (1979) included only a brief and mitigated positive evaluation of a lesbian community. It seems that throughout the 1970s, the lesbian community had already become so multi-faceted that a coherent in-group model was no longer available. One and a half decades later, Sheila Jeffreys (in Example E, 1994) was, rightly or wrongly, presented as hard-pressed to give convincing reasons for why someone should join a lesbian community. The author of the present text finally does not, perhaps cannot, describe such a community anymore, be it in positive or negative terms. Dominant patriarchal culture is still the point of reference.

Actions

The reader, referred to as 'you' or in imperatives, is seen as the actor in 47 processes and as goal of an action in an additional seven. These cover all five process types, with about half of all occurrences accounting for material processes. These are largely realized through imperatives, e.g., '[a]nalyze articles and pictures' (lines 49–50) or 'join a choir' (line 52). The list of imperatives in lines 41–56 clearly indicates an instructional perspective in that part of the text. The imperative 'write' deserves special attention, because it is repeated seven times. Since no mention is made of a text receiver, the focus is solely on the process of writing, thus confirming that writing can be a form of political practice and as such is particularly salient as a separatist practice. The 'broadened, demystified, less reverent view of publication' (Gregory 1991, p. 117) that one often finds in alternative publishing and writing is reflected in the advice not to 'try to write the way you're "supposed" to' (line 56). Identifying the act of writing as 'part of discovering yourself' (lines 56–7) echoes the main function of Puritan diaries (see earlier discussion) and, on a more secular note, shows how 'the writing in zines . . . works as a therapy session' (Sutton 1999, p. 170).

The second most frequent process type the reader is engaged in is relational, at 11 instances. These are mostly effected through rhetorical questions (e.g., '[a]re you sickened by the fact,' line 15). Interestingly, this process type is here not so much used to construct a (group) identity but rather to describe a negatively evaluated state that propels change. The starting point is dissatisfaction and repulsion, and accordingly, many of the relational processes can be recoded as covert mental processes (e.g., '[a]re you horrified by the fact,' lines 19–20). Change is indeed the central motif of the text, flagged up even in the present continuous of the title. The transition from one state to the other also triggers the unusually high number of material processes, which mostly denote activities undertaken to move from one identity to the other.

The reader features overwhelmingly as the actor in all processes, with the exception of the closing statement that 'the elements described above will help you to discover yourself' (line 58). This example also highlights another particularity of the text, namely the high number of reflexive processes, in which the reader is both actor and goal of the action. This dual role mostly maps out in material processes ('[y]ou can . . . surround yourself with your sisters,' lines 23–4) but also features in a verbal process ('[y]ou may be asking yourself,' line 7). This linguistic device embodies the belief that makes separatism so similar to ascetic religious movements, namely that women need to change their own consciousness and withdraw from the world. The reflexive processes are evidence that the separatist agenda is not primarily about changing the world but about changing oneself.

This change is largely one of consciousness, ironically referred to in Example E, but taken seriously in the present text. The process in the title itself can be analyzed as a covert mental process of gaining self-knowledge. Mental processes are also the drivers for change, e.g., 'if you think [society is] sick and wrong' (line 30). Likewise, the list of imperatives by which the author advises her reader how to change herself includes a number of overtly and covertly mental processes ('don't believe,' '[b]e critical,' '[a]nalyze' in lines 48–9). The endpoint of this process is encoded in two (covertly) behavioural processes at the beginning and the end of the text, thus keeping the goal in sight ('you will emerge into your new . . . identity,' lines 5–6 and 'you will find your inner lesbian separatist,' lines 59–60). The high-affinity epistemic modality gives the two processes the illocutionary force of promises.

In terms of their actions, women as a social actor group show a pattern similar to that of the reader, with material processes double the number of relational ones (six and three, respectively). However, they are not seen to engage in any mental or verbal processes and are also more often the goal of their own or other people's, notably men's, material actions. As such, they are represented as being 'sexually assaulted' (line 11), as 'being raped and beaten' (lines 17–18) and as 'mutilating and torturing themselves' (line 14). Women are seen as actors and goals only in negatively evaluated actions. It is only when a woman 'discover[s] [her]self' (line 58), i.e., her 'true' identity as a lesbian separatist, that evaluation becomes positive. In this new identity, women 'complete a higher level of education' (line 38), 'are enlightened' (line 39) and 'can live independently of males' (line 4). This feature realizes the proclaimed independence at the linguistic level.

Men as a group feature in 10 different actions, most of which encode stereotypically male activities and statuses. In material processes, men feature as raping and beating women (line 18) or as creating society, making laws and running governments (lines 28–9). Relational processes by definition see them in more static, but no less stereotypical roles, as 'leaders' and being 'responsible' (lines 31 and 32). However, while men are represented as brutalizing women, women in turn do not feature in material processes impacting on men. This stereotypical gender representation was already observed in Example B. The present text, too, thus re-inscribes the prevailing gender order, leaving separatist withdrawal as the only option to avoid harm.

Modality

Examples A and B were characterized by a high degree of deontic modality, a feature that was subsequently ascribed in Example E. In contrast to these earlier texts it draws on, modality in the present text is overwhelmingly epistemic. The only two examples of obligation and permission are the high-affinity 'you must educate yourself' (line 36), which is specified in 'you can watch one or two hours of TV a week' (line 46). This use of modality here reinforces the imperatives that are prominent elsewhere in the text. Granting permission in this way represents a condescending power gesture by which the author puts herself in the place of a parent controlling a child, i.e., the reader. Although the author of Example F was only twenty when she wrote the text, it may be this kind of attitude that kindles the metaphorical mother–daughter conflict observed in texts from the 1990s. However, the age of the authors of both Examples E and F show that the model of a community characterized by inter-generational strife oversimplifies reality. Returning to the present text, the author takes the sting out of her obvious condescension by remarking in brackets on her own TV consumption. By employing the first person singular for the first and only time throughout the text, the author provides a sharp contrast to the attitude she displays elsewhere, showing that she herself is not infallible. Along with the assumed shared knowledge about the TV series, the two parenthetic sentences are aimed at creating solidarity between author and reader and thus modify the previous authoritarian tone. They are therefore a politeness device used to do repair work in the simulated conversation between writer and reader.

The obligation conveyed in 'you must educate yourself' (line 36) indicates a shift from the expository and hortatory to the procedural. Up to line 35, the text largely explains, represents and seeks to persuade, as indicated by the anticipated questions, rhetorical questions and stark contrasts in evaluation. Another device contributing to the expository and hortatory nature of that stretch of text is epistemic modality. Right at the beginning, the phrase 'you too can be a lesbian' (line 3) bears the illocutionary force of a promise. The reader's possible reactions are further anticipated and responded to in '[y]ou may be asking yourself' (line 7), which implies that the reader is undecided about what to believe and can still be influenced. The argument for separatism is made by elaborating on the detrimental effects that patriarchal society has on women. The reader is directly addressed throughout, with the author suggesting thoughts and emotions to her which are encoded in rhetorical questions ('[a]re you sickened,' lines 15 and 17) and epistemic modality realized in adverbs ('[p]erhaps you've noticed,' line 11) and modal verbs ('you may be tired,' lines 14–15). Affirmation by the reader is assumed, which shows in the subsequent statement '[t]hen you can benefit from being a lesbian separatist' (lines 22–3). The promise is intensified to prediction in the high-affinity modals 'you will emerge' (line 5) and 'you will find your inner lesbian separatist' (lines 59–60), which together act as a bracket for the whole text. This textual function is reinforced by the author repeating the title almost verbatim at the very end of her text. Interpersonally, the reader is assured that following the author's advice will be in her own best interest.

Interdiscursivity

Example F is noteworthy for mixing a number of discourses and genres, in particular combining lesbian feminist discourse—and religious discourse as one resource that lesbian feminist writers draw on—with genres such as advertisements and self-help manuals. In doing so, the text illustrates that '[a]s historically specific organizations of language, discourses present themselves in the plural, coexisting within temporal frames, and instituting unpredictable and inadvertent convergences' (Butler 1990/1999, p. 184).

One trace of lesbian feminist discourse is the generic reference to 'women' or 'a woman' in lines 8–22. At several points in the text, the author switches from the general ('Lesbians are enlightened,' lines 38–9) to what is specific to the reader ('therefore your route to lesbianism is to become enlightened,' line 39). In the same vein, 'women' are juxtaposed with 'you' and 'your friend' (lines 17–20), depicting the personal as an effect of the political and thereby linguistically encoding a central tenet of

1970s feminism. As evidenced by Examples A and B, and parts of Example E, other linguistic devices adapted from lesbian feminist discourse are nominalization and abstract agency ('society has made it impossible for her,' lines 21–2 and 'oppressive ideas of our dominant culture,' line 50) as well as absolute quantifiers and declaratives ('[e]very man is responsible for the oppression against women,' lines 31–2). The all-encompassing nature of the author's mental model of the in-group also surfaces in the following statement, found on the website on which Example F was published: 'I personally believe every woman's life can be enriched by becoming a Lesbian Separatist.' By opening up the category 'lesbian' to all women, Examples A, B and F illustrate the observation that 'one could be "invited into" the imagined community' (Anderson 1983, p. 133).

Another feature of lesbian feminist discourse that could especially be observed in Example A is its own interdiscursive links with religious discourse. Further, it was argued earlier in this chapter that separatism is in many regards akin to a religious movement. In the present text, the central traces of religious discourse are the word forms 'enlightenment' and 'enlightened.' This is sometimes intensified through attribution ('profound enlightenment,' lines 3–4) and sometimes listed together with 'a series of epiphanies or revelations' (line 26). The latter in particular corroborates Stein's (1997, p. 218, n. 3) point about coming-out as epiphany and the coming-out story as conversion narrative. Traces of religious discourse could already be found in Example A, and taking up this device in order to integrate lesbian feminist discourse makes the text at hand an example of multiple interdiscursivity.

In stark contrast to the traces of lesbian feminist discourse, the author calls her text a 'self-help essay' (line 5) and promises the reader a 'few simple tips' (line 5). Traces of the procedural genre of the do-it-yourself manual show in lines 41–57, where they are combined with features of other, hortatory genres aiming to influence behaviour and beliefs (Longacre 1974). Thus, the goal orientation of procedural genres ('the elements described above will help you,' line 58) sits alongside features of hortatory genres such as focus on the addressee, encoded as second person ('when you read papers and magazines,' line 48) and a number of commands and suggestions ('[i]nvolve yourself in the arts . . . [y]ou can join a choir,' lines 51–2). In this part, the text paradoxically conveys both authority and solidarity.

The persuasive purpose of hortatory genres is most obviously manifested in advertisements, and indeed lines 7–24 draw heavily on this genre. Traces of this are anticipated questions by the reader, rhetorical questions, direct address, and the final offer of a positively evaluated lesbian separatism that is presented as an alternative to a negatively evaluated patriarchal society and a solution to a problem established in the text. The author seeks to gradually create *a*ttention, *i*nterest, *d*esire and consequently *a*ction in the reader, employing—perhaps unconsciously—the AIDA formula of product promotion. In a marketing context, action would mean the consumer buying a particular product. In the present context, action means the reader embracing the idea of a certain lifestyle and working towards its realization. The author makes unabashed use of promotional genres, something that the Leeds Revolutionary Feminists (Example B) had still ridiculed and rejected. In the late 1990s, however, we see a politically oriented lifestyle being advertised on the internet without a hint of irony.

The two discourses of lesbian feminism, on one hand, and the advertisement and self-help manual genres on the other are juxtaposed in the beginning, where 'a dedications [sic]' on part of the reader is coordinated with '[a] few simple tips' from the author (lines 4–5). Given the strictly anti-consumerist stance displayed in lesbian feminist discourse, mixing it with advertising genres seems bold to say the least. Such contradiction in texts can be brought about by several reasons: firstly, the narrative structure of the present text constitutes a progression from establishing the problem (women suffering under patriarchal conditions), constructing a certain reader reaction as logical ('If you don't like this society, . . . then you can't like the males who are the leaders of it,' lines 30–1), suggesting a solution and instructing the reader how to realize the solution. This basic structure requires features from different genres and discourses, which leads to hybridity. Secondly, the author may wish to target more readers than she could by staying within the confines of a particular discourse or genre. Given the political beliefs at the heart of lesbian separatism and separatists' aim to spread them, this is likely to be another reason for the marked interdiscursivity in the text. Thirdly, the author may face an 'ideological dilemma' (Billig 1988) which has her holding contradicting beliefs, values and attitudes in equal measure. In Example F, this is likely to be an unconscious motivation at best, given the explicit political stance of the author. Finally, hybridity and contradiction in texts can reflect social change. This reason seems most prominent, as the author takes a concept from 1970s discourse and transplants it into the context of the 1990s, in which consumerism and individualism had already largely taken over as societal values. The fact that the text was published on the internet is only the outward manifestation of this new context. The text's inherent contradictions show that the two contexts are largely incompatible.

Metaphor

Once again, we find the JOURNEY metaphor that is typically employed to conceptualize self-development and coming-out and is therefore also a stock element of religious conversion stories. The author realizes it when she promises that the reader 'will emerge into [her] new . . . identity' (lines 5–6) and when she speaks of 'your route to lesbianism' (line 39), although she elsewhere denies that forging such an identity could be 'a step by step process' (line 25).

The second central metaphor is that of ILLNESS (e.g., '[a]re you sickened by the fact,' lines 15 and 17). Although there are no realizations of this metaphor in Examples A and B, lesbian feminists are often presented as using it. Thus, lesbian feminist thought is said to centre on the idea that

> the self can overcome the noxious effects of socialization in a male-dominated culture [and that] there is a kind of contamination theory implicit in the structuring of lesbian-feminist relationships when it is felt that the more contact one has with men, the more one's inner strength and resourcefulness are sapped. (Wolf 1979, pp. 170, 171)

Likewise, the authors of Example D claim that anti-S/M lesbian feminists accused them of 'being contaminated by the patriarchy' (Example D, line 9). In the present text, the metaphor serves to intensify the negative evaluation of non-separatist existence.

There is, finally, a spatial metaphor CORE IS AUTHENTICITY, which is realized in the attribute 'inner' for the collocation 'lesbian separatist' (lines 1, 2–3, 59–60). Its elaborations include '[d]eep inside each woman' (line 2) and the idea that a woman's 'true' identity as a separatist can be 'discovered' (lines 25–6, 35–6, 57, 59–60). The attribute '[i]nner' presupposes the existence of an essential core of one's personality that is not constructed in discursive and other interaction, but can be revealed through changing one's consciousness. In an essentialist fashion reminiscent of the Radicalesbians' seminal pamphlet (Example A), a particular identity is therefore presupposed as inherent and authentic, to be discovered and enacted if one is to live to the full. All three metaphors—JOURNEY, ILLNESS and CORE—therefore serve to recontextualize lesbian feminist discourse.

Image of the Community

The model of collective identity constructed in Example F is very similar to that found in Examples A and B, and parts of Example E. Lesbian identity is defined along political lines, and the category is expanded to potentially include all women. (Note that none of the texts so far has problematized the concept of 'woman,' apart from the reference to 'transsexualism' in Example E.) Women then are the constitutive members of the in-group, the socio-cognitive representation of which also involves a script according to which women travel from one (collective) identity to another. Both the community itself and individual development of community membership are structured metaphorically, as BOUNDED SPACE and JOURNEY, respectively. In being so closely aligned with images of lesbian community found in earlier texts, Example F betrays an overall preservative strategy.

However, lesbian feminist discourse is mixed with promotional and self-help genres, leading to a conceptual clash in the text, which inadvertently transforms lesbian discourse and the model of collective identity that it transports.

Indeed, the whole text is strikingly heterogeneous, combining various discursive resources in order to convey models of identity and community from a specifically lesbian vantage point. This heterogeneity is also reflected by a break within the text which manifests itself in a change from explaining and persuading to instructing. The text is thus an excellent example of how an advocate of lesbian separatism—a movement which had its heyday in the 1970s—tries to adapt her beliefs and claims to the 1990s by choosing a modern medium of distribution (the internet) and by borrowing heavily from consumerist discourse. By 'selling' ideologically invested claims to the reader, Hanson reverses Bakhtin's statement that '[a]ny consumer good can . . . be made an ideological sign' (1929/1973, p. 10). The hybridity of the text further means that it straddles the normative and operative realms, constructing an ideal-type community while at the same time instructing potential members how to join.

The two texts that were analyzed in their socio-political and discursive practice contexts in this chapter are both characterized by contradiction and heterogeneity. The author of Example E enacts a conflict of identity models by scaling it down to an interview co-produced by representatives of two different views. Notably, the indirect and free indirect speech used throughout that text ascribes particular beliefs and linguistic behaviours to the interviewee which tend not to be reflected in the direct quotes. The author thereby exaggerates the differences between herself and the interviewee in order to construct a more clearly delineated in-group and transform models of a lesbian community.

Example F is equally heterogeneous and contradictory, although hybridity is there brought about by interdiscursively mixing features of lesbian feminist discourse with those of advertisements and self-help manuals. In doing so, the author inadvertently implements a transformative strategy, although her goal is likely to be the same as the interviewee's in Example E, i.e., to preserve a lesbian feminist model of collective identity. Nevertheless, the author of Example F singles out one woman, namely the reader, to make her case for separatism, just as in Example E, the author chooses to epitomize a conflict by representing two individuals. In that both authors explicitly (Example E) and implicitly (Example F) show themselves to be located in a socio-political context marked by increasing consumerism and individualism, they both represent the changing nature of lesbian discourses and models of collective identity. Since they overtly pursue different strategies, however, their texts are not only contradictory in themselves; the two authors, writing at roughly the same time, also contradict each other.

If anything, the fragmentation, individualization and commercialization of and within lesbian communities that was demonstrated in this chapter has intensified in the subsequent decade. The next and final chapter will trace this trend by analyzing two contemporary texts.

6　Consuming the Community
The 2000s

I believe in . . . individual responsibility [and] I would like to stress that
fact if I could.

(interview with Ingrid E. Barnes)

The last analysis chapter will investigate contemporary lesbian discourses
in mostly the US and, to a lesser extent, the UK and look at what mental representations of community they encode. To this end, I have chosen
two paradigmatic texts, one from an American nationwide magazine and
one from a blog. The first, a ranking of the '10 most powerful lesbians,'
is discussed as an example of how texts published in a commercial lesbian
mediascape incorporate societal values of corporatism and consumerism.
As such, it proposes a differentiated model of collective identity in which
appraisal of ideal-type in-group members is balanced with values of solidarity and group cohesion. The second text, an entry from a blog hosted by a
lesbian member of the US Republican party, is seen as a preliminary endpoint of lesbian discourses and their images of community, since the author
rejects the model of imagined communities as such and instead advocates
individualism. Together, the two texts are products of their socio-political
and discourse practice contexts, with the second text bringing some of the
features of the first text to their logical conclusion.

SOCIO-POLITICAL BACKGROUND:
ISSUES AND ARGUMENTS

The preceding chapter discussed the issue of separatism, which has been
described as 'the very antithesis of "lesbian chic"' (Doyle 1996, p. 179). Starting out as a mainstream media fad in the early 1990s, lesbian chic has since
been accepted as a dominant mode of self-representation in some lesbian discourses and communities. Originally, the term referred to the depiction of lesbians in the American, British and subsequently other European mainstream
media as feminine, style-conscious,[1] urbane and wealthy. The emphasis on
style and appearance in texts on lesbian chic in glossy women's magazines is

realized through key words and phrases such as 'chic Capital City life,' 'glamorous' and 'glossy' (D'Souza 1993, p. 5). Lesbian-themed fashion spreads first appeared in up-market women's magazines in the mid-1980s (O'Sullivan 1994, p. 80). The phenomenon got off the ground in the early 1990s, with lesbian characters appearing in TV soaps and lesbian imagery being used in advertising. Subsequent articles on lesbian life were published in both heterosexual women's magazines like *Elle, Vogue* and *Cosmopolitan* and daily newspapers such as the British *Guardian* and *Evening Standard*. It is difficult to trace the beginnings of, and reasons for, particular short-lived fashions in mainstream media. O'Sullivan (1994, p. 88) suggests that with the increasing spread of AIDS among the heterosexual population, lesbians came to be seen as healthy, safe and untainted by associations of disease. This is corroborated by Tennant and Cripps referring to lesbian sex as 'safe sex' (1994, p. 123). However, glossy women's magazines seldom went beyond a depiction of heterosexual women who had superficial lesbian experiences at parties. By referring to this behaviour as 'sweet, playful fun,' 'being girlie,' 'like going on holiday' and 'dabbling' (Tennant & Cripps 1994), these articles in fact reinforce the homophobic cliché of lesbian sexuality as being less than serious, a mere distraction from the 'real,' i.e., heterosexuality. Other journalists (D'Souza 1993, p. 5) even take up the pornographic idea of lesbianism as a voyeuristic titillation for men: 'declaring that one is glad to be gay might be the most hetero thing a woman can do.' Here, a political slogan is reinterpreted as mere flirtation.

The adaptation of lesbians by mainstream media is done at the expense of 1970s lesbian feminism, in that '[d]ogma and dungarees have been traded in for fashion and femme' (Ashton 1996, p. 158). The result is a split into 'good' and 'bad' lesbians. The dichotomy between the 1970s style lesbian and her chic counterpart is constructed by referring to the former as 'cropped, baggy, monochrome and self-censored' (Briscoe 1994, p. 10), 'the archetypal man-hating "diesel dyke"' (D'Souza 1993, p. 5), 'the short-haired "bulldyke"' (Kasindorf 1993, p. 33) and 'dungareed crop-haired wimmin' (Kaufmann 1996, p. 22). Such epithets help to form a dualism in which both images co-exist with very different evaluations. Consequently, lesbian chic is mainly about sex and consumption rather than identity, let alone politics. Here we can see how 'social transformation [is] replaced by a kind of personal transformation easily co-opted by consumer capitalism' (McElhinny 2004, p. 132).

Given this distorted picture painted by lesbian chic, it is unsurprising that most initial reactions from lesbians themselves were negative, often polemically so. Critics attacked what they perceived to be the key feature of lesbian chic, i.e., 'cheque-writing dykes who [look] suspiciously like the average Tory shithead's daughter' (Solanas 1993, p. 5). According to this view, lesbian chic is no more than a media-induced 'bimbo culture' (Healey 1996, p. 201). Critics further argue that lesbians are represented as isolated, de-contextualized individuals and are thus paradoxically, but by no means unintentionally, subjected to invisibility through visibility. The chic lesbian thus remains a phantasm, 'no real object, only the constitution of an "object" (signified) in discourse' (Fairclough 1995, p. 139). In the critics' line of argument, lesbian chic is 'less an enunciation of lesbian cultural power than a commodification of lesbianism' (Cottingham 1996, p. 2). While appearing to integrate lesbians into the mainstream, dominant discourses in fact once again constitute them as the Other. Indeed, the question remains in how far the images of 'lipstick lesbians' and 'designer dykes' are, or ever have been, reflections of lesbian life at a particular moment in history. Few critics of lesbian chic fail to mention the discrepancy between the media phenomenon and the reality of most lesbians, pointing out that 'life probably hasn't changed a great deal for your average lonely dyke in a Shropshire village' (Briscoe 1994, p. 10). This discrepancy between media representation and lesbian everyday life is particularly stark for poor lesbians. Indeed, the image of the chic lesbian is 'a complete joke to all working class or impoverished lesbians' (Solanas 1993, p. 5) as well as to older and/or black lesbians, one might add. Lesbians are also seen as being alienated from their own history, because the fact that 'political lesbianism paved the way for lifestyle lesbianism' (Stein 1992, p. 438) is denied.

Constructing an opposition between 1970s lesbian feminist style and contemporary lesbian chic represents a historically falsified view. In her article on lesbian supermodels, Kaufmann (1996, p. 22) reminds her readers that 'lesbianism [was] associated with hyperfemininity, a celebration of girlicity' at the turn of the nineteenth century and in the 1920s (and, to an extent, in the butch/femme culture of the 1950s and 1960s). In the period between the two world wars, lesbianism was overwhelmingly associated with an upper-class, bohemian lifestyle pursued in the epicentres of Berlin, New York and Paris. While the image of the financially independent émigrée and heiress, epitomized by stars such as Nathalie Clifford Barney or Tamara de Lempicka, hardly captured the reality of most 1920s women, these mythical figures represented, for at least parts of their life, lesbian wealth and glamour. After World War II, by contrast, it was working-class butches and femmes and, after them, lesbian feminists and their downward mobility who became the prototypical figures of lesbian historical narratives. The 1970s phenomenon of downplaying any gender markers is thus a relatively new one which should not be disconnected from its historical context. The celebrity culture propagated by many lesbian magazines, while a reflection of wider British and American culture, is not a recent invention either. Gever (2003) has traced lesbian stardom back to the 1920s and argued convincingly that even the lesbian movement of the 1970s, despite its emphasis on collective action and equality, brought forth its own 'stars' in the form of highly articulate, highly visible activists such as Jill Johnston or Rita Mae Brown (pp. 81–114).

The re-negotiation of femininity in lesbian discourse since the 1990s is to a degree inspired by lesbian chic (Kaufmann 1996, p. 24). In this context, radical feminist writers clearly regard lesbian femininity as unethical.

For instance, Penelope (1996) draws up a list of accessories and styles to be avoided by lesbians, bluntly stating that she 'can't respect a Lesbian who wears lipstick, dresses, paints her nails, reeks of perfume, and shaves her legs' (1996, p. 132). Penelope's account starts out with an autobiographical narrative of the trauma of enforced femininity and further states that lesbians, lacking the submission allegedly instilled by a heterosexual lifestyle, can never pass as straight and thus claim feminine privilege. What she does not consider is that hybrid signification, i.e., looking feminine but not passing as straight, may be the very point of lesbian femininity.

This hybridity and tension between straight style and lesbian life is what makes some queer theorists embrace lesbian chic as granting women flexibility and plurality in its rejection of any fixed, homogenizing identity. Lesbian chic's emphasis on traditional notions of femininity here meets the queer concept of imitation and parody. Semiotically speaking, the perceived tendencies of lesbian feminism to establish a hierarchy of oppression based on visibility—the less visible, the less oppressed—represent a 'reduction of whole systems of signifiers to a single privileged signifier' (Walker 1993, p. 869). From a queer point of view, the chic lesbian, while showing similar reduction, is a much more subversive figure since she adds a parodic twist to the question of signification. In a hegemonic discourse that assumes gender identity and gendered self-presentation to be an unproblematic effect of biological sex, the feminine lesbian becomes an illegible subject. In her case, the signifier is in a reverse relation to the signified; superficially, she looks straight, but actually she is not.

Lesbians themselves contribute to the marketization and commodification that lesbian chic represents with statements such as '[my girlfriend and I] go out shopping together and go out to clubs. I don't think that feminism means anything really to young dykes now . . . I've got my girlfriend, so I'm happy' (quoted in Ashton 1996, p. 166). A focus on consumption, brands and commodified identities pervades the discourse of lesbian chic. Marketing is in fact one of the most dominant discourses in late capitalist society, to the extent that not only products and services but also politics, lifestyles and, ultimately, the self, are branded and marketed. After all, capitalism discriminates exclusively on the basis of disposable income; as long as there is money to be made from a particular social group, be it teenagers, ethnic minorities or lesbians, every attempt will be made at packaging and marketing them. If lesbians are commodified for consumer use then a market has to be found for this particular product and the product has to be advertised. The ideal consumer is constructed as someone who can choose and if necessary change styles of living and loving (Maasen 1998, p. 93). Consumerist notions thus become key in a discourse which functions 'as a vehicle for "selling" goods, services, organizations, ideas or people' (Fairclough 1995, p. 138). The invasion by marketing concepts and, along with them, commodification and advertising, of areas not amenable to them can border on the dehumanizing, which is perhaps best shown in the cynicism of the following quotation (D'Souza 1993, p. 5): 'If last year's ultimate fashion accessory was having a baby, then this year's is having a lesbian affair.' If we think back to the 1970s notion of the lesbian nation (Johnston 1973), it seems that 'national identities have been challenged by consumer-based "branded" identities, cosmopolitanism, fandoms of popular culture "stars" and retreats to "lifestyle enclaves" within gated communities' (Longman 2006, p. 80).

Given the rising tide of consumerism within lesbian communities themselves, a version of lesbian chic has gradually become the dominant mode of self-representation in many lesbian media. Lesbians, too, participate in the 'discursively organized social space called femininity' (Talbot 1995, p. 144), either in a textually mediated form or materially, e.g., by enacting images marked as feminine in self-stylization (Luzzato & Gvion 2007). There is further evidence of female participation when lesbians interdiscursively weave naturalized, biologist and essentialist discourses into their own in an attempt to reclaim femininity. A striking example is Nightwind (1997), who maintains that '[femininity] is not a matter of social conditioning, [i]t is a matter of biology' and goes on to talk about 'the real nature of women' in what seems like a direct quote from hegemonic discourses on the subject. Her claim 'that men have . . . *used* our femininity . . . but I am denying that they *invented* it' is far from being common consent, however.

The professional and consumerist lifestyle many lesbians have embraced ever since the 1980s has clearly paved the way for accepting commodified lesbian chic as self-image. High-gloss publications such as *g3* and *Diva* in the UK or *Curve* and *girlfriends* in the US are not only filled with advertisements for jewellery, sex toys, DVDs, CDs and, above all, travel,[2] but also incorporate less obtrusive advertorials for designer fashion, clubs, bars and restaurants, and Christmas gifts. That these find a ready market can be seen in the personals in which women label themselves as 'professional' and 'femme' and boast their own house and car. This tendency is so widespread throughout the personals that it has already drawn satire: one woman, failing to meet the categories of 'slim, successful, rich, feminine' sarcastically describes herself as a 'freak [who will] probably put you right off' (*Diva*, March 2005, p. 92).

These ideals of consumerism and corporate femininity are the product of more than twenty years of historical development. In the 1980s, Thatcherite deregulation and Reagonomics ushered in a middle-class culture of personal equity investment, professional lifestyle and social conservatism on both sides of the Atlantic. As Faderman (1991, p. 275) notes, the reconstruction of society along the lines of consumerism and free market economics involved lesbians as well: 'Success, power, professionalism, which had been tools of the enemy in the eyes of the radicals, became signs of accomplishment to the . . . community of the '80s.' (Given the usual ten-year lag between the US and the UK, the changing paradigm took hold in many lesbian communities in Britain only in the 1990s.) Some lesbians have benefited substantially from the trend towards professional careers and private wealth creation.

With generally higher levels of education and fewer or no children, lesbians have for years been financially self-reliant and have had higher incomes than heterosexual women (Faderman 1991, p. 283), with an average income premium of 30 per cent in the 1990s (Berg & Lien 2002; see chapter 5, n. 14). While this still puts lesbians in a lower income bracket than straight men, the difference is remarkable and can only partly be explained with childlessness, a parameter that is in any case decreasing in importance as lesbian motherhood is increasing. Also, while lesbians show a higher proportion of university graduates because they do not expect to rely on a male income, they also show a tendency to take on low-skilled jobs. Clearly, economic independence from men is only half the story. Berg and Lien (2002, p. 407) speculate that there may be fewer career breaks even for lesbian mothers, pointing to the fact that lesbians are not subject to social pressures to fulfil hegemonic gender roles by staying at home when they have children, support rather than outshine men in their careers and generally identify as wives and mothers rather than independent professionals. Mental independence from these gender roles seems to be another crucial factor accounting for the income differential. Whatever the reasons, increased earnings usually bring the realization that creature comforts such as nice homes, travel and cars, once obtained, are hard to let go again. In the history of lesbian communities in the UK and the US, a professional re-orientation mirrored the more conservative social climate of the 1980s and the emergence of yuppies. This meant for lesbians that group identity became dependent on patterns of consumption (Chasin 2000, p. 15), especially of products and services such as rainbow jewellery or travel to particular destinations which are regularly promoted in lesbian media.

The trend towards consumerism went hand in hand with a gradual replacement of the ideal of a lesbian community with that of individualism and personal achievement. Perhaps no-one embraces the values of economic success and individualism more than conservatives. Indeed, right-of-centre views by lesbians in many regards take up the contemporary ideal of the wealthy, professional, feminine lesbian and carry it to its logical conclusion. Thus, gay conservatives proudly claim that '[u]nknown numbers of lesbians and gays have achieved economic success and reached the apex of their callings' (Lochhead 1993). The demarcation from a perceived 1970s kind of lesbian is also echoed in conservatives' statements, as evidenced in an email interview with Andrea Houghton of the Log Cabin Republicans, a gay and lesbian lobbying group within the US Republican party, who states that 'I don't have a problem with guys as many lesbians do. I am not fearful of them or dispise [sic] them.'

Next to a conservative agenda of small government, low taxes and a strong defence, the gay right in essence asks that gays and lesbians assimilate toward the heterosexual mainstream in exchange for acceptance and civil rights. As early as 1989, conservative gays in the US advocated to counter increased homophobia in the wake of the AIDS epidemic by building goodwill with heterosexuals through public relations that depicted 'well-adjusted' gays and lesbians and their desires as 'just a mirror image of straight love and sex' (Kirk & Madsen 1989, p. 46). In a similar vein, conservative gay men have called marchers at Gay Pride a 'public relations nightmare' (Bawer 1993, p. 156) and thereby reversed 1970s claims that 'the gay movement is a civil rights struggle and not a public relations campaign' (Morris 1977, quoted in Chasin 2000, p. 166).[3] As discussed previously, one way of building public good will is to adhere to hegemonic ways of gendered self-presentation. This assimilationist strategy is diametrically opposed to more in-your-face politics 'founded on the notion that it is straight society that will have to change its ideas and its attitudes toward lesbians and gay men before [they] change themselves to fit in with straight society' (Healey 1996, p. 183).

Gay (and, to a lesser extent, lesbian) conservatism is predominantly an American phenomenon, at least in its organized form. This is very likely due to the different socio-political contexts, not least the role of religion; while evangelical Christianity in particular plays a paramount role in much of US politics and public discourse, Britain is a secular country, in which Christian religion is often nominal and compartmentalized, having no effect on everyday life. As a consequence, the British government followed many other European countries and introduced civil partnerships for same-sex couples in 2005. Already in 2000, openly lesbian and gay service personnel had been admitted to the armed forces. Two of the main items on the conservative gay agenda have therefore been achieved already. As a consequence, there is no group within the British Conservative party that could be compared to the Log Cabin Republicans. Although lesbian and gay groups formed within all major British parties as early as 1976 (Hamer 1996, p. 199), the closest equivalent to the Log Cabin Republicans, Torch, seems to have dissolved after its chairman retired in 2004.

By contrast, opening state institutions such as marriage and the military to gay and lesbian people is the main campaigning issue of gay and lesbian conservatives in the US. For the Log Cabin Republicans, founded as a regional group in California in 1978, Andrea Houghton states that 'we did a survey last month [February 2005] [which showed] that women had the same priorities [as] men. That being the marriage issue.' Another member of the group, Tessa Borrodaile, underscores that 'government should encourage family structures that provide support for one another.' Unsurprisingly, this sentiment is regularly echoed by the leader of the British Conservative party, David Cameron, who explicitly includes civil partnerships in his call for 'strong, stable families' as a remedy to social problems. How close conservatives can be to the mainstream—or vice versa—shows in the fact that the three main campaign issues of the US gay and lesbian organization Human Rights Campaign are 'marriage, family, work life' (www.hrc.org).

The conservative enactment of dominant cultural values addresses the fundamental issue of whether gay and lesbian people are in fact a community in their own right or rather a loose affiliation of individuals and couples sharing a temporary interest in obtaining a certain set of civil rights. To paraphrase the (in)famous conservative Margaret Thatcher, is there still such a thing as society or are there only families and individuals? For some, liberation is necessarily tied to an understanding of community as counter-culture, if 'the movement is not to lose its revolutionary potential' (Wilchins 1997b, p. 69). In the spirit of the Radicalesbians' early manifesto (Example A), others hold that 'people with a common experience of stigma are *a people*. . . . oppression can be overcome only through the creation of an alternative identity. . . . It takes a community to liberate a person' (Goldstein 2003, pp. 22–3). By contrast, Bruce Bawer, a conservative gay author, stresses time and again that gays and lesbians should not identify as members of a group or community, because that would make it 'harder for many heterosexuals to see gays as individuals' (p. 32). Given the conservative value of individual responsibility and achievement, group identities are seen as

> blind[ing] people to both their individual qualities and to the human concerns and characteristics that they share with others; at its most extreme, such thinking can lead to unspeakable atrocities—slavery, holocausts—which are seen as justified because the victims all belong to a specific despised group. (Bawer 1993, p. 87)

Individualism, then, is seen as a defence against discrimination. This reverses the idea that communities have the power to liberate individuals and it therefore seems that gay and lesbian conservatism marks the endpoint of imagined communities. Paradoxically, the only group identities that are strongly promoted by conservatives are the family and national identity. As Ingrid E. Barnes, Hudson Valley, NY, chapter president of the Log Cabin Republicans, states in an email interview: 'I am an American first and foremost, lesbian second and black third.' In this context, it is crucial to note that '[f]or gay men and lesbians in the United States, assimilation is . . . also absorption into American identity' (Chasin 2000, p. 46).

According to a CNN exit poll of 13,660 voters after the 2004 presidential election, there was a slight majority for the Democrats among women voters (51 percent), while 23 percent of self-identified lesbian, gay and bisexual respondents had voted for the Republicans.[4] Although not indicated in the poll, this sizable minority must show significant differences between gay men and lesbians, if the marginal status of conservative lesbians is anything to go by. The following quote is typical of the female members of the Log Cabin Republicans:

> Coming out republican is harder than coming out gay [because] people's reaction is mostly of shock and dismay, specially other lesbians I know. It is almost like that coming out feeling, something you hide, don't talk about or lie about. . . . Many believe they have to be [D]emocrats, like it is part of being gay. (interview with Andrea Houghton)

Others corroborate that '[s]ome lesbians find a lesbian Republican offensive' (Tessa Borrodaile) and that 'it is typically easier for me to come out to Republicans/conservatives than it is for me to come out to the gay community' (Rachel D'Amico). In sum, they feel that '[i]t is tough being a Republican in the gay community' (Sarah Weber).

Conservative lesbians are further marginalized by the fact that the members and leaders of conservative gay organizations are mostly white, middle-class men. This is in fact an echo of the homophile movements of the 1950s and 1960s, which were not only overwhelmingly white, but also strictly middle to upper class, as evidenced by readership surveys of *The Ladder* lesbian magazine (Faderman 1991, p. 341, n. 31) and the UK magazine *Arena Three*, which in 1971 recorded 40 percent of its readership as professional, clerical and executive (Hamer 1996, p. 176). Working-class members of Daughters of Bilitis, who tended to be more interested in socials than in lobbying, actually split away from the organization to form their own groups (Wolf 1979, p. 51). The modern conservative emphasis on economic and professional achievement similarly incorporates middle-class values and upward social mobility. Gender representation is also remarkably skewed in conservative groups. As Robinson (2005, p. 3) has noted, '[f]or the most part . . . gay conservatism is a story about men and by men.' This is corroborated by the fact that only an average 5 to 10 percent of members of the various Log Cabin Republican chapter organizations are actually lesbians, with the national management team being 85 percent male and just 10 percent of chapter presidents being women (as of July 2007). As Rachel D'Amico conceded in an email interview: 'If gay republicans are a rare breed, then lesbian republicans are an endangered species' (see Example C, which used the same metaphor for another marginalized lesbian group). It needs to be stressed, however, that given the conservative value of individual achievement and rejection of any category membership, such under-representation of women as a group would not be perceived as a problem. Yet, it is seen as highly problematic by critics of conservatism, who point out that only people occupying unmarked normative identity positions can afford to reject group-related identities (Chasin 2000, p. 223). The criticism is that the respective groups are not only overwhelmingly male but also defined by masculine values, so much so that 'masculinism is what holds the conservative movement together' (Goldstein 2003, p. 75). The same author also ventures a psychological guess that gay conservatives strive for 'reconciliation with the father in the form of straight male society' (pp. 86–7).

This latter point reverses the metaphor, routinely used by gay and lesbian conservatives, that political activists of other convictions behave like children, irresponsibly relying on a parental government instead of taking control of their own lives, and forever seeing themselves as the victims of outward circumstances. For example, conservative lesbian writer Tammy Bruce demands that gay people 'stop looking to government for unconditional love and approval' and no longer act 'like children throwing a tantrum'

(2004). Another writer, Norah Vincent, likewise claims that many gay people have a tendency to 'act like children, spurning the "other," and demonizing anyone who doesn't mirror and reinforce our every whim' (2002). On a similar note, the group Gays and Lesbians for Individual Liberty doubts 'whether government should . . . protect us from our own foolishness' (Gays and Lesbians for Individual Liberty 2003). Discrediting out-group members as children is thus a common strategy in conservative discourse and will be further explored in the analysis of Example H.

Conservatives seem to feel very uneasy around politically more radical gays and lesbians. As Diana Chapman, former editor of *Arena Three*, states:

> You see, I am a deeply conservative person . . . and I didn't like that kind of brashness and anger [of the Gay Liberation Front]. As I say, I'd spent my life saying, "No, no, no; we're just like everybody else' and here were all these terrible people making out that we were not. (quoted in Hall Carpenter Archives 1989, p. 57)

Part of what renders radical lesbians and gays 'terrible' in the eyes of conservatives is their emphasis on the sexual aspect of lesbian and gay identity. Again, this can already be observed for 1950s and 1960s conservatives, who had little interest in the largely sexually defined lesbian subcultures of the time and indeed sought to distance themselves from bar culture in their attempt to appear respectable in the eyes of the straight majority (Wolf 1979, p. 18). Gay male conservatism in particular very much attempts to counter the (over-)sexualized (self-)image of gays (Robinson 2005, p. 16). The same holds true to some extent for lesbians, who are often depicted as particularly interested in the traditionally feminine—and conservative—values of marriage and family. Distracting attention away from sexuality is partly a reaction to a highly sexualized lesbian club scene, complete with strippers, explicit lyrics and flyers such as the one reproduced in Figure 6.1.

One result of backgrounding sexuality is that marginal sexual communities like transgendered persons, S/M practitioners, bisexuals, polyamorous lesbians, and butches are the first to be silenced by conservative discourses. As Butler observes (2004, p. 26), 'those who live outside the conjugal frame or maintain modes of social organization of sexuality that are neither monogamous nor quasi-marital are more and more considered unreal.'

The wish on the part of gay and lesbian people to adapt lifestyles that are traditionally connoted as heterosexual—including traditional gender identities and monogamous long-term relationships—is nothing new. In the early 1980s, Lorde and Star (1982, p. 69) already noted that '[m]uch of the gay white movement seeks to be included in the American dream.' Towards the end of the decade, Faderman observed that the 'appeal to homosexuals to blend in had some resurgence' and prophetically predicted that this 'may be a harbinger of more conservative times' (1991,

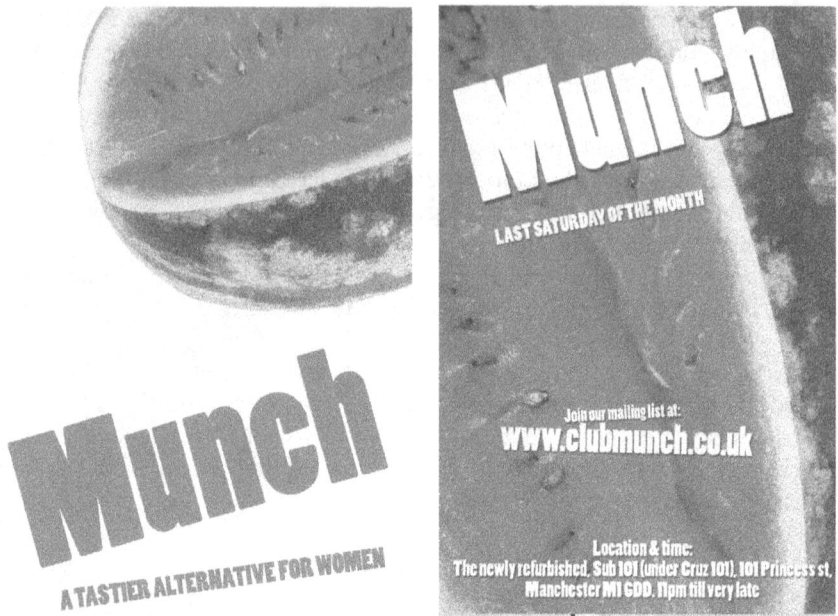

Figure 6.1   Flyer for Club Munch, Manchester/UK, 2007 (www.clubmunch.co.uk). Reproduced with kind permission by Club Munch.

p. 341, n. 31). If Johnston (1973) is right that the post-WWII history of the lesbian movements in America and Britain evolved 'from self hatred in guilt and secrecy to apologetic pleas for greater acceptance and greater sanctions' (p. 149), then the vocal contemporary form of gay and lesbian conservatism means that the wheel has come full circle. Granted, there are no outward indicators of self-hatred in the discourse of conservatives. However, their agenda is remarkably similar to that of the homophile organizations of the 1950s and 1960s such as Daughters of Bilitis in the US or Arena Three in the UK. As a former member of the latter organiza-tion stated: 'We were all concerned to present an image of normality and probity and the type of women that England would be proud of' (quoted in Hall Carpenter Archives 1989, p. 54). Respectability looms large, being seen as a way to achieving acceptance by heterosexuals and consequently gaining civil rights (Valocchi 1999, p. 64).

In his plea for 'a place at the table' (1993), Bawer asks for the inte-gration of gay people into a society that is inherently seen as good. In his seminal book, he argues that '[t]he excesses of the [gay] side fuel the [homophobic] rhetoric of the other' (p. 28) and thereby shifts the blame for homophobia to those who are at the receiving end of it. According to him, rather than alienate straight people, gays and lesbians need to educate them about homosexuality and lessen their prejudice (pp. 47–8). Semiotics are given a central role, because '[i]f the heterosexual majority ever comes to accept homosexuality, it will do so because it has seen homosexuals in suits and ties' (p. 51). This equation of heterosexual and corporate codes has prompted critics of the gay right to observe that 'gender conformity has returned as a marker of upward mobility . . . the business suit has become the *sine qua non* of gay male assimilation . . . [f]or lesbians, that means learning to be glamorous' (Goldstein 2003, pp. 8, 97). Likewise, Bawer's admiration for the 1993 March on Washington as 'eminently civilized, good-natured, orderly, peaceful, and tidy' (p. 219) has been interpreted as an expression of 'the illusion that stigma can be overcome by good behavior' (Goldstein 2003, p. 47). Respectability is communicated through dress and demeanour,[5] so that a semiotic code citing and reiterating the notion of traditional heterosexuality reifies it as inherently good and worth striving for, if not in lifestyle than at least in appearance.

To sum up the argument against assimilation:

> By gravitating towards mainstream communities, living in our nice houses with our partners, children and pets, we are no longer a threat to institutionalised heterosexism, and being lesbian or gay can be explained away as a sexual preference, rather than an open challenge to gender norms and heterosexuality. (Bindel 2004)

Given the historical links between the contemporary gay and lesbian right in the US and the pre-Stonewall homophile organizations, the question remains whether the conservatives' assimilationist agenda and rejection of any community beyond a local one represents the endpoint of lesbian communities as discussed in this book, or whether we are dealing with a swing of the pendulum that is going to be reversed in the course of time.

After outlining the main issues and arguments that can be observed in contemporary lesbian discourses—lesbian chic, consumerism and, for the US, lesbian conservatism—the next section will chart how these issues are related to, and how they impact on, discursive practices.

PRODUCTION, DISTRIBUTION AND RECEPTION OF TEXTS

The increasing commercialization of lesbian culture and lesbian media throughout the 1990s was not only in line with the then *zeitgeist*. It was also a corollary of cuts in public funding that caused the demise of many non-profit organizations and independent publishing. It also meant that lesbians re-oriented themselves toward mixed gay male and lesbian spaces (Healey 1996, p. 179) in order to tap into financial resources. For example, the nationwide UK magazine *Diva* was founded in 1993 as a glossy sister magazine of the *Gay Times,* which had already been running for ten years.

Ever since, the small lesbian lifestyle magazine market has diversified into magazines for 'sophisticated' (read: wealthy and over 35) lesbians (*Jane and Jane,* launched in the US in 2006), art and culture magazines (*Velvetpark,* launched in the US in 2002) and free magazines focusing on events listings and shopping (*g3,* launched in the UK in 2001, and *Dyke Life,* launched in the UK in 1999). As high-gloss, full-colour publications, these magazines typically feature many photographs and modular page layouts, perhaps in an attempt to align with the visual organization of web pages. In terms of content, they include sections on travel, fashion, relationships and sex, music, and careers. Each is accompanied by a website that provides further links to reader discussion and dating forums as well as shopping sites, with the latter mirroring the prominence of advertorials in the print versions:

> It's more of a glossy lifestyle approach and it feels like in order to get a magazine self-sustaining you have to go down this sort of glossy route because people don't seem to be interested in buying community news-letters and magazines . . . also I think the influence of the web has made it less likely. (interview with Gillian Eastham)

The readership of these magazines is typically urban and in the 20–35 age bracket, with a high disposable income (e.g., *g3* readers have an average yearly income of £32,704 [$65,151]; 'About us' 2007).

These publications are much more easily available then their predecessors, which were initially by subscription only and later also distributed through a network of women's bookshops, cafés and events. Given the demise of such independent enterprises, free glossy magazines are now available from mostly mixed lesbian and gay clubs and bars, an outlet which also reflects the young and urban target readership. Commercial magazines are also stocked by high-street bookshops and stationers, usually placed next to heterosexual women's glossies pushing the holy trinity of babies/marriage/diet. However, given the focus of some lesbian magazines on 'lesbian mums' and marriage/civil partnership, and their images of mostly white, often young, blonde women (see Figure 1.2), it seems that the gap is narrowing. As critics have remarked: 'One gets the impression that *Girlfriends* is about just that—mindless girlfriends who play with each other's hair and make-up, rather than with political ideas' (Yescavage & Alexander 1999, pp. 29–30).[6] Similarly, *Diva* magazine has been characterized by older lesbians as 'soft porn' with 'no politics in it at all' (interviews with Laura Donne and Lola di Marco). It seems that this mainstreaming of lesbian magazines is the price for an increased number of distribution channels and therefore more widespread reception. In addition, all publications are also available via the internet, although the for-sale magazines obviously only grant limited access to contents, redirecting the would-be reader to dating forums and shopping sites instead. Whether free or for sale, commercial magazines rely heavily on advertising, which tends to be for sex toys, travel and alcohol and as such ties in seamlessly with the editorial content.

It should not be forgotten, however, that non-profit publishing continues to exist at the local level, even though national magazines overtook local and regional ones in number, circulation and revenue already in the 1990s (Chasin 2000, pp. 75–6). One example of a local publication that has made it into the 2000s is the *Manchester Lesbian Newsletter*, which is collectively published by the Manchester Lesbian Community Project. It is made available through subscription and through non-commercial outlets such as the Lesbian and Gay Foundation—an organization whose building is home to various community projects—or municipal libraries. It is printed in two colours on non-gloss paper and on its six to eight pages addresses issues such as health, age, therapy and politics. It also lists community events and includes a small ads section, as indeed does the parallel e-bulletin. The editors state that '[a]ll adverts must be relevant to/aimed at lesbian and/or bisexual women in some way' and reserve the right to edit adverts that are not.[7] Adverts are one way of generating income for the publication, next to limited funding by public bodies such as Manchester City Council or the Neighbourhood Renewal Unit. Readers are urged to subscribe to the newsletter by email rather than post in order to save money, and the editors have also launched a donations scheme. The example of the Manchester Lesbian Newsletter illustrates the observation that

> [b]ecause most media companies not only create content but also have a hand in its distribution, alternative voices are also physically locked out of the public sphere [and] must circumvent the established distribution. . . . [They] rely totally on government intervention . . . or work to curry the favour of bookstore conglomerates and distributors. (Sutton 1999, p. 166)

Despite these structural difficulties, there are attempts to take community-based publishing to a nationwide scale, as evidenced by the 2004 launch of *Velvet,* a UK independent arts and literature magazine for and by lesbians.

While non-profit publications are struggling financially, their continued existence guarantees a varied media landscape. Next to this, there is also increased access to publications and a wider range of media now available for the distribution of lesbian discourses and texts. Although lesbian programming on local radio and TV stations started in the San Francisco Bay Area already in the late 1970s (Wolf 1979, p. 78), nationwide lesbian programming began only in the early to mid-1990s, with *OUT,* a gay and lesbian TV magazine (Hamer & Ashbrook 1994) and the weekly series *Dyke TV,* both broadcast by the BBC's Channel 4 and pioneering the trend in Britain. A decade later, there are no fewer than three full-time nationwide cable networks with lesbian and gay-themed content available in the US:

Here! (as in the slogan 'We're here, we're queer, get used to it'), launched in 2002, *Q Television* (as in 'queer') launched in 2004, and *Logo,* a channel owned by Viacom and launched in 2005 (Steinberg 2005). While the former two are subscriber-based and therefore more independent of advertising money, *Logo* has less independence but a wider reach. Given its reliance on advertisers, it is hardly a coincidence that *Logo* also has the least queer-connoted name. Political lesbian television is restricted to programmes rather than whole channels but has existed since 1993, in the form of New York-based *Dyke TV,* which is run on donations and grants.

In 2004, the debate on lesbian chic was rekindled by the advent of the first all-lesbian television series, *The L-Word,* on US and British screens. The arguments in favour and against were largely the same as ten years before, i.e., enthusiasm about increased visibility versus a critique of the overwhelmingly urban, affluent, white and feminine cast (Rosenduft 2005; see also Bindel 2006). The crucial difference to the mainstream media phenomenon of lesbian chic, however, lies in the fact that the series was written and produced by a lesbian, Ilene Chaiken. Although relying on the support of largely male-run TV networks and advertising accounts, phenomena like *The L-Word* can therefore not simply be dismissed as mere projections of heterosexual fantasies and fears of lesbians.

In line with lesbian chic's emphasis on conventional femininity, however, butch images are notably absent in the iconography of lesbian glossy magazines and TV channels, and it seems that gender conformity is the price that many lesbians are willing to pay for increased visibility in mainstream media (Warn 2005). Like much of contemporary lesbian discourse, the exclusion of lesbian masculinity, too, seems to hark back to pre-Stonewall days: early homophile groups of the 1960s worked through passionate debates on cross-dressing and its possible detrimental effects on broader acceptance (e.g., the 1964 discussions at the Minorities Research Group, the organization which published *Arena Three,* as quoted in Neild & Pearson 1992, pp. 41, 101–2). Those early organizations even imposed conventional dress codes for public appearances on their members (Phelan 1998, p. 193). Indeed, current images of lesbians seem to reflect the conviction that a woman quoted in Neild and Pearson (1992, p. 26) held in 1963: 'If you're going to sell a thing like lesbian, you've got to look like *Vogue.*'

The idealized lesbian characters of *The L-Word* series not only reflect the focus on femininity in much of lesbian self-representation, but also the ongoing reconceptualization of society in terms of business. Clearly, many characters approximate the ideal of corporate femininity, as can be seen in Figure 6.2.

Again, it is questionable how far these images bear any resemblance to contemporary lesbian life as it is presently lived in the UK and the US. As one letter writer asks about *The L-Word:* 'where is the . . . normalcy?' (Cindy 2005, p. 14). The pictures on the gossip pages of UK lesbian magazines—to say nothing of field observations—clearly illustrate that many

Figure 6.2 The L-Word, first series, 2004 (produced by MGM Entertainment). Reproduced from DVD (Region 2).

gay women continue to flaunt a style that is very different from the slick corporate femininity displayed on the pages and screens of lesbian media. There is also some anecdotal evidence that as a reaction to groups of heterosexual women increasingly roaming gay and lesbian clubs on weekend nights, some venues in Manchester/UK have adopted a policy of refusing entry for women who do not 'look gay' (Jayne 2007, p. 4). Meanwhile, the pictures of women working for national LGBT organizations betray a broad range, with some approximating corporate *masculinity* more than anything else.[8] Nevertheless, the ideal, at least for the more affluent part of the lesbian community, continues to be corporate femininity. An example of this is Citypink, a group of London-based lesbian professionals formed in January 2004, which offers a 'network for gay women professionals.' The fact that 'professionals' functions in nominal usage and is modified by 'gay women' in attributive use clearly indicates that the women's identity is first and foremost as professionals. This notion is further underscored by the information that they meet at 'sophisticated, elegant and exclusive venues' and by the list of sponsors including all the major investment banks. The network also has an explicit dress code, reflected in the website's visuals. Contrary to the demographic links between ethnicity and wealth, the same visuals also feature a black woman in a prominent position (Citypink 2005).

This visual code is reminiscent of the images on the website of the Log Cabin Republicans (www.logcabin.org). Not only does the picture slide show on the landing page feature only couples, in contrast to for instance the British organization Stonewall, which also depicts single individuals and groups (www.stonewall.org.uk). On the Log Cabin Republican website, those couples are further depicted in business attire, with lesbian couples also shown in domestic settings. All age groups are represented, but one looks in vain for pictures of people of different abilities or body sizes. Finally, almost all African Americans who are depicted are at the very light-skinned end of the spectrum. On the whole, the website reflects a scale of images of femininity, ranging from the domestic to the corporate, while conventional masculinity is never questioned. Clearly, women are expected to either stay in the domestic sphere or aspire to male-defined areas such as business. Together, this implicit devaluation of women and the value apparently placed on physical attributes such as ability, slimness and fair skin, combine into a marketable image of lesbians and gays that in no way offends conventional tastes and beliefs. The Log Cabin Republicans' website is therefore the perfect visual reflection of the organization's assimilationist agenda.

Along with websites, blogs, e-magazines and discussion forums are important channels of distributing texts by lesbian and gay conservatives. This is likely to be an effect of the minority position of conservatives, especially in lesbian communities. For example, among the seven interviews and articles covering the 2004 presidential election in the April 2005 issue of *Curve,* only one presents a conservative standpoint. The tokenistic gesture is underscored by the title of the opening piece to the feature, 'How to survive four more years,' which tacitly assumes that the re-election of George W. Bush was a negative event for lesbians. Other articles centre on words and expressions like 'doom and gloom,' 'pain' and 'blues,' while the closing commentary asserts that lesbians and others in the gay community need to 'sever all and any ties we might have to . . . those queer Republicans like the Log Cabinites,' also referred to as 'Log Cabin sycophants' (Brownworth 2005, p. 62). Similarly, a pre-election article in *Girlfriends* magazine (Rostow 2004) talks about 'the conservative and the gay voters' (p. 15) and thereby constructs gays and conservatives as two opposed groups. In this context, it is worth noting that the Log Cabin Republicans decided not to endorse Bush Jr. as presidential candidate, because of the president's campaign to amend the constitution to state that marriage would have to be between persons of opposite sexes. This move was regarded by the Republican gay and lesbian lobbying group as going 'against the party's core principles of smaller government and personal freedom' (Log Cabin Republicans n.d.).

As a result of limited space in lesbian and gay print media, gay and lesbian conservatives use blogs and online forums to distribute their texts, next to radio shows. This strategy has a remarkable impact, e.g., the well-known conservative gay writer Andrew Sullivan boasted 1.5 million visits a month to his blog in mid-2003 (Robinson 2005, p. 43), and conservative lesbian journalist Norah Vincent enjoys similar recognition. It is also in online publishing that conservative opinions are most represented; thus, the queer-themed website Planet Out regularly reports on the activities of the Log Cabin Republicans in its news section. Online texts are characterized by a high degree of interconnectedness, with websites incorporating hyper-links to other websites, e-magazines including discussion forums and comments on blogs routinely quoting from, and linking to, other blogs. These connections lend cohesion to a discourse and it is thus no surprise to find a significant amount of intertextuality in lesbian conservative discourse. This includes the aforementioned metaphor of political opponents as children, and the claim that they revel in their self-constructed 'victimhood' (e.g., Bawer 1993, p. 36; Bruce 2004; Lochhead 1993) but also negatively connoted keywords such as 'groupthink' (e.g., Vincent 1996, 2002) and the vilification of left-leaning lesbians as totalitarian, the 'orthodoxy' (e.g., Vanasco 2001; Vincent 1996), the 'Gay Gestapo' (Bruce 2004), the 'Gay Inquisition' (Paglia 2002),[9] a replacement of 'the Catholic Church of the 1950's as the new unassailable bastion' (Gossett 2004) and 'fascist gays' (Paglia 2001). The epithet 'fascist' was already used in the 1980s debates on sexual identities and practices (see Chapter 4; Faderman [1991, p. 235] further quotes a woman as describing the debating behaviour of lesbian feminists as 'the language of revolution [combined with] the procedure of the inquisition'). The conservative in-group, on the other hand, is given neutral to positive attributes such as 'independent' (e.g., Bruce 2004; see also the online Independent Gay Forum), 'moderate' or 'mainstream' (e.g., Lochhead 1993) and 'libertarian' (e.g., Paglia 2002; see also the group Gay and Lesbians for Individual Liberty).[10]

To reflect the important role of glossy magazines and online publishing for contemporary lesbian discourses in the US and the UK, the two examples that are analyzed in the following are taken from these two media (see Chapter 2 and glossary for technical terms). As for topics, the first example represents what links lesbian chic to conservative thinking, namely the increasing importance of consumerism and corporate lifestyles as an ideal. Lesbian media and lesbian communities have increasingly focused on money and career matters. Thus, we now have gay career guides (Snyder 2003) and a rising number of networks of gay and lesbian professionals. *Curve* magazine featured its first annual careers special in November 2004, following *Girlfriends* magazine's annual special on lesbian-friendly employers and career advice launched in 1999. Similar features regularly appear in Pride magazines across the UK, e.g., the 2005 issue of London Pride (Swan 2005). Extracts from the *Curve* special issue make up Example G. This particular text was chosen because the editorial of the magazine issue in which it appears explicitly mentions *Fortune* business magazine, and Example G is to a large extent visually and linguistically modelled on that publication. The text is therefore a prime instance of pursuing a transformative strategy by introducing other genres into lesbian discourse. Because this is not explicitly claimed but rather implicitly illustrated by way of an example, the transformation is effected in the operative rather than the normative realm. The analysis will show how this incorporation of business media text types makes for a differentiated model of lesbian collective identity in which the value of individual achievement is balanced by the textual construction of solidarity between members of an imagined community.

EXAMPLE G: 'THE 10 MOST POWERFUL LESBIANS' (BLOCH 2004) (EXTRACTS)

Reproduced with kind permission by the editor.

1 When 'you're fired!' becomes the country's favorite catchphrase you know
2 you're in trouble. Curve comes to the rescue with this handy and, dare we
3 say, comprehensive guide for working girls everywhere.
4 Surely you've heard of the really big power lesbians, like Hilary Rosen (the
5 former chief executive of the Recording Industry Association of America
6 who took down Napster) and Megan Smith (the former CEO of PlanetOut
7 who currently works at Google). But what about other sisters in business,
8 government and industry who excel in their careers and give some of their
9 success back to the community? From gals who've been in the boardroom
10 forever to some up-and-coming working women, these lesbians give 9 to 5 a
11 good name, which is why we anoint them (in no certain order) to our 10 Most
12 Powerful Lesbians list.
13 1. Finally, a Bush we can identify with: Linda Bush, founder and former CEO
14 of SafeRent, the first credit-profiling model in the country, recently became
15 chief operating officer at the Gill Foundation, a Colorado-based philanthropic
16 organization dedicated to securing equal opportunity for all people regardless
17 of sexual orientation or gender identity. With an endowment of approximately
18 $200 million, the Gill Foundation is the country's largest funder of LGBT
19 organizations. . . .
20 3. When lesbian mom Kathy Levinson, former president and chief operating
21 officer of eTrade, was asked to donate a big chunk of change to the No on
22 Knight Campaign (the group that campaigned against the California initiative
23 that defines marriage as valid only between a man and a woman), her
24 decision was such a big one that it inspired a case paper at Harvard Business
25 School. But Levinson has long been involved in women's, LGBT and Jewish
26 causes: She's responsible for making Charles Schwab one of the first major
27 companies to offer benefits to same-sex partners and was instrumental in
28 establishing a domestic-partner registry in Palo Alto, California. In 2000,
29 Levinson launched the Lesbian Equity Foundation of Silicon Valley, which
30 explores the intersections between sexual orientation, gender and Judaism.
31 . . .
32 7. 8. Speaking of power couples, Joan Garry, who worked at Showtime and
33 helped launch MTV back in 1981, is now executive director of the Gay and
34 Lesbian Alliance Against Defamation. GLAAD announced last summer that
35 it would be teaming up with Logo, the new digital television network
36 targeting queer viewers, to broadcast the 2005 GLAAD Media Awards, which

37   celebrate fair and accurate representations of the LGBT community in
38   media and entertainment. One key consultant and programmer over at Logo is
39   none other than Eileen Opatut, former senior vice president of programming
40   and production at Food Network—and Garry's life partner. Talk about
41   networking.

This extract was taken from a list of the ten most powerful lesbians in US for-profit and non-profit businesses, which is explicitly modelled on the lists published regularly in *Fortune* business magazine (Fortune Global 500, Fortune Most Powerful Women in Business, Fortune Best Employers etc.; for a comparison of Example G with the Fortune Most Powerful Women in Business list, see Koller forthcoming). The issue's careers special further includes a list of the top 15 companies for lesbians, portraits of entrepreneurs and their companies, a report of workplace discrimination on the grounds of sexual orientation as well as two humorous and critical comments, respectively, on the lack of high-powered careers for women and on female poverty. It is the latter pieces in particular which show traces of feminist thought. Likewise, 1970s values are reflected in the selection criteria for the 15 best companies, as these are ranked according to not only diversity management, but also general ethical behaviour (environmentally friendly operations, no animal testing, minimum wages for all workers etc.). As such, the whole feature, and also Example G, draws on a range of genres and their typical characteristics, integrating them into lesbian discourse to advance a model of a lesbian community that embodies the values of corporatism and individualism.

Although careers and corporate lifestyles only became reported on in the lesbian media in the late 1990s, lesbian entrepreneurship and, with it, wealth creation can be recorded as early as the late 1970s:

> In the City of Berkeley there was an association of lesbian entrepreneurs in the late 1970s. . . . On the one hand, there were all those lesbian collectives and then there was that influx of lesbian entrepreneurs. And they all joined forces. (interview with Ina Feder)

Wealth loomed large on the lesbian radar in that pivotal figure of the 1980s, the yuppie: Stein (1997, p. 123) reports that by 1987, organizations for lesbian professionals had—along with those for lesbian mothers—come to dominate the San Francisco community. This points to two new ideal types in the lesbian community, mothers and businesswomen, who embody two different notions of femininity. Both types are represented in Example G.

Social Actors

Social actors can be divided into collectivized representations of the lesbian community, the collective 'we,' 'you,' the reader, and six specific women.

Of these, references to 'lesbians,' 'women,' 'sisters' and 'girls/gals' are most frequent at eight instances, while the first person plural ('we') and the second person ('you') are used three times each. Most individual women are referred to only once, with the exception of Joan Garry, who is referred to twice, and Kate Levinson, who is mentioned four times, including the anaphoric pronoun 'she.'

As a collective actor, 'we' refers to the editors of *Curve* magazine twice, being juxtaposed with the name of the magazine (line 2) and one of its features ('our . . . list,' lines 11–12). This collective social actor addresses the reader directly in the opening to the whole feature ('you know you're in trouble,' lines 1–2), where *Curve* magazine is set up as a benefactor of the reader ('Curve comes to the rescue,' line 2) in order to foster reader loyalty and raise interest in the careers special. Direct address continues in the first lines of the part on lesbians in business ('[s]urely you've heard,' line 4), which presupposes shared knowledge and thereby further fosters the relation between magazine and readers. The relationship then finally culminates in the inclusive 'we,' which refers to both the writer and the reader ('a Bush we can identify with,' line 13).

The portrayed women are referred to collectively as 'the 10 most powerful lesbians' in the salient space of the headline. Individually, they are mentioned formally or semi-formally by (first and) last name, or by job title, a feature that is also typical of business magazine articles. Other labels relate, literally or metaphorically, to family and private life ('sisters in business' in line 7, 'lesbian mom' in line 20 and 'life partner' in line 40). In Example G, this feature contrasts with more public labels. Although the two means of reference can be juxtaposed, they do not merge: *lesbian* qualifies only private roles ('lesbian mom' rather than 'lesbian executive director'), and sexual identity is thus connected with the private sphere. This corroborates the observation that 'the very categories of lesbian and work mirror the private and public dichotomy' (McElhinny 2002, p. 120). It further flies in the face of early feminist claims that the personal is political, and it is therefore questionable whether the label 'sisters' (line 7), which originated in the same context, is more than just a nod to lesbian feminist history.

As a group, the lesbian community is invoked by the neutral label 'lesbians' four times and specified as 'working women' (line 10) once. An alternative label is 'girls'; reference is made not only to 'working girls' (line 3) but also to the even more informal 'gals' (line 9). This indicates closeness between the writer and the portrayed women, a relation which is extended to the reader. Familiarity is afforded by all social actors being part of an imagined lesbian community, explicitly invoked in lines 9 and 37. Such a community is conceptualized as a sisterhood, although the modification here is to 'sisters in business' (line 7). Nevertheless, the closeness between writer and reader, their familiarity with the portrayed women and their embeddedness in an imagined community conveys the importance of solidarity and community spirit, even if some women are singled out as particularly successful members of the community.

Evaluation

The nature of rankings demands positive evaluation of the women selected to be worthy of inclusion (unless the ranking is a 'black list'). As a consequence, the unabashedly positive evaluation of the women occasionally becomes celebratory. In this, hyperbole, especially superlatives and intensifiers, are used prominently ('most powerful lesbians' in 11–12, 'really big power lesbians' in line 4). Verb connotations are another evaluation device, as in 'who excel in their careers' (lines 8) or 'we anoint them' (line 11). Positive evaluation can also work indirectly, by linking the woman with a company that is ascribed superlative attributes ('the country's largest funder' in line 18, 'one of the first major companies' in lines 26–7).

Interestingly, lesbian executives become more important the more they are noticed by, and connected with, mainstream business—witness the dropping of names like 'Napster' (line 6), 'Harvard Business School' (lines 24–5) and investment bank 'Charles Schwab' (line 26), which are only indirectly related to the women. It seems that the measure of success is appraisal by mainstream society and especially business, an attitude which is also reflected in modelling the ranking on that of a business magazine.

Actions

The three types of action realized most frequently—material, behavioural and relational—each occur six times. The widest spread of process types can be recorded for the collective social actor 'lesbians' etc., who engage in all three kinds of actions ('these lesbians give 9 to 5 a good name,' lines 10–11, "sisters . . . who excel in their careers,' lines 7–8 and 'gals who've been in the boardroom,' line 9). The first person 'we' features in material, behavioural and verbal processes, while Kathy Levinson, who is portrayed in rather more detail than the other women in the extract, is the actor in material, sayer in verbal and, most frequently, carrier of attributes in relational processes (e.g., 'Levinson has long been involved' or '[s]he's responsible,' lines 25 and 26). In most actions, the collective and individual social actors indeed carry out actions; only twice do we find them as the goal or target of someone else's action (e.g., 'Kathy Levinson . . . was asked,' lines 20–1). In the other example, the actor is the first person plural ('we anoint them,' line 11), maintaining the community as the locus of action.

The relatively high number of behavioural and relational process types overall make for an altogether rather static representation of the women's actions, which is in sharp contrast to the dynamic, forceful activities that businesspeople are usually shown to be engaged in by business magazines. Another contrast to that format is the absence of interviews with the women, which translates into a lack of verbal process types and intertextuality in general. This dearth of first-hand information is to some extent compensated for by information about the organizations the respective women work for. These are mostly quoted and paraphrased from the websites of the respective organizations (www.gillfoundation.org, http://www.glaad. org/events/mediaawards/index.php), which could indicate restricted access to the women and their organizations. If this is indeed the case, then *Curve*'s attempt to emulate *Fortune* business magazine is constrained by the lesbian magazine's less powerful position in terms of discourse access.

Modality

Being largely narrative and expository, the text features only a very low amount of modality; in fact, there are only two instances ('[s]urely you've heard' and 'a Bush we can identify with,' lines 4 and 13). Both of these serve to foster in-group solidarity by assuming shared knowledge and presupposing shared political values and beliefs. Apart from meeting the interpersonal metafunction, modality in the text further serves the ideational metafunction in that it represents corporate lesbians as widely known role models and conservatism as opposed to lesbian identity. This latter move echoes the magazine's post-2004 election special (mentioned previously) and contributes to the marginalization of conservative lesbians, while the construction of corporate role models reinforces corporate lifestyles as an ideal for lesbians to aspire to.

Interdiscursivity

The text shows traces from three different discourses. These are, in declining order of importance, corporate, domestic and lesbian feminist discourses. The first one, corporate discourse, is of course inevitable, given the topic; however, it is most frequently invoked throughout the text and accompanied rather than challenged by the other two. Expressions like 'you're fired!' (line 1), 'careers' (line 8), 'boardroom' (line 9) and '9 to 5' (line 10) all invoke the public sphere of office and corporate life, as indeed do the numerous job titles used as attributes for the portrayed women. The noun compound 'power couples' (line 32) acts as a hybrid combining the public sphere of the office with the private sphere of the home. The same effect is achieved by ranking two couples in the list (numbers five and six [omitted from Example G] as well as seven and eight). This also accounts for the occurrence of 'life partner' in line 40, where the first half of the compound specifies what kind of partner is being referred to. Incidentally, this shows that the word 'partner' for one's companion or lover—widely used, especially among same-sex couples—is actually a term transferred from the public sphere of business to the private domain of domestic relationships. A similar blurring of the public and the private is effected by the double attribution of Kathy Levinson as both 'former president and chief operating officer at eTrade' and 'lesbian mom' (lines 20–1). The latter seems somewhat unmotivated, given that her motherhood is not referred to again and is not shown as impacting on her professional role. Its occurrence in the text can perhaps best be explained as reference to another ideal type, that of the mother. The juxtaposition of both lesbian-as-mother and lesbian-as-executive is a reflection of changes in the wider societal context, where a relatively recent role for women is now that of the successful professional. While this change looks as if the range of self-realization and self-expression has been broadened for women, this impression is illusionary; if women's magazines and self-help books are anything to go by, the 'ideal woman' is expected to be lover, mother and professional in equal measure and with equal success, while the same demands are not made on men, for whom there is no domestic ideal type. The adoption of a dual ideal of mother and professional in a lesbian text therefore represents a rather uncritical acceptance of dominant, if only partly traditional, gender roles.

The blurring of the business and domestic spheres through interdiscursivity moreover presents the public as private, thereby reversing the classical feminist dictum that the personal is political. Indeed, traces of lesbian feminist discourse pale by comparison, being restricted to 'sisters in business' (line 7) and 'community' (lines 9 and 37). While the notion of community still plays a pivotal role in the text—witness the alignment of writer, reader and individual women as discussed previously—the expression 'sisters in business' is another hybrid, this time of lesbian feminist and corporate discourses, and as such seems little more than a modified, possibly ironic reference to earlier lesbian discourses (see Examples A and B).

The whole text is interdiscursive on a macro-level, imitating as it does a text type originating in business magazines. While there will be an overlap between the readerships of business magazines and lesbian magazines, the genre imported from the business magazine format may well be alien to, and unexpected by, most readers of lesbian magazines and hence requires careful introduction and adaptation, e.g., through interdiscursivity at the micro-level. This kind of recipient design draws on context models relevant for interacting with the target readership (van Dijk 2006a, pp. 170–3), with the aim being to present the sphere from which the text type was imported, i.e., the corporate world, as the goal of lesbian ambitions.

Metaphor

Perhaps the most striking feature of the text is that it makes hardly any use of metaphors other than spatial ones to refer to social actors. These are UP IS GOOD ('up-and-coming working women,' line 10) as well as BIG IS POWERFUL ('big power lesbians' in line 4, 'her decision was such a big one' in lines 23–4). The latter in particular can be seen as a strategy of positive evaluation in a business context. Positive evaluation is also conveyed through the expression 'we anoint them' (line 11), while the kinship term 'sisters' (line 7) is a nod at earlier discourses. However, one of the defining characteristics of business magazines, the use of flamboyant metaphors (Koller 2004), is conspicuously absent. This shows that while the author of the text seeks to emulate business magazines, she does so only to a certain extent, whether intentionally or not.

Image of the Community

The basic conflict between individual and community, freedom and belonging, pervades contemporary lesbian discourses, which have come to represent diametrically opposed socio-cognitive representations of identity. In the present text, the two models are reconciled by constructing the ideal of 'sisters in business . . . who excel in their careers and give some of their success back to the community' (lines 7–9). Here, American values of good citizenship are integrated into a model of lesbian community. The definite article ('the community') indicates that the community is presupposed as a given, while the modified reference to 'sisters' taps into earlier models of lesbians as closely related to each other. One possible interpretation is that this is a reflection of 'pro-business forms of feminism hijacking models of self-expression from an earlier, progressive period of the movement' (Butler 2004, p. 175). An alternative reading may allow for mildly ironic overtones, but still see the author as feeling comfortable in invoking sisterhood. This reading is motivated by contrasting the present text with writings of conservative authors, who claim that 'it is excessive to speak, as some do, about gay "brotherhood"' (Bawer 1993, p. 37). In Example G, community cohesion is also seen to be fostered by bringing writer, reader and the individual women together through assumed shared knowledge and use of the first person plural ('we' in line 13). Despite the corporatist nature of Example G, and the focus on consumption in the magazine as a whole, it seems that discourse participants are not 'more lost or homeless in their consciousness simply because the social organizing objects in question happen to be commercial' (Muniz & O'Guinn 2001, p. 415). On the other hand, the text as such elevates individual women and evaluates them in intensely positive terms, by combining verb connotation, metaphor and intensifiers ('really big power lesbians,' line 4). The overall image is that of 'local girls make good,' of individuals who are nurtured by a community, rise above the masses but never forget to whom they owe their success. This is set up as an ideal that members of the lesbian community can aspire to. The juxtaposition of corporate with domestic roles points toward a colonization of the private by the public (Fairclough 2003, p. 33) as well as to a reduction of one's direct community to the private sphere, i.e., to partner, family and friends. Nevertheless, there is still a strong imagined community.

By contrast, the last text, Example H, solves the tension between individual and community in favour of the former. Writings by lesbian conservatives show a scale of presupposing a community to questioning and ultimately abolishing it, with the present text representing a middle ground. It criticizes the notion of social categories based on sexual identity and instead foregrounds the value of individualism. In that the author comments on an everyday example to do so, her text can be located in the operative realm. The analysis will demonstrate how she uses linguistic devices such as personal pronouns for social actors and sarcasm to prioritize individual rather than collective identity.

EXAMPLE H: 'I FEEL LEFT OUT' (BARNES 2002)

Reproduced with kind permission by the author.

1 I feel left out!
2 Two weeks ago a lesbian group calling itself Lesbians for Liberty held a kiss-
3 in at Madison Square Garden. Why did they have a kiss-in? And why wasn't I
4 invited? Well it seems that many lesbian sisters have nothing better to do with
5 their Friday night than to stir up what amounts to childlike behavior. But we
6 have to hear from kids now don't we?
7 It seems that the Lesbians for Liberty are quite peeved at the Liberty
8 management because [they] have not paid attention to all the 'lesbians' that
9 attend Liberty games. In an email, which by the way I did not receive and I'm
10 quite miffed, the ladies stated, 'are you tired of the W.N.B.A. and the New
11 York Liberty denying that lesbians are packing Madison Square Garden week
12 after week for women's basketball games?' They go on to claim that
13 management refuses to acknowledge the lesbians in the crowd. Now, I don't
14 know about anyone else but one of the stereotypes of lesbians is that they are
15 probably packing Madison Square Garden for 'every' sport. But I digress
16 so I'll get to the point.
17 The point is this, so what? For anyone who has been to a Liberty basketball
18 game it is quite obvious that there are lesbians there, but so are a variety of
19 souls. There are the little kids in jerseys of their favorite players. There are
20 blacks, whites, Hispanics, old people, young people, gangsta boys etc. So I
21 ask you this, why should lesbians be singled out for acknowledgement? Just
22 because they are lesbians? I don't think so. How about if we single out the
23 black lesbians and the Hispanic lesbians? How about if we single out the
24 grandmother who got a courtside seat as a present for her birthday? How
25 about if we single out the white male who brought his young daughter to see
26 women play professional basketball? How about if we single out the poor
27 souls in the nose bleed sections who wish they had courtside seats where all
28 the kissing is going on? How about we single out the hard workers serving
29 these lesbians in club seats for holding down a job?
30 Why do we insist on having celebrities and sports figures speak for us? So
31 what if we don't get a Liberty player to sit a top [sic] a float on gay pride

32 day? So what if Liberty management doesn't do a shout out to lesbians in the
33 crowd? These women are not here to raise flags or engage in kiss-ins, sit-ins
34 or the like. They are here to PLAY basketball. That is what they are getting
35 paid for. That is what we are paying money to watch, not to hear them talk
36 about their favorite lesbian bar on gay pride day. I go to watch them win and
37 work on their rebounding game. I go to yell at them for not boxing out. And I
38 go to drink a beer or two and relax with friends. Am I missing something here?
39 So, here are my suggestions for the Lesbians for Liberty. First, go and enjoy
40 the game. Enjoy the diversity that surrounds you. Second, understand that
41 basketball, football, baseball, and golf players are just that, players. They are
42 not activists, they are not spokespersons for any one group that enters MSG
43 they are professional players there [to] do their job and hopefully win a game or
44 two. Third, if you really want something to argue about how about suggesting
45 to management that Richie Adubato have the ladies work on their rebounding
46 skills because the lack of it is killing them? Fourth, how about protesting for
47 more endorsements and more pay for the women? But then these would
48 be logical issues to fight for, wouldn't they? See you at courtside ladies!

This final example was published as an entry on the author's blog, which has, at the time of writing (July 2007) moved from www.iebarnes.com to http://notyourtypicalnegro.blogspot.com/, with entries stretching back no further than 2006 at the new address. As mentioned previously, the author serves as the Hudson Valley, NY, chapter president of the Log Cabin Republicans and as such also granted me an email interview. Besides her professional life, her function as chapter president of a Log Cabin Republican chapter and maintaining her blog, she is active writing letters to various (online) gay magazines. As is its nature, the blog provides a commentary on current events from the writer's perspective and allows for readers' comments, although no comments were posted for Example H.

Social Actors

The roots of blogs lie in the diary, which effects a prominent use of the first person singular ('I'). Blogs are therefore in many ways the perfect format for a writer who espouses the values of individualism. While we could see the writer referring to herself already in Examples C and E, neither of those used the first person singular so persistently as does the present text. Indeed, the specific 'I' is not only given salience by being headlined, but also occurs 12 times, as often as the genericized 'players,' alternatively referred to as '[t]hese women' (line 33), 'the ladies' (line 45) or, in more general terms, 'celebrities and sports figures' (line 30). This is complemented by five references to the basketball teams' management and coach as well as six references to increasingly specific members of the audiences. Most references, however, are made to lesbians as a group, divided almost equally between 'lesbians' in general and the group 'Lesbians for Liberty,' also addressed as 'ladies' (lines 10 and 48) and called 'lesbian sisters' (line 4). Both 'ladies' and 'sisters' already featured in earlier examples; while the former was used at the end of Example C ('Ladies, is there a conservationist in the house?,' Example C, line 64) to index a tongue-in-cheek old-fashioned gallantry of the butch author, 'sisters' was used seriously in Examples A, B and F ('her "straight" . . . sisters,' Example A, line 16; 'our heterosexual feminist sisters,' Example B, line 3; 'you can . . . surround yourself with your sisters,' Example F, lines 23–4), and with mildly ironic overtones in Example G ('sisters in business,' line 7). In the present text, irony has intensified to sarcasm by ascribing 'childlike behavior' (line 5) to the women referred to as 'sisters.' In fact, they are no longer 'sisters' on par with the author but 'children' who the author cannot take seriously.

The lesbian activists are addressed directly, by means of the second person ('you' in lines 44 and 48) and imperatives ('go and enjoy the game' in lines 39–40, 'understand that . . . players are just that,' lines 40–1), with the final salute in the text combining the various devices for direct address ('See you at courtside ladies!,' line 48). Next to the first person singular, the text also includes a somewhat ambiguous first person plural ('we have to hear from the kids' in lines 5–6, '[h]ow about if we single out' in lines 22–8 and 'we are paying money to watch' in line 35). While the first 'we' refers to anyone but the lesbian activists, denoted as 'kids' in the phrase, the five occurrences in 'we single out' seem to be a generic 'we.' Finally, the 'we' who pays to watch basketball is anyone in the audience, including both the author and the lesbian activists. The most multi-faceted use of the pronoun occurs in line 30: 'Why do we insist on having celebrities and sports figures speak for us?' Paradoxically, the author here uses a pronoun including herself to depict a form of behaviour that she takes issue with. This might indicate that she still considers herself—however grudgingly and tentatively—as a member of a wider community. Her point echoes one made by Norah Vincent, only that the latter effects a crucial shift from first to third person when asking: 'When will dykes grow up enough not to need groupie handholding to keep them going?' (Vincent 2002).

The text as a whole shows a shift from first person singular to first plural and back; thus, the 'I' features most prominently in lines 1–16 and 36–8, where it is set in opposition to an out-group. The out-group of lesbian activists is mostly represented through reported speech, i.e., by quoting an email from them directly (lines 10–12) and indirectly (lines 12–13). (Incidentally, the direct quote employs the same rhetorical question—'[a]re you tired of'—that was used as a persuasive device in Example F, line 18.) The 'we' then becomes central, in all its ambiguity and shifting referential range, in lines 22–35, before the 'I' makes its re-entry in lines 36–8. This oscillating between 'I' and 'we,' individual and community, can be interpreted as the linguistic reflection of the basic conflict that conservative lesbians have with other, more left-leaning lesbians.

One very diverse social actor group is the members of the audience that are specifically mentioned, and it is their very diversity that is used to refute the demand that any one group be singled out for official acknowledgement. The argumentation first juxtaposes 'lesbians' (line 21) as a group with a more or less random list of other groups such as 'blacks, whites, Hispanics, old people, young people, gangsta boys etc.' (line 20), before narrowing it down to 'the black lesbians and the Hispanic lesbians' (lines 22–3). Finally, the author proceeds from narrowly defined groups to specific individuals ('the grandmother,' 'the white male,' lines 23–4 and 25) and thereby effects a shift from community to individual. By doing so, she re-instantiates conservative values of individualism in the face of liberal requests for group recognition.

By highlighting particular members of the audience at a basketball game at Madison Square Garden, the author further evokes a prototypically American scene. Considering her statement in the interview that she identifies as 'an American first and foremost' and her assertion that 'gay Republicans will continue to live as principled Americans' (Barnes 2004b), we can link her invocation of the all-American audience to the Americana that Vanasco (2005) lists when she reclaims the allegedly oxymoronic 'gay American' as her identity. In that text, the author not only links Gay Pride to Independence Day but crucially characterizes the all-American lifestyle with a set of attributions ('we have jobs and cousins and roots in home-towns,' 'we are assimilated') as well as behaviours ('we ride the bus,' 'we go camping,' 'we send our mom flowers'), including consumption ('we buy iPods, 'we want yards and fireplaces and granite countertops and Jacuzzi tubs'). The intersections between lesbian identity, American identity and consumer identity are also hinted at in Barnes' text. The move from the political in the form of a social group to the personal in the form of individuals is backed up by financial arguments: to paraphrase lines 34–6, basketball players cannot represent a group because that is not what they are paid to do and it is not what the individual members in the audience pay for when buying their tickets.

So far, then, we can say that the text constructs an out-group in the form of lesbian activists demanding recognition as a group. In contrast to earlier examples, however, Example H does not go on to set up an in-group in return; rather, and despite some oscillation between individual 'I' and communal 'we,' the alternative to the community is presented as what Lochhead (1993) has referred to as 'thousands of individuals.'

Evaluation

The out-group of lesbian activists is evaluated in unanimously negative terms, through comparison, ridicule, sarcasm, parody and overall trivialization. In lines 28–9, the list of individuals in the audience to be singled out ends with 'the hard workers serving these lesbians in club seats.' Compared to the conservative values of 'stability and family, hard work and education and thrift and honesty' (conservative gay journalist Jonathan Rauch quoted in Lochhead 1993), the lesbian activists appear downright frivolous, living off someone else to engage in what the author regards as their 'childlike' (line 5) behaviour. Another implicit comparison is drawn at the end of the text, where the author directly addresses the activists with suggestions of what to campaign for (lines 46–7). She ends with the sarcastic remark '[b]ut then these would be logical issues to fight for' (lines 47–8), insinuating that the activists are illogical and perhaps even incapable of rational thought. This ties in with the attribute 'childlike' and is linked to the claim, propounded in many texts by lesbian conservatives, that serious politics are made at the national level, in dialogue with powerful elites. Whether one sees this political thrust as evidence of '[gay conservatives'] devotion to the powerful' (Goldstein 2003, p. 42) or as *realpolitik,* the fact remains that opposing allegedly irresponsible and silly left-of-centre activist with perceived responsible and 'grown-up' conservative politics is pervasive in many texts by lesbian conservatives. Thus, Lochhead (1993) contrasts 'gay ghettos' with 'the center of national discussion in Washington,' while Vincent (2002) hopes that lesbians will 'be ready for prime time in Washington' once they 'graduate from the clubby small time of softball teams, meatless potlucks and womyn's folk festivals.' This cliché of the 1970s lesbian feminist is also invoked in another blog entry by Barnes herself, where she sarcastically comments on one Democrat senator's dismay at a Schwarzenegger speech by asking if 'all of her [the senator's] politically correct lesbian friends come and bring hummus [to a potluck supper] to soothe the pain?' (Barnes 2004a). The positive attribute 'logical' as the opposite of leftwing activists' behaviour echoes Paglia's description of a TV debate that involved gay conservatives and liberals: 'Sullivan and Vincent . . . seemed thoughtful, centered, anchored. . . . [T]heir language was considered and their tones measured' (Paglia 2002). This contrasts sharply with her perception of 'screeching gay activists' (Paglia 2001).

In the present text, sarcasm combines with parody when the author imitates the perceived victim mentality and childish, sulking behaviour of the out-group. This starts with the very title of the piece. While positioning oneself as being excluded from comments and emails is a typical feature of blogs (see lines 1, 3–4, 9–10), it here also serves a function specific to a contemporary lesbian discourse, namely to make fun of the perceived behaviour of activists and thereby refute their—and indeed any—model of imagined communities. This reading is corroborated by the author's claim to be 'quite miffed' (line 10), which links back to the members of the Lesbians for Liberty group being 'quite peeved' (line 7). Ridicule is also built up in lines 22–9, where ever longer sentences refer to ever more specific groups and subsequently individuals that could be singled out for official recognition.

This strategy makes the initial demand that lesbians be acknowledged as a group in the audience seem absurd.

Next to all the sarcasm and ridicule, however, there are also serious and constructive suggestions in the last paragraph of the text. As far as the Log Cabin Republicans as a whole are concerned, their argumentation strategy at the policy-making level is very much characterized by a focus on the positive. For example, the lobbying group ran a $1 million TV advertising campaign against the Marriage Protection Act, which would have meant a change in the US Constitution to codify marriage as between a woman and a man only. The slogan developed for the campaign called on politicians to 'save the Constitution' against 'anti-family amendments,' thus tapping into classical conservative values rather than explicitly opposing the proposed amendment along the lines of 'say no to . . .'. This argumentation strategy illustrates Lakoff's (2002) observation that one of the reasons for continued Republican success in US elections (prior to the mid-term elections of 2006, that is) is the relentless focus on the positive, while the Democrats rather negate the arguments of their political opponents. Since negation is frame-preserving—to quote the title of another of Lakoff's books (2004), 'don't think of an elephant' makes you do just that—the Democrats inadvertently help spread Republican ideas.

On the whole, negative out-group evaluation in the text is achieved through sarcasm, ridicule and parody, as well as through implicit comparisons with positive in-group markers. Like so many of the other examples, the present text, too, relies on an 'us vs. them' dualism with negative out-group and positive in-group attribution to construct its evaluative stance.

Actions

Unlike many of the previous examples, Example H is characterized by a high number of material processes. In fact, this is the one most frequent type, at 30 instances, and even if we deduct those that could be recoded as overtly material but covertly mental ('Liberty management . . . have not paid attention,' lines 7–8) or verbal ('Liberty management doesn't do a shout out,' line 32), we are still left with 25 material processes. While this is unusual in the context of the other examples in this book, it is not remarkable in general, especially not for spoken texts, whose features are transferred to computer-mediated text types. To be sure, there are still a fair number of relational actions, namely 14 overt ones, including two that are covert mental processes ('[they] are quite peeved' and 'I'm quite miffed,' lines 7 and 9–10). This is partly an effect of stating what the basketball players are (not), according to the author ('[t]hey are not activists, they are not spokespersons,' lines 41–2), and it partly stems from identifying members of the audience ('[t]here are the little kids in jerseys,' line 19). Incidentally, the latter example shows that it is justified to conflate relational with existential process types, as pure existential processes are extremely rare in pragmatic terms (Ryder 2007); when the author mentions that '[t]here are blacks, whites, Hispanics' (lines 19–20), this statement is not made to inform the reader that those groups exist, but to modify the importance of lesbians in the context of the basketball game.

The mental process in the title ('I feel left out,' line 1) points towards the encoding of beliefs, attitudes and emotions that are at stake whenever notions of community and identity are negotiated. Thus, the author states her beliefs and doubts ('I don't know about anyone else' and 'I don't think so,' lines 13–14 and 22) and also explicitly asks the activists she addresses to 'enjoy the game' (lines 39–40) and 'understand that . . . players are just that' (lines 40–1). The relative prominence of this process type shows that the argument is ultimately about mental models and the emotions that attach to them. These models have to be textually mediated, i.e., encoded, distributed and received via texts of various sorts, which together make up discourses on community. Accordingly, we find nine overt (e.g., 'the ladies stated,' line 10) and another five covert verbal processes (e.g., 'I'll get to the point,' line 16).

Obviously, the number of times a social actor is referred to can be lower than the number of actions they are seen performing, because the actor can be implied in elliptic sentences ('[s]ee you at courtside,' line 48). One effect of doing so is to increase the prominence of the writer. On the other hand, the mismatch between number of times the activist group is mentioned and the actions allocated to them is accounted for by the four imperatives the author directs at them (e.g., 'go and enjoy the game,' lines 39–40). This again strengthens the author's position as she sets herself up as being in the position of instructing the others. The first person singular and the out-group also engage in the widest range of process types, making them the two most differentiated social actors in the text. The first person singular ('I') is most often portrayed as the actor, featuring as goal only once ('why wasn't I invited?,' lines 3–4) for the 14 actions that she is seen performing. By contrast, the lesbian activists are in the role of actor/carrier of an attribute twice ('held/have a kiss-in,' lines 2–3) and also feature twice as the goal of someone else's action ('hard workers serving these lesbians,' line 28–9, and 'see you at courtside,' line 48).

In sum, the various ways of representing actions supplement the parameters of social actors and evaluation in constructing a relatively weak, negatively connoted out-group in contrast to a strong self. All earlier examples—with the notable exception of Example G—relied on out-group constructions to communicate models of identity, albeit more or less explicitly so; Example C only hinted at the lesbian feminist out-group in abstract terms ('the current trend of lesbian literature,' Example C, lines 7–8). Even where the conflict was between two individuals, as in Example E, either woman was constructed as a representative of a certain model of lesbian identity. The novel strategy in Example H is to set the self up in opposition to a group, precisely *because* that group seeks recognition as a community.

Modality[11]

Modality in the text is divided almost equally between epistemic, deontic and mixed forms, where the latter mean that the same clause is marked for both modalities. While the one instance of epistemic modality can be neglected for the overall argument ('lesbians . . . are probably packing Madison Square Garden' in lines 14–15), deontic modality does contribute to characterizing the out-group. After evaluating the activists' behaviour as 'childlike' (line 5), the author states that 'we have to hear from kids' (lines 5–6). In the context of Example H, this not only invokes anti-authoritarian stances to education, regarded by conservatives as a historical mistake with far-reaching social consequences (Bruce 2003). The deontic modal 'have to' also conveys an obligation imposed from outside, rather than the speaker's own will, thus constructing the out-group ('kids') as a nuisance or necessary evil. The second instance of deontic modality is couched in a question ('why should lesbians be singled out for acknowledgement?,' line 21) which relates back to the activists' demand for official recognition, calls it into question and subsequently refutes it.

Mixed modality can be found in the two conditional clauses of the text. The first of these ('If you really want something to argue about how about suggesting,' line 44) provides an epistemic frame within which mild obligation is implied in 'how about suggesting.' Note that the 'how about' construction here echoes the list of sarcastic questions in lines 22–9, recoding them as serious suggestions. This strategy is employed once more in lines 46–7 ('how about protesting for more endorsements'). The second conditional is elliptic ('[b]ut then these would be logical issues to fight for', lines 47–8), and while we cannot be certain what would complete it, we can infer that a complete conditional may be something like 'these would be logical issues to fight for, if only you could bring yourselves to fight for them.' Semantically speaking, the modal 'would' is epistemic, because it presents the addressee with a possibility. Pragmatically, however, the intended meaning is deontic, representing as it does a conditional request. This interpretation is also suggested by the imperatives preceding the elliptic conditional clause.

While scarce throughout the text, modality thus helps to further evaluate the out-group in negative terms, refute their demands for recognition as a group and indeed their model of a lesbian community, and present the author as instructing them in what for her are more constructive politics.

Interdiscursivity

Apart from the intertextuality of the quoted and paraphrased email (lines 10–13), the text also features interdiscursivity, i.e., the integration of other discourses and genres. As a blog entry, the text is typical of many forms of computer-mediated communication in that it incorporates features of spoken genres such as a high number of material process types and also discourse markers more familiar from spoken language such as 'well,' 'now,' 'so' (lines 4, 13, 39) to indicate the beginning of a new section or introduce an argument.

Two discourses that the author recontextualizes are those of grassroots political activism and of lesbian feminism, brought into the text by particular lexical items. While the first of these, 'kiss-in' (line 3) is probably taken over from the activists' use of the term, it is reworked into a question ('[w]hy did they have a kiss-in?,' line 3) and then both refuted and ridiculed by being lumped together with expressions from the same discourse ('to raise flags or engage in kiss-ins, sit-ins or the like,' lines 33–4). Related to this is the expression 'lesbian sisters,' which is taken from lesbian feminism and as such is used sarcastically and evaluated negatively ('it seems that many lesbian sisters have nothing better to do,' line 4). Interdiscursivity then is mainly used to underscore ridicule and sarcasm as a strategy of degrading the out-group and refuting their beliefs, values and practices.

Metaphor

The two most noteworthy metaphoric expressions in the text are the two kinship terms 'sisters' and 'kids' in lines 4 and 6. As mentioned previously, the first is used sarcastically, referring to a model that is associated with lesbian feminism, an ideology that the author refutes. The fact that the same social actors, lesbian activists, are called 'kids' in the next sentence (line 6) betrays the author's actual image of them, not as equals but as irritating minors. The metaphor of leftist gay and lesbian activists as children is very much elaborated on in gay and lesbian conservative discourse. Some examples were already provided in the section on issues and arguments; here are some more to show how typical Example H is of the discourse it is embedded in:

> the government authority . . . that gay leftists dream of in their nanny-care utopia of cradle-to-grave socialism (Paglia 2002);

> [gay leftists are] fanatics . . . who are still nursing childhood wounds and who cling to 'the movement' as a consoling foster family (Paglia 2002);

> [gay activists] confuse liberation with childish abandon, as if no responsibility went along with it (Bawer 1993, p. 172);

> a fringe group of gay protest-junkies who have to have everything (stamping foot on the ground) NOW! NOW! NOW! . . . I'm . . . not searching for the government's approval in order to make up for whatever it was I didn't get from mommy or daddy (Scott 2005).

The author herself, when asked in an email interview about her view of non-conservative lesbians, said that she saw them 'as two-year-olds who want all the attention and never grow up to assume their rightful place as responsible adults.'

It indeed seems that '[t]he developmental metaphor that associates radicalism with childishness and moderation with maturity is a fixture in the writings of all the new gay conservatives' (Robinson 2005, p. 12). Yet, discrediting opponents by metaphorically referring to them as children actually has a long tradition in conservative discourse. In particular, assimilationist lesbians have often belittled more radical thought and action as immature, as for instance in the following letter published in UK magazine *Sappho* in 1978: 'proclaim your sexuality to the Universe as childlike you shriek for acceptance and approval (or is it martyrdom?)—but don't knock us well-adjusted gays by calling us cowards!' (quoted in Kitzinger 1987, p. 111).

This feature of conservative gay and lesbian discourse contradicts Lakoff's (2002) claim that the main metaphor that conservatives use to conceptualize the government is that of the STRICT FATHER, whereas liberals rather metaphorize it as a NURTURING PARENT (see also Goatly 2007, pp. 383–8). Rather, gay and lesbian conservative writers 'reject any higher secular authority' (Gays and Lesbians for Individual Liberty 2003) and demand that the notion of government as whatever kind of parent, or of the community as an *ersatz* family, be abandoned altogether because it stands in the way of individual responsibility. The metaphoric concept of GOVERNMENT AS FATHER is even ascribed to leftists and refuted explicitly; as Bawer (1993, p. 187) claims, radical gay activists 'assail the government petulantly as father figure.' Others go so far as to reject any government intervention in individuals' lives, including the demand for marriage—a main item on the agenda of US lobbying groups—as a wish to be acknowledged by a 'Mommy or Daddy . . . [s]ociety' (Bruce 2004). Again, we can see that lesbian and gay conservatives do not engage in debate by offering a counter-model equal to that proposed by their opponents—a different metaphor, say, or a different kind of community. Instead, they completely reframe the debate by refuting metaphoric concepts of government altogether and by abandoning the idea of any community and embracing individualism instead. As Goldstein (2003) observes, using a culture-specific metaphor, gay conservatism is 'not just another tribe in the ever-expanding queer nation; it's a highly articulate attempt to secede from that confederation' (p. xi).

It was noted earlier that the title is part of the author's strategy to parody and ridicule the out-group. It is worth looking at in terms of metaphor, too, though: Butler posits—albeit in a different context—that 'the compelling metaphors of the spatial distinctions of inner and outer . . . remain linguistic terms that facilitate and articulate a set of fantasies' (1990/1999, p. 170). From a cognitive semantics perspective, we may wish to add that metaphors are also, even primarily, cognitive phenomena, which are expressed on the surface level of language. This expression in turn helps set up, and feeds into existing, mental models that capture the image of community as a bounded space. Boundaries can soon become limitations and indeed, Norah Vincent revisited the question of lesbian identity in a text titled 'Beyond Lesbian' (Vincent 1996). The spatial metaphor here denotes lesbianism, understood as a political concept, as limiting, even marginalizing because it confers minority status to lesbians as a group. Seen in connection with that earlier piece, the title of Example H is sarcastic not only by imitating the perceived behaviour of lesbian activists but also because we can infer that the author actually *prefers* to be left out of any imagined community, the very notion of which she rejects.

IMAGE OF THE COMMUNITY

The question for the final part of the analysis then is not so much what an image of a lesbian community the text communicates, but if the concept of an imagined community is still upheld at all. The discourse of conservative lesbians shows a range of stances on this. It seems to be common consent that any lesbian community is more diverse than gay activists would have it; as Vanasco (2001) puts it, 'we are not a monolithic movement . . . [w]e are a culture, a people, with diverse ideas, beliefs and opinions.' Does this mean then that there is still a community? For some writers there seems to be, as suggested by their unproblematic references to 'the community,' where a definite article presupposes its existence: e.g., 'there is not a consensus in the gay community about [marriage]' (Bruce 2004). At the other end of the scale, Norah Vincent crystallizes the fundamental question about the individual's relation to any community when stating that 'there is an urgent question . . . a question the so-called "lesbian community" does not ask: Who am I?' (Vincent 1996). Not only is the self here contrasted with the community, but the author also distances herself from the latter with the dual strategy of ascribing and scare quotes.

Example H can be located in the middle range of the scale. There are indications that the author still regards herself, however tentatively, as part of a wider imagined community. This is mostly encoded in the change between first person singular and plural in the text as a whole, where the 'we' is paradoxically seen to make demands that the author rejects ('[w]hy do we insist on having celebrities . . . speak for us?,' line 30). In almost every other respect, however, gay activists and their belief in a lesbian community are weakened, ridiculed and refuted, notably through negative evaluation and sarcasm, through number and types of actions ascribed, through deontic modality and through sarcastic labelling in interdiscursive and metaphoric terms.

In her previously mentioned text, Vincent (1996) asks '[w]hat does it mean to be a lesbian?' and thereby echoes Example A, which started out (line 1) by asking 'What is a lesbian?' In a stark contrast to the answer given in the early manifesto, which laid the foundations for political lesbianism ('[a] lesbian is the rage of all women condensed to the point of explosion,'

Example A, lines 1–2), the conservative author of the later text defines lesbianism as 'primary sexual and emotional attraction to women.' Lesbianism is no longer a political agenda, a lifestyle or the defining characteristic of a community. Stripped of all additional, and ideologically loaded, meanings, the term has become neutral. What sense of community there is, is not grounded in this 'primary emotional and sexual attraction' but expressed in friendships between individuals (mentioned by both Vincent and Barnes; line 38 in Example H), in the conservative emphasis on family and nation as communities, and in the paradox of a group of people believing in individualism or, with regard to the internet as the preferred distribution channel for conservative lesbian discourses, an online community denouncing the notion of imagined community. In that some contemporary writers abolish all models of an imagined community, texts by lesbian authors have gone from following a constructive strategy (Example A) to pursuing a destructive strategy (Example H). One can bemoan that the very idea of a lesbian community has ceased to exist in the latest turn that lesbian discourse has taken and accuse conservatives of reducing the meaning of 'lesbian' *ab nihilo*. Yet their rejection of the lesbian community, while extreme at times, not only robs the individual of the safety of communal bonds but also frees her from having to accept a group identity and the concomitant lifestyle and ideology in exchange for such safety. To return to the terminological point of conservatism and libertarianism (see n. 10), the authors of the texts investigated around Example H indeed wish to conserve traditional values and by doing so return to pre-Stonewall discourses and practices. But they also seek to liberate the individual of what can sometimes be the fetters rather than the support of the group. In this sense, we have reached an endpoint in lesbian discourses and the images of community that they construct and transport. Where the proverbial lesbian goes from here is uncertain, but if conservatives/libertarians are to be believed, she will be equipped with the best of the past and free to make her own way from now on. And freedom has always been a thing of terrifying beauty.

This final analysis chapter has investigated contemporary lesbian discourses, mostly in the US, showing how the wider societal values of corporatism, individualism and consumerism impact on both the production, distribution and reception of texts by lesbian authors as well as on the socio-cognitive representations of collective identities that are constructed and negotiated in those texts. Again, the described trends are paradigmatic rather than representative of all local lesbian communities and discourses. However, models of imagined lesbian communities are changing, incorporating new values and ideal-type members—such as the successful businesswoman—rather than prototypes (see Examples A and C). Some lesbian authors, e.g., the one of Example G, balance these new features of the model with older ones such as in-group solidarity. Nevertheless, the logical conclusion of consumption of products and services as a practice granting in-group membership, and of the individualism related to it, can be observed in Example H. This is one of a number of texts that radically reframe lesbian discourses and the representations of community that they transport. Indeed, the last example in this book throws into sharp relief the ambiguity of the word 'consumption': while it has connotations of joy and access, it is also synonymous with obliteration. Example H anticipates a lesbian community that has been consumed and therefore has ceased to exist.

7 Conclusion
Changing Images, Changing Communities

> I remember and I always think that it is important to keep the memory but I would also say that these twenty years were twenty very long years.
>
> (interview with Vera Vaizek, 1997)

Given the development of this book, ten years have elapsed since my interview partner commented on how long twenty years can seem when one looks at the changes in images of lesbian community. The first text analyzed, Example A, dates back to 1970, and in the nearly 40 years since, lesbian communities, discourses and texts in the UK and the US have changed almost beyond recognition. In the last pages of this book, I will provide a summary of the overall findings, comment on how a critical discourse analysis helps trace historical changes and flag up some possible future research in the area of language and sexual identity.

In this book, I have explored the changing images of a lesbian community as they were conveyed in texts by self-identified lesbian authors in Britain and the US between 1970 and 2004. Going through the decades, I have outlined the wider socio-political contexts that gave rise to particular issues and arguments that were vital for lesbian discourses at their respective times. I have further shown how the same contexts impacted on practices of discourse production, distribution and reception in lesbian communities, and I have analyzed eight texts from four different decades in linguistic detail to show what models of collective identity were represented and how. Lesbian communities have never been homogeneous, and therefore the analyzed texts are paradigmatic but not representative of lesbian life at the time. Indeed, their analysis shows how myths about lesbian communities at particular points in time are created that do not reflect the complexity of collective identity: for instance, neither were all lesbians in the 1970s necessarily feminists, nor were those that were feminists as asexual as particular narratives would have it. Moreover, the generational conflict that forms the dominant narratives for the 1990s is not always reflected in authors of a certain age subscribing to a particular brand of politics. The texts from the respective decades are linked interdiscursively in the sense that the later examples reiterate, recontextualize and on occasion reject elements of the earlier texts, the discourses they instantiate and the mental models those discourses transport. An added complication is the fact that British and American communities show only partial overlap due to wider cultural differences, while similar developments do not happen at the same time. Nevertheless, some general tendencies can still be observed, even if these did not evolve in as linear a fashion as a historical account might suggest.

If we return to the original research questions, these asked:

- what images of a lesbian community have been transported in lesbian discourses after 1970 in Britain and the United States;
- how this change can be traced in non-fictional, lesbian-authored texts;
- why these images have changed.

Looking first at the question of what images have been communicated, we can see that the image of community in the analyzed texts first shifted from the notion of a safe haven and endpoint of personal development (Example A) to the model of a group under attack from outside, which led to enforced homogeneity within (Example B). The model started to be differentiated at the turn of the 1970s/1980s, with authors who felt that their individual and collective identities were denied in the paradigmatic lesbian feminist discourse of the 1970s demanding to be acknowledged (Examples C and D). The model communicated is still that of one community—especially in Example D—albeit a more differentiated one. The rifts deepened, however, when a new generation coming out in the 1990s brought about a metaphorical mother–daughter conflict within the community (Example E) and recontextualized older models (Example F). The value of individualism, which had first surfaced in the 1980s, came to fruition twenty years later, showing in a transformed image that positioned individuals as ideal-type members of a lesbian community (Example G) or even reduced the community to personal social networks, ultimately denying the notion of an imagined community altogether (Example H).

Proceeding to the question of how this change in collective identity models can be traced in texts, we need to distinguish between the realms that texts are located in, the overall discursive strategies that their authors pursue and the linguistic devices they employ to implement a particular strategy. As for realms, we can see a change at the turn of the 1980s/1990s, after which texts were increasingly located in the operative rather than normative realm (the exception to this being Example C). This is what one would expect to find in the historical development of collective identity, models of which are first proposed by normative texts and then exemplified and negotiated in operative texts. On a related note, discursive strategies change from constitutive in the early days of the period under investigation (Example A) to reproductive/preservative (Example B), to reproductive and transformative, as in Example C, which seeks to preserve an older model of identity and thereby transforms the one predominant at the time the text was written. Transformative strategies prove persistent for some time to come (Examples D, E and G), and although Example F seeks to preserve lesbian feminist models of community, its hybrid, interdiscursive nature shows so many traces of discourses dominating the 1990s that the text inadvertently transforms the images of community. At the preliminary endpoint of the development, we find destructive strategies at work in texts that refute the notion of an imagined community altogether (Example H).

In the texts, there is a noticeable shift away from men and society as collective and abstract social actors; these can, however, be found in early texts (Examples A and B) and in texts that recontextualize lesbian feminist discourse (Examples E and F). Likewise, the actor group set apart from men, i.e., lesbians, and women in general, are genericized in the same texts, with a generic singular in Example A. While demarcation of the in-group against that particular out-group seems to have lessened in importance, demarcation within the lesbian community became increasingly constitutive for the formation of in-group identity. This is mirrored in a tendency to use the first person plural ('we') as exclusive, referring to particular sub-groups (Examples B, C, D) rather than a community imagined as homogeneous (Example A). (Example D combines both uses.) Increasing individualization and a move away from the 'we' shows in the use of the third person singular ('she') in Examples C, E and G, in direct address via the second person ('you') in the later texts (Examples F, G, and H) and indeed in the emergence of the first person singular ('I') in Examples C, E, F and H, with Example G showing an institutional 'we' that refers to the author. (In Example B, the use of both first person singular and second person are due to the simulated dialogue.) With the notable exception of Example G, all texts establish an out-group. The author of Example C, however, only hints at the out-group of lesbian feminist in abstract terms and is alone in not evaluating the out-group negatively; all other texts that feature an out-group do so to some extent. Interestingly, this is not mirrored by an equally pervasive positive evaluation of the in-group, which only shows in Examples A, C and G, and in modified form in Example B. While negative out-group and positive in-group representation is to be expected, the relative dearth of the latter is astounding and may point towards an undifferentiated model of the collective self or, worse still, internalized homophobia.

The actions that the aforementioned actors are engaged in vary, with relational process types cutting across all texts, with both out-group and in-group members being defined by that feature. Some texts are particularly amenable to verbal processes, especially those that simulate or represent spoken and quasi-spoken interaction (the latter, e.g., being computer-mediated forms of communication), as do Examples B, D, E and H. As for material processes, most of the texts that represent or recontextualize lesbian feminist discourse (Examples A, B and F) not only feature men or society as a salient social actor, but also ascribe great power to that group in that they are seen as the actors whose material, often violent, actions impact on lesbians, and on women in general. (Example F has women acting on themselves in reflexive processes.) While the symbolic and/or physical violence that many men continue to inflict on women cannot be disputed—and that this should be so is an outrage—the predominant representation of women as powerless behavers rather than actors still reinscribes a victim role. That role is only abandoned in the contemporary examples (Examples G and H). Self-victimization is also at work in Examples D and E, where the in-group and the author, respectively, are at the receiving end of others' material and verbal actions. Lastly, mental processes are mostly reserved for the in-group, and the model of them thereby contains affective components, which do not tend to be included in models of the out-group. Next to such affective aspects, the models of collective identity also include values and beliefs, which are conveyed through deontic and epistemic modality, respectively. Unsurprisingly, deontic modality is linked to the normative realm, with texts in the operative realm featuring deontic modality only in indirect forms or as ascribed to out-group members (Examples E and H). (Example A includes deontic modality in the remainder of the text that follows the excerpt reproduced in Chapter 3.) Epistemic modality, on the other hand, is particularly strong in texts with hortatory genre elements (Examples F and G), where it serves to build solidarity with the reader and have her identify with the in-group.

Other ways in which changing images are communicated in texts are interdiscursivity and metaphor. These devices are closely related in that metaphor can act as a vehicle for features from another discourse domain (see Koller 2004, pp. 38–41 for an in-depth discussion). Thus, one trace from religious discourse is the JOURNEY metaphor (Examples A and F), although this can be realized without religious overtones as well (Example E). Likewise, revolutionary rhetoric is in Example B characterized by use of the WAR metaphor, which again can also be used without invoking that discourse domain (Example D). Different realizations of the FAMILY metaphor are to be found across texts, where the serious, ironic or sarcastic reference to other lesbians as 'sisters' is a trace of lesbian feminist discourse (Examples F, G and H). Other realizations of that particular metaphor include non-egalitarian models such as the implied mother–daughter conflict that we could observe in Example E, or the denigration of the out-group as children that is typical of conservative discourse (Example H). Cognitively, the FAMILY metaphor serves to scale down an imagined community to a more concrete level; in this function it can also be found in the discourses of nationalists and large corporations. Just as metaphors can be ascribed to others—e.g., the ILLNESS metaphor in Example D—traces from other discourses can be used to convey sarcasm in certain texts but used seriously in others. A case in point is advertising discourse, which is used ironically, if not sarcastically, in Examples B and C, but seriously in a later text (Example F), reflecting the ongoing commercialization of lesbian communities.

After having outlined the changes in images of a lesbian community and summarized how they are effected in and through texts, the final question is why these changes have taken place. Reasons are economic, political and ideological, and as such trickle down from the wider social formation to lesbian communities, also impacting on the discursive practices observed there. Economic changes are first and foremost the commercialization and commodification that can be observed in late capitalist societies, bringing with them a surge in promotional genres and their colonization of discourses other than marketing, branding and advertising (Fairclough 2003). As a result, not only products and services, but also events, ideas, social groups and individuals are now regarded as marketable. Together with cuts in public funding, this increased focus on for-profit operations has led to a decline of independent publishing and independent booksellers and a concomitant assimilation of images and identities to those found in mainstream discourses. Most publishing needs to be commercially viable these days, and therefore relies on advertising, which reinforces commercialization and mainstreaming. Political changes tie in with the decrease in public funding, leading to more centralized activities at the expense of small grassroots groups, projects and publications that could act as a site for alternative collective identities. As a result, we find an increasing assimilation to mainstream discourses, practices and values within lesbian communities. These economic and political changes are reflections of deeper ideological changes that foster the values of financial success and upward mobility and bring prestige to all things corporate. As nation states increasingly shift responsibilities to the private sector, they ultimately bring about individual rather than collective social actors.

Problematic though they are in their foreclosure of alternative models, these developments also have positive effects. After all, they bring about self-responsibility and individual freedom, even if taking liberties is only permissible within the dominant ideological framework. Also, some local lesbian communities have made a virtue of necessity and shown remarkable creativity and inventiveness in securing funds. The focus on individual self-expression coincides, at least in Britain, with a consensus in public discourse, if not in everyday life on the street, that homophobia is not congruent with modern pluralist societies. Direct textual effects of these changes are the increase of the author's voice as an individual, collective identity formation that relies less on out-group vilification and more on positive in-group evaluation, and a representation of lesbians as self-determined actors. As a paradigmatic example of contemporary lesbian discourses, Example G encapsulates all of these features, along with a focus on corporate lifestyles and individual success, which is, however, reliant on, and accountable to, a strong imagined community. While one text is of course not sufficient evidence for a wider change, it in many ways linguistically encodes the values discussed herein and is, at the very least, an indicator of a changing focus. The most positive effect of this representation is that it overcomes the focus on out-groups and the in-fighting that is typical of most other texts analyzed in this book. This is paramount, because negative out-group construction within an imagined lesbian community eats up energy reserves that are badly needed to tackle the lingering marginalization of, and discrimination against, lesbians in society at large.

As can be seen from this summary, a detailed linguistic analysis lies at the heart of this book. In answering *what* images of community are to be found in lesbian discourses, *how* they are constructed and negotiated in discourse and *why* the images have changed over time, such an analysis provides an essential complement to historical and sociological accounts elaborating on the 'what' and the 'why.' If the preceding chapters have focused on the 'how,' this was done to elaborate and supplement such previous studies (e.g., Faderman 1991; Neild & Pearson 1992; Hamer 1996; Stein 1997) and to make a case for why linguistic analysis is necessary if one is to gain as complete an account as possible. Critical discourse analysis (CDA) enables the researcher to uncover the formation and negotiation of (collective) identity as it emerges through textual interaction in context. In its socio-cognitive and discourse-historical versions, it further throws light on the intricacies of the discursive communication of cognitive models, showing non-linear developments and historical relations between texts. To illustrate, the more programmatic a text is, in terms of its functional genre, the more predictable are its structures. However, genre conventions and genre-specific purpose do not determine, they only favour, certain linguistic features. Language use still reflects a selective choice of certain features at the expense of others for the sake of representing aspects of the world from a particular perspective. To give an example, this is clearly demonstrated when comparing Example B with Example F: both texts embody separatist positions that were regarded as extreme and controversial at the time. However, while the later example shows clear interdiscursive links with the earlier one, it also incorporates linguistic features that are typical of text types such as self-help books and advertisements, which had become dominant genres in 'Western' societies by the 1990s. This shows the wider socio-historical impact on linguistic choice, demonstrates the dynamic nature of genres over time and illustrates how one and the same purpose (here: persuading readers to adopt a particular lifestyle) can be realized with quite different linguistic means. Although Butler's claim that 'you never receive me apart from the grammar that establishes my availability to you' (1990/1999, p. xxiv) is perhaps too close to a discourse idealism that disregards material practices, it is still true that the image of a community, however conceptualized, is clearly constructed, reiterated and challenged in discourse. The approach advocated and exemplified in this book is therefore useful to a diachronic study of the discursive construction and cognitive structure of collective identities in general.

Future discourse-analytical studies into lesbian identity formation and negotiation will hopefully address the gaps in this book, most importantly the discursive construction of individual and collective sexual identities in non-'Western' cultures. Further, the discourse-historical approach could fruitfully be applied to other historical periods to complement accounts from other disciplines (e.g., Boswell 1980; Faderman 1985). As sketched in Chapter 2, much of the research on lesbian discourse to date has been on spoken texts, and a CDA perspective could here be complementary to discursive psychology and conversation analysis to investigate how 'membership of specific social groups, based on sexuality and lifestyle choices, [is signalled] through language' (Sauntson & Kyratzis 2006a, p. 1). Finally, discourse-analytical studies could look in more detail at the interrelations between mainstream and lesbian discourses. And of course, all these foci of interest can intersect across cultures, times, text types and discourses.

As mentioned at the beginning of this chapter, the work on this book has taken ten years all in all. Even within that time span, lesbian discourses and images of lesbian community have changed noticeably, with the emergence of gay and lesbian conservatism as the latest development. The attempt of writers in that tradition to replace a model of an imagined community with socio-cognitive representations of individual identities seems like both a cyclical return to times before the 1970s and a preliminary endpoint in the construction, reproduction and transformation of community models. However, proclamations that we have reached 'the end of history' are rarely if ever correct, history having a habit of going on rather stubbornly. Sexual and other identities, both individual and collective, will continue to be formed cognitively and discursively and to be communicated in texts. It will be worth the while to see where the heterogeneous group loosely affiliated under the label 'lesbian'—less a cohesive nation than a federation of states—is in another ten years' time and how any collective identity maps out in different social, economic and cultural contexts. To quote the old slogan, lesbians are always and everywhere. Future research will have to address where and what they are exactly, and how.

Glossary

This glossary contains some basic definitions of technical linguistic terms as they are used in this book. A substantial amount of research has been done on each of them, to which the interested reader is asked to refer.

adjacency pairs
Two subsequent turns in a conversation in which the first conventionally prompts the second. Examples are question–answer, greeting–greeting or request–permission/refusal.

anaphora
Personal pronouns, like 'she,' 'they,' 'it,' or demonstrative pronouns, e.g., 'that,' which refer back to a person or entity mentioned earlier in the text. Because they refer to something, these pronouns are → deictic. Anaphora are the opposite of → cataphora and are one way of creating → cohesion.

cataphora
The opposite of → anaphora; personal pronouns, like 'she,' 'they,' 'it,' or demonstrative pronouns, e.g., 'that,' which refer forward to a person or entity mentioned later in the text. Because they refer to something, these pronouns are → deictic. Cataphora are one way of creating → cohesion.

coherence
The → semantic links between propositions in a text which ensure that the text can be processed as a meaningful whole. See → cohesion.

cohesion
The → syntactic links between the grammatical elements in a text which make a text hang together as a whole. See → coherence.

collocation
The tendency for two words, or collocates, to co-occur routinely in the language use of a particular → discourse community, e.g., 'lesbian feminist.'

Corpus linguistic methods can establish the statistical significance of these word partnerships. One effect of collocation is that the evaluation usually attached to one collocate rubs off on the other, leading to certain semantic preferences. See → connotation.

conditional clause

Part of a sentence that constructs a hypothetical or counter-factual scenario, usually in the form of an 'if'-clause. These scenarios can be more or less close to actual reality as perceived by the speaker.

connotation

The evaluative meaning that usually accrues to a word, e.g., 'weakness' is conventionally evaluated as negative. The tendency for words to co-occur in the language use of a → discourse community (→ collocation) is one way of effecting connotation. To illustrate, 'to admit' routinely co-occurs with negatively connoted words (e.g.,'to admit a mistake') so that in homophobic discourse, it can be used to derogate lesbian and gay people, e.g., 'she admitted to being gay,' where 'gay' accrues negative connotations by being linked to 'admit.'

deictic, deixis

Deixis is the quality of a text to refer to, usually, a time or a thing outside itself, as in '*that girl* never asked me out.' Also the quality of elements within a text to refer to each other. See → anaphora, → cataphora, → cohesion.

discourse (count noun)

Discourses are ways of representing an aspect of the world from a particular perspective, e.g., a conservative discourse on family. Discourses are instantiated in → texts.

discourse (mass noun)

Discourse is language use as social practice. Through discourse, i.e., the accumulation of → texts in a social domain, speakers and writers establish, reinforce or challenge their social positions vis-à-vis each other and negotiate their values, beliefs, attitudes and goals.

discourse community

A group of people who relate to each other by sharing a set of values and → texts produced from a similar perspective, in a similar style or on a particular topic. Discourse communities can self-identify as such or be identified by the researcher. Discourse communities can, among other factors, be constituted by a certain shared identity of their members, e.g., a lesbian discourse community. As all communities, they can be local or imagined.

discourse marker

Mostly found in spoken → texts, discourse markers indicate the beginning or end of a conversation, or the transition of one stretch of talk to the next. Examples are 'well then,' 'right' and 'so.' Discourse makers are often used with phonetic features such as vowel lengthening, or rising or falling intonation. They are one way of creating → cohesion.

discourse practice, discursive practice

The more or less conventionalized ways in which spoken and written → texts are produced, distributed and received within a → discourse community. Discursive practice involves questions of power in that the social roles of particular members of the discourse community grant them privileged access to text production and reception. Members of a discourse community can also be restricted in what kinds of texts they can produce or receive. For example, secretaries in most institutions are requested to distribute the agenda of a meeting in advance and take the minutes during the meeting but are not normally expected to contribute to the meeting in any other way.

ellipsis

The omission of one part of a sentence or clause, leaving the reader to infer the omitted elements. For example, 'see you later' is the highly conventionalized elliptic version of 'I will see you later.'

format

A medium such as a magazine or website that combines different → genres, e.g., a magazine combines editorial, interviews, feature articles and adverts.

genre

Genres are ways of classifying → texts according to a set of formal or functional features that they share. This classification can be done on formal grounds, grouping together texts with similar features (e.g., articles) and/or distributed via particular media (e.g., TV dramas). Genre can also be defined functionally (e.g., the persuasive function of advertisements), including the intended effects that a text in a particular genre is to have on its recipients (e.g., thrillers as meeting an entertainment function). Seen as such, genres have a communicative purpose and therefore (re)produce relations between producers and recipients of texts. Another approach to classifying texts is to group them by the → discourse practices surrounding them. See → text type.

hypotaxis

A quality of → syntax by which sentences contain many sub-clauses. Hypotaxis is a typical feature of formal written → texts, especially in an academic context. See → parataxis.

illocutionary force

The function that a → speech act is endowed with by the speaker, e.g., a promise. As such, illocutionary force (re)constructs the relations between speakers. Speaker intention and recipient interpretation can differ, e.g., a promise can be interpreted as a warning; see → perlocutionary effect.

interdiscursivity

The integration of different → discourses and → genres in a → text.

intertextuality

References to other → texts in a text, either in the form of direct quotes or of → reported speech.

metafunctions (ideational, interpersonal, textual)

In systemic-functional grammar, clauses are seen as simultaneously meeting three different metafunctions of language: the ideational function, which represents reality as it is perceived by the speaker or writer, the interpersonal function, in which text producers and recipients negotiate their relation to each other, and the textual function of structuring → texts. For example, 'it is only her view that counts for her' represents a person from a particular perspective (ideational), while also encoding the speaker's evaluation of that person (interpersonal). Finally, the example also structures the rest of the text in implying a complement such as 'and no-one else's.' The concept of metafunctions can also be applied to → metaphor use, to whole texts and to → discourse.

metaphor

The cognitive operation by which one entity is conceptualized in terms of another, and the result of that operation in the form of a mental model. For example, a mental model for argument can be metaphorically structured as war. The cognitive operation leading to such a model has been theorized as either a mapping from a source domain (here: war) to a target domain (here: argument), or as a blending of two input-spaces that share some generic structure. In order for a metaphor to emerge, the two concepts in question need to share some semantic features, the so-called ground of the metaphor. Any combination of domains or spaces is partial, in that only particular features will be mapped, or will enter into a blend, e.g., in ARGUMENT IS WAR, utterances are conceptualized as weapons but speakers are not usually given metaphorical ranks of military hierarchy. Conceptual metaphor at the cognitive level is realized in language as → metaphoric expression. Metaphor is one means of achieving → interdiscursivity, and can be theorized to meet the three → metafunctions.

metaphoric expression

The realization of a → metaphor at the level of language or any other sign system (e.g., visuals). For example, 'I am at a crossroads now' is the metaphoric expression realizing the metaphor LIFE IS A JOURNEY.

metonymy

A cognitive operation by which one entity is conceptualized in terms of one of its aspects or parts. The latter phenomenon is also known as synechdoche or pars pro toto; an example is the sexist reference to women in terms of body parts, accessories or pieces of clothing. Reversely, a part of an entity can be conceptualized in terms of the whole entity, e.g., 'the police did not come in time,' where 'police' stands for individual members of the police force. As with → metaphor, the linguistic realization of metonymic concepts can be used for rhetorical purposes.

modality

A function of language by which speakers and writers can express degrees of likelihood (epistemic modality), obligation and permission (deontic modality), or ability and volition (dynamic modality). Modality can be expressed by various linguistic devices, including modal verbs (e.g., 'may,' 'can,' 'should'), adverbs (e.g., 'probably') and relational → process types (e.g., 'I am convinced that. . . . ').

parataxis

A quality of → syntax by which sentences contain few sub-clauses. Parataxis is a typical feature of informal spoken → texts. See → hypotaxis.

perlocutionary effect

The interpretation that a speech act is given by its recipient, e.g., a warning. Speaker intention and recipient interpretation can differ, e.g., the utterance 'I'll be back' can be intended as a promise but be interpreted as a warning, depending on who says it to whom and under what circumstances. Like → illocutionary force, perlocutionary effect (re)constructs the relations between speakers.

pragmatic, pragmatics

Pragmatics is the study of language as it is used in communication. The pragmatic function of language refers to its affordance to make the speaker seem polite, to prompt certain behaviours in others or to save one's own face.

process types

In systemic-functional grammar, any actions that are encoded in language are classified into different process types. These are: material processes, in which an actor brings about a change in the outward flow of events, often impacting on a goal (e.g., 'she accepted the job offer'); behavioural processes that do not impact on the behaver's surroundings ('she worked'); mental processes which encode cognitive processes, knowledge and feelings (e.g., 'she had very much wanted to get a job offer'); verbal processes that encode communicative actions (e.g., 'she told her boss that she was going to resign') and relational processes that encode identification or attribution (e.g., 'she is the best candidate for the job,' 'she has a good set of qualifications'). A final process type identified in systemic-functional grammar is existential processes, which refer to the existence of an entity (e.g., 'her dream job did exist after all').

reported speech

A form of → intertextuality by which text or talk by someone else is not quoted directly but referred to in indirect speech (e.g., 'she said that she was angry') or free indirect speech, which re-enacts someone's thoughts or speech (e.g., 'she could barely find words for how angry she was'). A text producer can also report the → perlocutionary effect that someone else's utterances have had on them, e.g., 'she attacked me viciously.'

semantic, semantics

Semantics is the study of meaning in language, from a formal or functional point of view.

speech act

A spoken utterance seen from a functional point of view. Speech acts can be broadly divided into statements, questions and requests.

syntactic, syntax

Syntax is the structure that sentences have, and the study thereof. See → hypotaxis, → parataxis.

text

A self-contained instance of language use that hangs together as a meaningful whole. Texts can be spoken or written and differ vastly in length, but most refer to something outside of them. They can be classified into → genres and are the concrete instantiations of → discourse.

text type

The term is here used to refer to a formally defined → genre.

transitivity

The grammatical system by which social actors are labelled and shown to be engaged in different → process types. Analyzing a text for transitivity shows who is represented as a grammatical actor and who is the goal of that action, and in what kinds of actions who takes which role.

Notes

NOTES TO CHAPTER 1

1. Each chapter is preceded by a quote from one of the interviews I conducted to gain supplementary background knowledge on lesbian discourses and communities; see Chapter 2.

NOTES TO CHAPTER 2

1. Selected accounts of film as a medium of lesbian discourse/discourses on lesbians can be found in Weiss (1992), Olson (1994), Whitelaw (1996), Halberstam (1998b, pp. 175–230) and Schmidt (2005). Several essays in Hamer and Budge (1994) also address lesbian film(s).
2. Julia Penelope Stanley later called herself Julia Penelope, abandoning the name of her father as a political gesture.
3. Note that the term 'actor' denotes a participant in a material process and is therefore different from 'social actor,' which refers to any individual or group represented in the text, whether engaging in an action or being at the receiving end of it.
4. Following the notational conventions of cognitive metaphor theory, conceptual metaphors will in the following be indicated by small capitals.

NOTES TO CHAPTER 3

1. Clashes between gay men and lesbians in LGBT rights organizations have also been recorded for the 1960s homophile organizations (Hamer 1996, pp. 195–6), and tensions continue to ail cooperation to this day.
2. For the debate between radical/revolutionary and socialist feminists, see *McCabe (1980; the revolutionary position) and *Lesbian Left (1977; the socialist position). While both radical and socialist feminists 'call for . . . radical transformations of political systems' (McElhinny 2004, p. 131), the latter focus on capitalism rather than patriarchy as the root cause of social inequality.
3. For an excellent and thorough analysis of the intertextual formation evolving around this dictum, see Hark (1996, pp. 110–23).
4. See Wolfson (1993, p. 93): 'The first recorded use of the phrase was in 1975, when an American lesbian organisation . . . described its progress in an "intellectually and politically correct way"'. However, Wolfson fails to specify the organization or the text in which the phrase occurred, and Suhr and Johnson

(2003) indeed point out that the term is much older, dating back to 1793. In its current pejorative sense of 'dogmatic,' the term was first recorded in 1935, although 'the more immediate context for "PC" was undoubtedly Maoism with its central importance for the New Left politics of the 1960s' (Suhr & Johnson 2003, p. 9).

5. Indeed, especially Rich's text gained such importance that it was seen by some as still valid decades later. For example, Cameron (1992) not only continues the intertextual chain starting with Rich's text but also attempts to adapt it for lesbian political discourse of the 1990s.

6. If the notion of the 'woman identified woman' was intended as a persuasive device to recruit new members to the lesbian feminist cause, it surely was effective. As one 'old gay' woman—i.e., one who had been out before Stonewall—observed, heterosexual feminists joined in such numbers as to virtually constitute the lesbian feminist movement of the 1970s (Cordova 1978, p. 19, quoted in Stein 1997, p. 43).

7. *Lesbians Rising (1977) provide a clear example of the difficulties lesbian students faced when trying to publish a newsletter on a university campus.

8. Note the hedging devices in this quote ('if you will,' 'as it were'), which indicate that the speaker is using the metaphor consciously (Cameron & Deignan 2003).

9. Typically enough, the lesbian porn magazine *on our backs,* published intermittently between 1984 and 2006, not only reversed the title of the lesbian feminist paper *off our backs* but also resexualized the Radicalesbians' definition by stating that 'a lesbian is the lust of all women condensed to the point of explosion.'

10. One of the members of the group was Sheila Jeffreys, who features again in Chapter 5.

11. It was this new invisibility under feminist auspices that saw many feminist projects in Germany and Austria in the 1990s being attributed as 'for and by women and lesbians.' Inevitably, this juxtaposition, which placed 'lesbian' on the same level as 'woman' rather than as a sub-category, drew much scorn from outside but also from within the lesbian community.

12. Fascism and patriarchy are explicitly equated by Friesen (1998), who speaks of 'the fascist state of male dominance.'

CHAPTER 4

1. Exclusion of disabled women was also effected, albeit unwillingly, through non-accessible publications: 'There's also a great need for more information and books in Braille and on tape for blind lesbians' (Hall Carpenter Archives 1989, p. 70). At the time of writing (2007), physical space has become more accessible but there is still widespread exclusion from discursive space.

2. But see Faderman (1991, pp. 171–2) and Healey (1996, p. 44) for sexual flexibility in butch/femme communities.

3. This detail is particularly ironic if one considers that the difficulties a butch faces when going to the women's toilet are a central topic in lesbian narratives, conversation and literary fiction (e.g., Buttgereit 1997; Munt 1998).

4. Despite her stated radical feminist position, Kitzinger (1987, p. 147) delivers a passionate defence of butch/femme and calls for a political analysis of these identities that acknowledges their complex nature.

5. Arguments about sexual practices and identities were not limited to the Anglo-American sphere. Ebner (2005) reports similar tensions in Austrian

feminist groups in the 1980s, and also relates how S/M-themed pictures by lesbian artists were stolen from an exhibition in Salzburg.

6. A similar dynamic developed at a lesbian march in London in 1984 (Healey 1996, pp. 97–8).

7. Evidence that (gay) male imagery is still going strong was provided by porn magazine *on our backs*' twentieth anniversary issue (June 2004): of a selection of 52 pictures published since the magazine began, 15 feature male props such as strap-on dildos and beards, or enact gay male practices like blow jobs through glory holes and uniform fetish scenes. However, male props are sported by femme models as well, calling into question the criticism that 'sex radicals' simply emulate men.

8. Naiad Press re-published a number of lesbian pulp novels in the 1980s, while a second wave of ironic-nostalgic recovery began in 2002 with the re-publications by Cleis Press. At the time of writing (2007), lesbian pulp has been thoroughly commercialized in the form of merchandise ranging from fridge magnets to mouse pads. Lesbian pulp novels have also been collected in several anthologies (Zimet 1999; Stryker 2001; Forrest 2005).

9. Hoagland, who otherwise argues against S/M as a feminist sexual practice, concedes that '[l]esbian sadomasochists [who] complain that wimmin in the anti-pornography movement who accept money from the right and otherwise align themselves with reactionary interests are collaborating in the cooptation of feminism . . . are correct' (1982, p. 153; see also Butler 1993, p. 23; Case 1988/1999, p. 187).

10. The links between various political causes such as women's liberation, animal rights and environmentalism are illustrated by the Greenham Common anti-missile protests in the UK after 1983 (see also Chapter 5). Moreover, the author of Example C has long been active as a trustee and volunteer with the British Cats Protection charity.

11. Faderman (1991, pp. 150–5) provides a harrowing account of homophobia in the US military in the 1950s.

12. Jones' (2007) ethnographic study of a lesbian walking group corroborates love of the 'great outdoors' as a lesbian identity marker, although her informants replace the image of the lone ranger conquering nature with the feminist model of women as a group interacting with nature.

13. However, hyperfemininity can be linguistically indexed in femme speech, e.g., by using marked feminine suffixes, as in 'photographerette' and 'authorette' ('Welcome to Aphrodite' n.d.).

14. Other gay and lesbian places in 1960s London, Brighton and Manchester are mentioned in Neild and Pearson (1992, pp. 47–8, 59).

15. Lesbian porn magazines *Bad Attitude* and *on our backs* encountered similar problems when they were first launched in 1984; only a few gay male bookstores across the US would agree to sell it, and almost all women's bookstores refused to do so (Cassidy 2004, p. 29). The same held true for its UK equivalent, *Quim,* which was published between 1989 and 1995 (Healey 1996, pp. 144, 184–5).

16. In the Bank of English (BoE) online sampler (available at http://www.collins.co.uk/Corpus/CorpusSearch.aspx), 'admit' collocates with the following lexical items denoting what one can admit to, in decreasing order of significance: manslaughter, charges, mistake, responsibility, theft, guilt, murder, assault, offences, error, conspiracy, stealing, robbery. The BoE sampler includes 56 million words of contemporary written and spoken British English. The data comes from the Bank of English corpus jointly owned by HarperCollins Publishers and the University of Birmingham. In 2007 the corpus stood at 500+ million words.

17. In the Bank of English sampler (see n. 16), 'accuse' collocates with the following lexical items denoting what one can be accused of, in decreasing order of significance: hypocrisy, wrongdoing, conspiring, corruption.

18. Healey (1996, p. 173) makes an interesting claim that the often explicitly sexual images used for safe sex campaigns desensitized many lesbians to pictures that would previously have been criticized as pornographic.

NOTES TO CHAPTER 5

1. At a stylistic level, writers in post-structuralism in general, and queer theory in particular, are notorious for their tendency to use scare quotes to signal their distance from any concept that hegemonic discourses construct as natural. They thus deliver a neat illustration of Sontag's claim that '[c]amp sees everything in quotation marks . . . [it's] not a woman, but a "woman"' (1964/1994, p. 280).

2. Nevertheless, Butler observes 'a certain comedy that emerges when "queer" becomes so utterly disjointed from sexual practice that every well-meaning heterosexual takes on the term' (1993, p. 124).

3. The latter image is subsequently called 'an unfortunate comparison' (Dixon 1988, p. 78).

4. Lesbian feminist/separatist discourse here links up with pre-bourgeois discourse, which did not recognize any divide between public and private either. Privacy itself can be regarded as a construct of nineteenth-century bourgeois discourse.

5. Todmorden, a Yorkshire town in the North of Britain, is known for its sizable lesbian population.

6. From a radical feminist angle, calling separatism 'atheist' in its fixation on men would be an instance of the 'equivalence theory, whereby the thinking and behaviour of the radical is said to resemble . . . the ideologies of the radical's political opponents, [and which] is another technique whereby radical ideologies are often discredited' (Kitzinger 1987, p. 127).

7. A final, ironic corroboration of the close discursive and cognitive links between separatism and religious fundamentalism is the anecdotal evidence that many lesbian separatists later became evangelical Christians leading a conventional heterosexual life (quoted in Stein 1997, p. 116).

8. This process of unlearning is referred to by many separatist writers such as killa-man (1974), Penelope (1990) and Shulman (1983, p. 54), who speaks of 'an enormous effort at unlearning everything that I had learned.'

9. The same metaphor can be found in a reader's reaction to the paper by the Leeds Revolutionary Feminists (see Example B), of whom Sheila Jeffreys was a member: 'This isn't a vanguard cadre group with a five-year apprenticeship and an entrance exam, it's a liberation movement, for all women' (Onlywomen Press 1981, p. 11).

10. The negative evaluation of herself as an out-group representative was indeed perceived by the interviewee, who referred to the article as 'hostile' and as a 'bowdlerised account,' which included 'not words I used, just [the interviewer's] interpretations' (Jeffreys 2007).

11. The one exception to this is celebrity interviews.

12. The author of Example E, Carol Ann Uszkurat, wishes the reader to note that at the time of writing (2007), she no longer identifies as a lesbian and sees her move in that direction as caused by a mixture of factors that include being sexually abused as a child and having a mother who suffered from mental illness. She further wishes to remark that she has not gone

back to heterosexuality but rather sees herself as too damaged to engage in healthy intimacy with either sex. She is relieved to be where she is at. Carol Ann Uszkurat has also developed a Christian faith and was accepted into the Catholic Church in 2006.

13. In the late 1990s, almost all of the lesbian separatists present on the internet stated that they used old computers and included assistance on old-fashioned systems on their homepages.

14. The author's claim about educational levels in lesbians presents only a partial truth. For the period 1991–6, Berg and Lien (2002) have established that lesbian full-time workers in the US had 'both more graduate degrees and more school dropouts per capita than . . . heterosexual females' (p. 399). Despite being more likely to work in low-skilled jobs, lesbians nevertheless enjoyed an earnings premium of between 13 and 47 percent when compared with their straight female colleagues (p. 411).

NOTES TO CHAPTER 6

1. Ironically, Spears (1985, p. 323) gives a meaning of 'dikey [as] "ultrafashionable"'.

2. The importance of travel to gay lifestyles shows in the fact that several airlines offer particular gay-targeted services as well as in the existence of the International Gay and Lesbian Travel Association (IGLTA). Founded in 1983, it describes itself as a '900 plus member strong and growing organization of gay, lesbian and community friendly travel professionals,' bringing together travel agencies, tour operators, airlines, car rental companies, accommodation services and tourist boards (IGLTA 2002). As a special-interest LGBT organization, it is rivalled only by the two sports associations Gay Games and Outgames.

3. See also activist Gloria Steinem's dictum that 'what we are attempting is a revolution, not a public relations movement' (Steinem 1978, quoted in Faderman 1991, p. 213).

4. Available <http://us.cnn.com/ELECTION/2004/pages/results/states/US/P/00/epolls.0.html> (accessed 12 August 2007).

5. Such straight acting can be inadvertently undermined: Faderman (1991) features a picture of a 1960s picketing which shows lesbian and gay demonstrators decked out in conventional dresses and ties. Ironically though, their body posture is hilariously butch and camp.

6. To be fair, it has to be mentioned that *Girlfriends* was twinned with lesbian porn magazine *on our backs* and may have taken a deliberately conservative stance to enable the two magazines to cover a wider market between them.

7. When I served as participant liaison for Vienna Pride in the latter half of the 1990s, I attempted to implement a similar policy that the contributions of all groups in the annual Pride march should be directly relevant to lesbian and gay people. This was on more than one occasion met with stunned silence by commercial participants, who then usually explained that they would put some drag queens on their float.

8. For examples, see <http://www.thetaskforce.org/about_us/board_of_directors> (National Gay and Lesbian Task Force, USA) and <http://www.hrc.org/Content/NavigationMenu/Press_Room/Liz_Seaton.htm> (Human Rights Campaign, USA). All websites accessed 12 August 2007. Interestingly, the two main UK organizations, Stonewall and Outrage, do not feature photos of executives on their website.

9. Whether Camille Paglia can be regarded as a conservative is a moot point. As a self-defined 'libertarian' and voter for the Green party, she is referred to as a

conservative by the more centrist members of the Log Cabin Republicans, while the more staunchly conservative ones question her credentials as one of them.

10. Note that in American political discourse, 'libertarian' needs to be distinguished from 'liberal,' although the two would be largely convergent in European usage. Yet, 'liberal' in the US political landscape denotes persons and opinions left of centre.

11. I am grateful to Costas Gabrielatos for helping me with parts of this section of the analysis.

Bibliography

'About us' (2007) Available: <http://www.g3mag.co.uk/joomla104/content/view/54/41/#Aboutus> (accessed 12 August 2007).

Abrams, D. (1999) 'Social identity, social cognition, and the self: the flexibility and stability of self-categorization,' in D. Abrams and M.A. Hogg (eds) *Social Identity and Social Cognition,* Oxford: Blackwell.

Ammer, C. (1999) *Fighting Words: from war, rebellion, and other combative capers,* 2nd edn, Chicago: NTC Publishing.

Anderson, B.R. O'Gorman (1983) *Imagined Communities: reflections on the origin and spread of nationalism,* London: Verso.

Anderson-Minshall, D. (2005) 'Trend-spotting: think pink,' *Curve,* October: 25.

Anthonissen, C. (2008) 'The sounds of silence in the media: cencorship and self-censorship,' in R. Wodak and V. Koller (eds) *Communication in the Public Sphere* (Handbook of Applied Linguistics 4), Berlin: de Gruyter.

Ashton, C. (1996) 'Getting hold of the phallus: "post-lesbian" power negotiations,' in N. Godwin, B. Hollows and S. Nye (eds) *Assaults on Convention: essays on lesbian transgressors,* London: Cassell.

Askehave, I. and Swales, R. (2001) 'Genre identification and communicative purpose: a problem and a possible solution,' *Applied Linguistics,* 22(2): 195–212.

*Aspen (1979) 'Consciousness raising,' *Revolutionary and Radical Feminist Newsletter,* 2: 24–5.

Atkinson, T. (1974) *Amazon Odyssey,* New York: Links.

———. (1982) 'Why I'm against S/M liberation,' in R.R. Linden, D.R. Pagano, D.E.H. Russell and S.L. Star (eds) *Against Sadomasochism: a radical feminist analysis,* San Francisco: Frog in the Well.

Augoustinos, M. and Walker, I. (1995) *Social Cognition: an integrated introduction,* London: Sage.

Austin, J.L. (1962) *How to Do Things with Words,* Oxford: Clarendon.

Ayres. T. and Saxe, L. (1988) 'Politics, vision and play: some thoughts on the lesbian separatist conference,' *Lesbian Ethics,* 3(2): 106–15.

BAAL (British Association for Applied Linguistics) (2007) 'Recommendations on good practice in Applied Linguistics.' Available: <http://www.baal.org.uk/good_practice_draft.doc> (accessed 12 August 2007).

Bainton, R.H. (1970) *The Reformation of the Sixteenth Century,* Boston: Beacon Press.

Baker, P. (2005) *Public Discourses of Gay Men,* London: Routledge.

Bakhtin, M. (1929) *Marxism and the Philosophy of Language;* trans. L. Matejka and I.R. Tutnik (1973), New York: Seminar Press.

———. (1986) *Speech Genres and Other Late Essays;* trans. V.W. McGee, Austin: University of Texas Press.

Barnes, I.E. (2002) 'I feel left out.' Available <http://iebarnes.com/main/view/2020814a.html> (accessed 30 March 2005).

———. (2004a) 'Girlie-men and not so girlie-women.' Available <http://iebarnes.com/main/view/20040720.html> (accessed 30 March 2005).

———. (2004b) 'Principles, first and foremost.' Available <http://iebarnes.com/main/view/200400908.html> (accessed 30 March 2005).

Barrett, R. (2002) 'Is queer theory important for sociolinguistic theory?,' in K. Campbell-Kibler, R.J. Podesva, S.J. Roberts and A. Wong (eds) *Language and Sexuality: contesting meaning in theory and practice,* Stanford: CSLI.

Bawer, B. (1993) *A Place at the Table: the gay individual in American society,* New York: Poseidon Press.

Baxter, J. (2003) *Positioning Gender in Discourse: a feminist methodology,* Basingstoke: Palgrave.

Bellah, R.N., Madsen, R., Sullivan, W.M., Swindler, A. and Tipton, S.M. (1985) *Habits of the Heart: individualism and commitment in American life,* Berkeley: Perennial Library.

Bender, D. and Due, L. (1994) 'Coming up butch,' in L. Burana, Roxxie and L. Due (eds) *Dagger: on butch women,* Pittsburgh: Cleis Press.

Berg, N. and Lien, D. (2002) 'Measuring the effect of sexual orientation on income: evidence of discrimination?,' *Contemporary Economic Policy,* 20(4): 394–414.

*Bev Jo, Strega, L. and Ruston, N. (1990) *Dykes Loving Dykes,* Oakland: published by the authors.

Bhatia, V.K. (1993) *Analyzing Genre: language use in professional settings,* London: Longman.

Billig, M. (1988) *Ideological Dilemmas: a social psychology of everyday thinking,* London: Sage.

Bindel, J. (2004) 'Location, location, orientation,' *Guardian,* 27 March. Online. Available: <http://www.guardian.co.uk/print/0,3858,4888064–103425,00.html> (accessed 12 August 2007).

———. (2005) 'The ugly side of beauty,' *Guardian Weekend,* 2 July: 38–41.

———. (2006) 'From dysfunctional dyke to designer doll,' *Guardian,* 12 June. Online. Available: <http://www.guardian.co.uk/print/0,,329502269–103680,00.html> (accessed 12 August 2007).

Bloch, J. (2004) 'The 10 most powerful lesbians,' *Curve,* 14(7): 24–6.

Bornstein, K. (1994) *Gender Outlaw,* New York: Routledge.

Boswell, J. (1980) *Christianity, Social Tolerance, and Homosexuality: gay people in Western Europe from the beginning of the Christian era to the fourteenth century,* Chicago: University of Chicago Press.

Bourdieu, P. (1991) *Language and Symbolic Power;* trans. G. Raymond and M. Adamson, Cambridge, MA: Harvard University Press.

Bright, S. (2004) 'Working girl,' *on our backs,* June/July: 30–1.

Briscoe, J. (1994) 'Lipstick on her collar,' *Sunday Times,* 5 June: 10.

Brown, B. (1995) 'The art of the impossible: some thoughts on lesbian separatist political strategy.' Available: <http://www.efn.org/~b_brown/b_brown.html> (accessed 22 June 1998).

———. (1997) 'Welcome, cranky dykes. Others beware.' Available: <http://www.efn.org/~b_brown/b_brown.html> (accessed 22 June 1998).

Brownworth, V. (1975) 'Butch/femme, myth/reality or more of the same?,' *Wicce,* 4: 7–10.

———. (2005) 'Our history is now,' *Curve,* 15(2): 62.

Bruce, T. (2003) *The Death of Right and Wrong: exposing the Left's assault on our culture and values,* Roseville, CA: Prima Lifestyle.

———. (2004): 'Respecting marriage and equal rights,' *FrontPageMagazine.com*, 25 February. Available: <http://www.frontpagemag.com/Articles/PrintBLE. ASP?id=12339> (accessed 2 June 2005).

Brunet, A. and Turcotte, L. (1986) 'Separatism and radicalism: an analysis of the differences and similarities'; trans. L. Happner, *Lesbian Ethics*, 2(1): 41–9.

Bucholtz, M. and Hall, K. (2004) 'Theorizing identity in language and sexuality research,' *Language in Society*, 33: 469–515.

———. (2005) 'Identity and interaction: a sociocultural linguistic approach,' *Discourse Studies*, 7(4–5): 585–614.

Burana, L., Roxxie and Due, L. (eds) (1994) *Dagger: on butch women*, Pittsburgh: Cleis Press.

Butler, J. (1990/1999) *Gender Trouble*, 2nd edn, New York: Routledge.

———. (1991) 'Imitation and gender insubordination,' in D. Fuss (ed.) *Inside/Out: lesbian theories, gay theories*, New York: Routledge.

———. (1993) *Bodies That Matter: on the discursive limits of 'sex,'* New York: Routledge.

———. (1997) *Excitable Speech: a politics of the performative*, New York: Routledge.

———. (2004) *Undoing Gender*, New York: Routledge.

Buttgereit, S. (1997) 'Der Eintritt ins Austreten: Butches im Spiegel des Toilettenbesuchs [Stepping out: butches going to the bathroom],' in S. Kuhnen (ed.) *Butch/Femme: eine erotische Kultur* [Butch/Femme: an erotic culture], Berlin: Querverlag.

Califia, P. (1981) 'A personal view of the history of the lesbian S/M community and movement in San Francisco,' in Samois (eds) *Coming to Power*, Boston: Alyson.

Cameron, D. (1992) 'Old het?,' *Trouble & Strife*, 24: 41–5.

——— and Kulick, D. (2003) *Language and Sexuality*, Cambridge: Cambridge University Press.

——— and Kulick, D. (2005) 'Identity crisis?,' *Language & Comunication*, 25: 107–25.

Cameron, L. (2003) *Metaphor in Educational Discourse*, London: Continuum.

——— and Deignan, A. (2003) 'Combining large and small corpora to investigate tuning devices around metaphor in spoken discourse,' *Metaphor & Symbol*, 18(3): 149–60.

Carraher, D., Cox, S., Daake, E., Gagne, M., Good, P., McManmon, J. and O'Connor, M. (1996) '"Generation X," the "Third Wave," or just plain radical: reviewing the reviewers of Catherine MacKinnon's *Only Words*,' in D. Bell and R. Klein (eds) *Radically Speaking: feminism reclaimed*, London: Zed Books.

Case, S.-E. (1988) 'Towards a butch-femme aesthetic,' in F. Cleto (ed.) (1999) *Camp: queer aesthetics and the performing subject*, Edinburgh: Edinburgh University Press.

———. (1998) 'Making butch: an historical memoir of the 1970s,' in S.R. Munt and C. Smyth (eds) *Butch/Femme: inside lesbian gender*, London: Cassell.

Cassidy, C. (2004) 'Opening Pandora's box,' *on our backs*, June/July: 28–9.

Chasin, A. (2000) *Selling Out: the gay and lesbian movement goes to market*, New York: Palgrave.

Chenier, E. (2004) 'Lesbian sex wars,' in C.J. Summers (ed.) *glbtq: an encyclopedia of gay, lesbian, bisexual, transgender, and queer culture*, Chicago: glbtq. Online. Available: <http://www.glbtq.com/social-sciences/lesbian_sex_wars.html> (accessed 12 August 2007).

Chilton, P. (2005) 'Missing links in mainstream CDA: modules, blends and the critical instinct,' in R. Wodak and P. Chilton (eds) *A New Agenda in (Critical) Discourse Analysis* (Discourse Approaches to Politics, Society and Culture 13), Amsterdam: Benjamins.

Chirrey, D.A. (2003) '"I hereby come out": what sort of speech act is coming out?,' *Journal of Sociolinguistics*, 7(1): 24–37.

Chouliaraki, L. and Fairclough, N. (1999) *Discourse in Late Modernity*, Edinburgh: Edinburgh University Press.

Chryssochoou, X. (2003) 'Studying identity in social psychology: some thoughts on the definition of identity and its relation to action,' *Journal of Language and Politics*, 2(2): 225–41.

Cindy (2005) Letter to *Curve*, 15(6): 14.

Citypink (2005) 'Welcome to Citypink.' Available: <http://www.citypink.co.uk/home.aspx> (accessed 12 August 2007).

Clarke, I., Kwon W. and Wodak, R. (forthcoming) 'The anatomy of management practice: a discourse-historical perspective,' *Journal of Management Studies*.

Cohen, C.L. (1986) *God's Caress: the psychology of Puritan religious experience*, New York: Oxford University Press.

Connell, R.W. (1995) *Masculinities*, Berkeley: University of California Press.

———. and Messerschmidt, J.W. (2005) 'Hegemonic masculinity: rethinking the concept,' *Gender & Society*, 19(6): 829–59.

Cook, G. (2001) *The Discourse of Advertising*, London: Routledge.

Cordova, J. (1978) 'Ticket to Lesbos: who qualifies?,' *Lesbian Tide*, May–June: 19.

Core, P. (1984) 'Camp: the lie that tells the truth,' in F. Cleto (ed.) (1999) *Camp: queer aesthetics and the performing subject*, Edinburgh: Edinburgh University Press.

Cory, D.W. (1965) 'The language of the homosexual,' *Sexology*, 32(3): 163–5.

Cottingham, L. (1996) *Lesbians Are So Chic . . . That We Are Not Really Lesbians at All*, London: Cassell.

Cox, R.W. (1993) 'Gramsci, hegemony and international relations,' in S. Gill (ed.) *Gramsci, Historical Materialism and International Relations* (Cambridge Studies in International Relations 26), Cambridge: Cambridge University Press.

Creet, J. (1991) 'Daughter of the movement: the psychodynamics of lesbian S/M fantasy,' *Differences*, 3(2): 135–56.

Cunningham, J. (1996): 'Bad language,' in L. Mohin (ed.) *An Intimacy of Equals: lesbian feminist ethics*, London: Onlywomen Press.

Damrosch, L. Jr. (1985) *God's Plot and Man's Stories: studies in the fictional imagination from Milton to Fielding*, Chicago: University of Chicago Press.

Davis, K. (1981) 'Introduction: what we fear we try to keep contained,' in Samois (eds) *Coming to Power: writings and graphics on lesbian S/M*, Boston: Alyson.

Dawson, M. (2007) 'Zines!,' *Mule*, winter/spring: 14.

Day, C.L. and Morse, B.W. (1981) 'Communication patterns in established lesbian relationships,' in J.W. Chesebro (ed.) *GaySpeak: gay male and lesbian communication*, New York: Pilgrim Press.

De Cillia, R., Reisigl, M. and Wodak, R. (1999) 'The discursive construction of national identities,' *Discourse & Society*, 10(2): 149–73.

Dixon, J. (1988) 'Separatism: a look back at anger,' in B. Cant and S. Hemmings (eds) *Radical Records: thirty years of lesbian and gay history*, London: Routledge.

Doyle, G. (1996) 'No man's land: lesbian separatism revisited,' in N. Godwin, B. Hollows and S. Nye (eds) *Assaults on Convention: essays on lesbian transgressors*, London: Cassell.

D'Souza, C. (1993) 'Love me, love my doppelgänger,' *Sunday Times*, 7 February: 5.

Duggan, L. (1992) 'Making it perfectly queer,' *Socialist Review*, 1: 11–31.

Dworkin, A. (1979) *Pornography: men possessing women*, New York: Perigree and Smith.

Ebner, M. (2005) '"Die Bilder, sie wachsen": Artikulationen lesbischer Identitäten in der Frauenszene der 1980er' [Growing images: evaluating lesbian identities in the women's community of the 1980s], in A. Brunner, I. Rieder, N. Schefzig, H. Sulzenbacher and N. Wahl (eds) *Geheimsache Leben: Schwule und Lesben im*

Wien des 20. Jahrhunderts [Classified lives: gays and lesbians in 20th century Vienna], Vienna: Löcker.

Edwards, D. and Potter, J. (2001) 'Discursive psychology,' in A. McHoul and M. Rapley (eds) *How To Analyse Talk in Institutional Settings: a casebook of methods*, London: Continuum.

Eisenstein, Z.R. 'Connections between class and sex: moving toward a theory of liberation,' paper presented at the annual meeting of the American Political Science Association, 1973.

Faderman, L. (1985) *Surpassing the Love of Men: romantic friendship and love between women from the Renaissance to the present*, London: Women's Press.

——. (1991) *Odd Girls and Twilight Lovers: a history of lesbian life in twentieth-century America*, New York: Penguin.

Fairclough, N. (1992) 'Discourse and text: linguistic and intertextual analysis within discourse analysis,' *Discourse & Society*, 3(2): 193–217.

——. (1995) *Critical Discourse Analysis*, London: Longman.

——. (2003) *Analysing Discourse: textual analysis for social research*, London: Routledge.

Farrell, R.A. (1972) 'The argot of the homosexual subculture,' *Anthropological Linguistics*, 14: 97–109.

Fellegy, A.M. (1995) 'Patterns and functions of minimal response,' *American Speech*, 70: 186–98.

Flowerdew, J., Li, D.C.S. and Tran, S. (2002) 'Discriminatory news discourse: some Hong Kong data,' *Discourse & Society*, 13(3): 19–45.

Forrest, K.V. (2005) *Lesbian Pulp Fiction: the sexually intrepid world of lesbian paperback novels 1950–1965*, San Francisco: Cleis Press.

Forster, J. (1984) 'Sappho: history now—a pioneer in its day,' *GLC Women's Committee Bulletin*, 17: 30–1.

Foucault, M. (1972a) *The Archaeology of Knowledge and the Discourse on Language*; trans. A.M. Sheridan Smith, London: Pantheon.

——. (1972b) *Die Ordnung des Diskurse* [The Order of Discourse]; trans. W. Seitter (1991), Frankfurt a.M.: Fischer.

——. (1976) *Sexualität und Wahrheit 1: der Wille zum Wissen* [Sexuality and Truth: The will to know]; trans. U. Rauff and W. Seitter (1977), Frankfurt a.M.: Suhrkamp.

Friesen, F. (1998) 'Lesbian separatist?.' Available: <http://www.intergate.bc.ca/personal/fran/separatism.html> (accessed 22 June 1998).

Frye, M. (1978) 'Some reflections on separatism and power,' *Sinister Wisdom*, 6: 30–9.

Fuss, D. (1989) *Essentially Speaking: feminism, nature and difference*, New York: Routledge.

Gardiner, J. (2002) *From the Closet to the Screen: women at the Gateways Club, 1945–1985*, London: Pandora.

Gays and Lesbians for Individual Liberty (2003) 'What is GLIL?.' Available: <http://www.glil.org/history.html> (accessed 12 August 2007).

Gellner, E. (1997) *Nationalism*, London: Phoenix.

Georgalou, M. (2006) 'The discursive construction of national identity in media sport: the case of Greece at Euro 2004,' unpublished MA dissertation, Lancaster University/UK.

Geraldine T. (1988) 'Practising separatism,' *Lesbian Ethics*, 3(2): 3–5.

Gever, M. (2003) *Entertaining Lesbians: celebrity, sexuality, and self-invention*, London: Routledge.

Gilliambardo, R. (1966) *Society of Women: a study of a women's prison*, New York: Wiley.

Gloria G. (2001) 'Queer durch: Körperpolitik in Österreich am Beispiel Transgender: von Lesbenknaben, phallischen Frauen, Genderbenders, ÜberläuferInnen des

Geschlechts' [Queercuts: Austrian body politics and the example of transgender. Of lesbian boys, phallic women, genderbenders and defectors], in W. Förster, T.G. Natter and I. Rieder (eds) *Der andere Blick: lesbischwules Leben in Österreich* [The Other View: Lesbian and gay life in Austria], Vienna: MA 57.

Goatly, A. (2007) *Washing the Brain: metaphor and hidden ideology* (Discourse Approaches to Politics, Society and Culture 23), Amsterdam: Benjamins.

Goldstein, R. (2003) *Homocons: the rise of the Gay Right,* London: Verso.

Gossett, S. (2004) 'Media bias through the eyes of a gay journalist.' Available <http://www.aim.org/sherrie_blog_entry_2411_0_18_0_C/> (accessed 2 June 2005).

Grady, J. (1997) 'Foundations of meaning: primary metaphors and primary scenes,' unpublished thesis, University of California Berkeley.

Gramsci, A. (1971) *Selections from the Prison Notebooks;* trans. J. Matthews, London: Lawrence & Wishart.

Grech, C. (1998) 'Plunger: Weil wir das Recht haben, gehört zu werden' [Plunger: because we have a right to be heard], A. Baldauf and K. Weingartner (eds) *Lips, Tits, Hits, Power? Popkultur und Feminismus* [Pop Culture and Feminism], Vienna: folio.

Gregory, G. (1991) 'Community publishing as self-education,' in D. Barton and R. Ivanič (eds) *Writing in the Community,* London: Sage.

Groocock, V. (1996) 'Chelsea girls,' *Diva,* 16: 42–3.

Gulston, L. (1980) 'Butch,' *Sequel,* 15: 8–10.

Halberstam, J. (1998a) 'Between butches,' in S.R. Munt and C. Smyth (eds) *Butch/Femme: inside lesbian gender,* London: Cassell.

——. (1998b) *Female Masculinity,* Durham, NC: Duke University Press.

Hall Carpenter Archives Lesbian Oral History Group (1989) *Inventing Ourselves: lesbian life stories,* London: Routledge.

Halliday, M.A.K. (1976) 'Anti-languages,' *American Anthropologist,* 78(3): 570–84.

——. (1978) *Language as Social Semiotic: the social interpretation of language and meaning,* London: Edward Arnold.

——. and Matthiessen, C.M.I.M. (2004) *An Introduction to Functional Grammar,* 3rd edn, London: Edward Arnold.

Hamer, D. and Ashbrook, P. (1994) 'OUT: reflections on British Television's first lesbian and gay magazine series,' in D. Hamer and B. Budge (eds) *The Good, the Bad, and the Gorgeous: popular culture's romance with lesbianism,* London: Pandora.

——. and Budge, B. (eds) (1994) *The Good, the Bad, and the Gorgeous: popular culture's romance with lesbianism,* London: Pandora.

Hamer, E. (1996) *Britannia's Glory: a history of twentieth-century lesbians,* London: Cassell.

Hanson, C. (1998) 'Finding your inner lesbian separatist.' Available: <http://www.geocities.com/Athens/9884/separatist.html> (accessed 12 August 2007).

Hark, S. (1996) 'Magisches Zeichen: die Rekonstruktion der symbolischen Ordnung im Feminismus' [Magical sign: The Reconstruction of the symbolic order in feminism], in S. Hark (ed.) *Grenzen lesbischer Identitäten* [Boundaries of Lesbian Identities], Berlin: Querverlag.

Hart, N. (1996) 'From an eroticism of difference to an intimacy of equals: a radical feminist lesbian separatist perspective on sexuality,' in L. Mohin (ed.) *An Intimacy of Equals: lesbian feminist ethics,* London: Onlywomen Press.

Harvey, K. (2000) 'Describing camp talk: language/pragmatics/politics,' *Language and Literature,* 9(3): 240–60.

——. and C. Shalom (1997) (eds) *Language and Desire: encoding sex, romance, and intimacy,* London: Routledge.

Healey, E. (1996) *Lesbian Sex Wars,* London: Virago.

Hennessy, R. (2000) *Profit and Pleasure: sexual identities in late capitalism,* New York: Routledge.

Higgins, R. (1995) 'Murder will out: gay identity and media discourse in Montreal,' in W. Leap (ed.) *Beyond the Lavender Lexicon: authenticity, imagination and appropriation in lesbian and gay languages,* New York: Gordon and Breach Press.

Hoagland, S.L. (1982) 'Sadism, masochism, and lesbian-feminism,' in R.R. Linden, D.R. Pagano, D.E.H. Russell and S.L. Star (eds) *Against Sadomasochism: a radical feminist analysis,* San Francisco: Frog in the Well.

——. (1987) 'Lesbian separatism: an empowering reality,' *Gossip,* 6: 24–36.

Hollibaugh, A. and Moraga, C. (1981) 'What we're rolling around in bed with: sexual silences in feminism: a conversation toward ending them,' *Heresies,* 12: 58–62.

Hunt, M. (1981) 'Report of a conference on feminism, sexuality and power: the elect clash with the perverse,' in Samois (eds) *Coming to Power,* Boston: Alyson.

IGLTA (International Gay and Lesbian Travel Association) (2002): 'About IGLTA.' Available: <http://iglta.org/about.cfm> (accessed 12 August 2007).

Irigaray, L. (1985) *This Sex Which Is Not One;* trans. C. Porter and C. Burke, Ithaca: Cornell University Press.

Jayne (2007) Letter to *Out Northwest,* 67: 4.

Jeffreys, S. (1989) 'Butch and femme: now and then,' in Lesbian Herstory Group (eds) *Not a Passing Phase: reclaiming lesbians in history, 1840–1985,* London: Women's Press.

——. (1990) *Anticlimax: a feminist perspective on the sexual revolution,* New York: New York University Press.

——. (1994) *The Lesbian Heresy: a feminist perspective on the lesbian sexual revolution,* London: Women's Press.

——. (1996) 'Heterosexuality and the desire for gender,' in D. Richardson (ed.) *Theorising Heterosexuality,* Buckingham: Open University Press.

——. (2003) *Unpacking Queer Politics: a lesbian feminist perspective,* Cambridge: Polity.

——. (2007) 'Reproducing interview with me.' E-mail (24 July 2007).

Jeffs, L. (2005) 'Under the skin,' *Diva,* June: 32–4.

Johnson, M. (1987) *The Body in the Mind: the bodily basis of meaning, imagination, and reason,* Chicago: University of Chicago Press.

Johnston, J. (1973) *Lesbian Nation: the feminist solution,* New York: Simon & Schuster.

——. (1975) 'Are lesbians "gay"?,' *Ms,* 3: 12, 85–6.

Jones, D. (1990) 'Gossip: notes on women's oral culture,' in D. Cameron (ed.) *The Feminist Critique of Language: a reader,* London: Routledge.

Jones, L. 'Identity construction in a lesbian community of practice,' paper presented at the Gender and Language Research Group, Lancaster University/UK, March 2007.

Jones, R. 'Sex, power and the internet,' paper presented at Sociolinguistic Symposium 16, Limerick/Ireland, July 2006.

Kappeler, S. (1992) 'Entpolitisierung durch Identitätspolitik?' [Depoliticization through identity politics?], *Kofra: Zeitschrift für Feminismus und Arbeit,* 10: 3–12.

Kasindorf, J.R. (1993) 'Lesbian chic: the bold, brave new world of gay women,' *New York Magazine,* 19: 29–37.

Katz, J.N. (1996) *The Invention of Heterosexuality,* New York: Plume.

Kaufmann, T. (1996) 'Feminine charms,' *Diva,* October: 22–4.

Kaur, S. (forthcoming) 'The performance, construction and co-construction of gender in computer-mediated communication,' unpublished thesis, Lancaster University/UK.

Kennedy, E.L. and Davis, M.D. (1993) *Boots of Leather, Slippers of Gold: the history of a lesbian community,* New York: Routledge.

Kenyon, F.E. (1968) 'Studies in female homosexualities 4: social and psychological aspects and 5: sexual development, attitudes and experience,' *British Journal of Psychiatry,* 114: 1342.

KhosraviNik, M. 'Actor, action, argumentation: towards an amalgamation of CDA methodological categories in the representation of social actors,' paper presented at the Second Linguistics and English Language Postgraduate Conference, Lancaster University/UK, July 2007.

killa-man of the C.L.I.T. Collective (1974) 'Trying hard to forfeit all I've known,' in S.L. Hoagland and J. Penelope (eds) *For Lesbians Only: a separatist anthology*, London: Onlywomen Press.

Kirk, M. and Madsen. H. (1989) *After the Ball: how America will conquer its fear and hatred of gays in the '90s*, New York: Doubleday.

Kitzinger, C. (1987) *The Social Construction of Lesbianism*, London: Sage.

———. (2002) 'Doing feminist conversation analysis,' in P. McIlvenny (ed.) *Talking Gender and Sexuality*, Amsterdam: Benjamins.

——— and Wilkinson, S. (1994) 'Virgins and queers: rehabilitating heterosexuality?,' *Gender & Society*, 8(3): 444–63.

——— and Wilkinson, S. (1995) 'Transitions from heterosexuality to lesbianism: the discursive production of lesbian identities,' *Developmental Psychology*, 31(1): 95–104.

Koller, V. (2003) 'Metaphor clusters, metaphor chains: analyzing the multifunctionality of metaphor in text,' *Metaphorik.de*, 5: 115–34. Online. Available: <http://www.metaphorik.de/05/koller.pdf> (accessed 12 August 2007).

———. (2004) *Metaphor and Gender in Business Media Discourse: a critical cognitive study*, Basingstoke: Palgrave.

———. (forthcoming): 'CEOs and "working gals": the textual representation and cognitive conceptualisation of businesswomen in different discourse communities,' in K. Harrington, L. Litosseliti, H. Sauntson and J. Sunderland (eds) *Language and Gender: theoretical and methodological approaches*, Basingstoke: Palgrave.

Kopperschmidt, J. (2000) *Argumentationstheorie zur Einführung* [Introduction to Argumentation Theory], Hamburg: Junius.

Köveceses, Z. (2002) *Metaphor: a practical introduction*, Oxford: Oxford University Press.

———. (2005) *Metaphor in Culture: universality and variation*, Cambridge: Cambridge University Press.

Kress, G. (1989) *Linguistic Processes in Sociocultural Practice*, Oxford: Oxford University Press.

Kristeva, J. (1986) *The Kristeva Reader*; ed. T. Moi, trans. S. Hand and L.S. Rondiez, Oxford: Blackwell.

Kuhnen, S. (ed.) (1997) *Butch/Femme: eine erotische Kultur* [Butch/Femme: an erotic culture], Berlin: Querverlag.

Kulick, D. (2000) 'Gay and lesbian language,' *Annual Review of Anthropology*, 29: 243–85.

Lakoff, G. (1993) 'The contemporary theory of metaphor,' in A. Ortony (ed.) *Metaphor and Thought*, 2nd edn, Cambridge: Cambridge University Press.

———. (2002) *Moral Politics: how liberals and conservatives think*, 2nd edn, Chicago: University of Chicago Press.

———. (2004) *Don't Think of an Elephant: know your values and frame the debate*, White River Junction, VT: Chelsea Green.

——— and Johnson, M. (1980) *Metaphors We Live By*, Chicago: University of Chicago Press.

Land, V. and Kitzinger, C. (2005) 'Speaking as a lesbian: correcting the heterosexist presumption,' *Research on Language and Social Interaction*, 38(4): 371–416.

Laporte, R. (1971) 'The butch-femme question,' in J. Nestle (ed.) (1992) *The Persistent Desire: a femme-butch reader*, Boston: Alyson.

Lazar, M. (2005) *Feminist Critical Discourse Analysis: gender, power and ideology in discourse,* Basingstoke: Palgrave.

Leap, W. and Boellstorff, T. (eds) (2004) *Speaking in Queer Tongues: globalization and gay language,* Urbana: University of Illinois Press.

Leck, G.M. (1995) 'A lavender-tongued reliably-queer lesbian does language on language,' in W. Leap (ed.) *Beyond the Lavender Lexicon: authenticity, imagination and appropriation in lesbian and gay languages,* New York: Gordon and Breach Press.

Leeds Revolutionary Feminists 'Political lesbianism: the case against heterosexuality,' paper presented at Revolutionary/Radical Feminist Conference, Leeds, September 1979; reprinted in *Wires,* 81: 25–8; and also in Onlywomen Press (eds) (1981) *Love Your Enemy? The debate between heterosexual feminism and political lesbianism,* London: Onlywomen Press.

Legman, G. (1941) 'The language of homosexuality: an American glossary,' in G.W. Henry (ed.) *Sex Variants: a study of homosexual patterns,* New York: P.B. Hoeber.

Lemon, G. and Patton, W. (1997) 'Lavender blue: issues in lesbian identity development with a focus on an Australian lesbian community,' *Women's Studies International Forum,* 20(1): 113–27.

*Lesbian Left (1977) 'Lesbianism as a model of feminism,' in *Lesbian Left: a collection of papers,* no place given: published by the authors.

*Lesbians Rising (1977) 'A lesbian free press means a lesbian culture,' *Lesbians Rising,* no issue number given: n.pag.

Lettice (1987) 'Separatism,' *Gossip,* 6: 107–10.

Liang, A.C. (1997) 'The creation of coherence in coming-out stories,' in A. Livia and K. Hall (eds), *Queerly Phrased: language, gender, and sexuality,* New York: Oxford University Press.

——. (1999) 'Conversationally implicating lesbian and gay identity,' in M. Bucholtz, A.C. Liang and L. Sutton (eds) *Reinventing Identities: the gendered self in discourse,* New York: Oxford University Press.

Linden, R.R. (1982) 'Introduction: against sadomasochism,' in R.R. Linden, D.R. Pagano, D.E.H. Russell and S.L. Star (eds) *Against Sadomasochism: a radical feminist analysis,* San Francisco: Frog in the Well.

——, Pagano, D.R., Russell, D.E.H. and Star, S.L. (eds) (1982) *Against Sadomasochism: a radical feminist analysis,* San Francisco: Frog in the Well.

Lip editors (1993) 'Editorial,' *Lip,* December: 4.

Livia, A. (1995) '"I ought to throw a Buick at you": fictional representations of butch/femme speech,' in K. Hall and M. Bucholtz (eds) *Gender Articulated: language and the socially constructed self,* New York: Routledge.

——. (1996) 'With gossip aforethought,' in L. Mohin (ed.) *An Intimacy of Equals: lesbian feminist ethics,* London: Onlywomen Press.

——. (2002a) '*Camionneuses s'abstenir:* lesbian community creation through the personals,' in K. Campbell-Kibler, R.J. Podesva, S.J. Roberts and A. Wong (eds) *Language and Sexuality: contesting meaning in theory and practice,* Stanford: CSLI.

——. (2002b) 'The future of queer linguistics,' in K. Campbell-Kibler, R.J. Podesva, S.J. Roberts and A. Wong (eds) *Language and Sexuality: contesting meaning in theory and practice,* Stanford: CSLI.

Lochhead, C. (1993) 'The third way,' *Independent Gay Forum.* Available <http://www.indegayforum.org/news/show/26774.html> (accessed 12 August 2007).

Log Cabin Republicans (n.d.): 'Talking points: why it's okay being a gay Republican.' Available <http://www.logcabin.org/logcabin/talking_points_whyitisokay-beingagayGOP.html> (accessed 12 August 2007).

Longacre, R.E. (1974) 'Narrative versus other discourse genres,' in R.M. Brend (ed.) *Advances in Tagmemics,* Amsterdam: North-Holland.

Longman, L. (2006) 'The social psychology of nationalism: to die for the sake of strangers,' in G. Delanty and K. Kumar (eds) *The Sage Handbook of Nations and Nationalism,* London: Sage.

Lorde, A. and Star, S.L. (1982) 'Interview with Audre Lorde,' in R.R. Linden, D.R. Pagano, D.E.H. Russell and S.L. Star (eds) *Against Sadomasochism: a radical feminist analysis,* San Francisco: Frog in the Well.

Luzzato, D. and Gvion, L. (2007) 'The coming of the young and sexy lesbian: the Israeli urban scenario,' *Social Semiotics,* 17(1): 21–41.

Maasen, S. (1998) *Genealogie der Unmoral: zur Therapeutisierung sexueller Selbste* [The Genealogy of Immorality: or the therapeutization of sexual selves], Frankfurt a.M.: Suhrkamp.

MacKinnon, C. (1993) *Only Words,* Cambridge, MA: Harvard University Press.

Maher, M. and Pusch, W. (1995) 'Speaking "out": the implication of negotiating lesbian identity,' in W. Leap (ed.) *Beyond the Lavender Lexicon: authenticity, imagination and appropriation in lesbian and gay languages,* New York: Gordon and Breach Press.

Malešević, S. (2006) 'Nationalism and the power of ideology,' in G. Delanty and K. Kumar (eds) *The Sage Handbook of Nations and Nationalism,* London: Sage.

Marty with the help from the dykes of S.E.P.S. (1983a) 'Popular separatist-baiting quotes and some separatist responses,' in S.L. Hoagland and J. Penelope (eds) (1988) *For Lesbians Only: a separatist anthology,* London: Onlywomen Press.

———. (1983b) 'Relating to dyke separatists: hints for the non-separatist lesbian,' in S.L. Hoagland and J. Penelope (eds) (1988) *For Lesbians Only: a separatist anthology,* London: Onlywomen Press.

*McCabe, T. (1980) 'Why revolutionary feminism?,' *Revolutionary and Radical Feminist Newsletter,* 5: 6–16.

McElhinny, B. (2002) 'Language, sexuality and political economy,' in K. Campbell-Kibler, R.J. Podesva, S.J. Roberts and A. Wong (eds) *Language and Sexuality: contesting meaning in theory and practice,* Stanford: CSLI.

———. (2004) '"Radical feminist" as label, libel, and laudatory chant,' in R.T. Lakoff, *Language and Woman's Place,* 2nd revised and expanded edn, ed. M. Bucholtz, Oxford: Oxford University Press.

McIlvenny, P. (2002a) 'Critical reflections on performativity and the "un/doing" of gender and sexuality in talk,' in P. McIlvenny (ed.) *Talking Gender and Sexuality,* Amsterdam: Benjamins.

———. (2002b) 'Introduction: researching talk, gender and sexuality,' in P. McIlvenny (ed.) *Talking Gender and Sexuality,* Amsterdam: Benjamins.

McKee, A. (2002) 'I don't want to be a citizen (if it means I have to watch the ABC),' *Media International Australia,* 103: 14–23.

Meredith, J. (1982) 'A response to Samois,' in R.R. Linden, D.R. Pagano, D.E.H. Russell and S.L. Star (eds) *Against Sadomasochism: a radical feminist analysis,* San Francisco: Frog in the Well.

Miller, P. (1961) *The New England Mind: the seventeenth century,* Boston: Beacon Press.

Moonwomon, B. (1986) 'Towards the study of lesbian speech,' in S. Bremner, N. Caskey and B. Moonwomon (eds) *Proceedings of the First Berkeley Women and Language Conference,* Berkeley: Berkeley Women and Language Group; reprinted in A. Livia and K. Hall (eds) (1997) *Queerly Phrased: language, gender, and sexuality,* New York: Oxford University Press.

———. (1995) 'Lesbian discourse, lesbian knowledge,' in W. Leap (ed.) *Beyond the Lavender Lexicon: authenticity, imagination and appropriation in lesbian and gay languages,* New York: Gordon and Breach Press.

Moonwomon-Baird, B. (1996) 'Lesbian conversation as a site for ideological identity construction,' in N. Warner, J. Ahlers, L. Bilmes, M. Oliver, S. Wertheimer and M. Chen (eds) *Gender and Belief Systems,* Berkeley: Berkeley Women and Language Group.

Moraga, C. (1983) *Loving in the War Years,* Boston: South End Press.

Morgan, R. and Wood, K.L. (1995) 'Lesbians in the living room: collusion, co-construction and co-narration in conversation,' in W. Leap (ed.) *Beyond the Lavender Lexicon: authenticity, imagination and appropriation in lesbian and gay languages,* New York: Gordon and Breach Press.

Morris, C.L. (1977) 'Anita has the right to speak, however,' *Sentinel,* 5 May: 7.

Morrish, E. (1997) '"Falling short of God's ideal": public discourse about lesbians and gays,' in A. Livia and K. Hall (eds) *Queerly Phrased: language, gender, and sexuality,* New York: Oxford University Press.

—— and Leap, W. (2006) 'Sex talk: language, desire, identity and beyond,' in H. Sauntson and S. Kyratzis (eds) *Language, Sexualities and Desires: cross-cultural perspectives,* Basingstoke: Palgrave.

—— and Sauntson, H. (2007) *New Perspectives on Language and Sexual Identity,* Basingstoke: Palgrave.

Moscovici, S. (1988) *The Invention of Society: psychological explanations for social phenomena;* trans. W.D. Halls (1993), Cambridge: Polity Press.

—— (2000) *Social Representations: explorations in social psychology,* Cambridge: Polity Press.

Muniz, A.M. and O'Guinn, T.C. (2001) 'Brand community,' *Journal of Consumer Research,* 27: 412–32.

Munt, S.R. (1998) 'Orifices in space: making the real possible,' in S.R. Munt and C. Smyth (eds) *Butch/Femme: inside lesbian gender,* London: Cassell.

National Lesbian and Gay Survey (eds) (1992) *What a Lesbian Looks Like: writings by lesbians on their lives and lifestyles,* London: Routledge.

Neild, S. and Pearson, R. (1992) *Women Like Us,* London: Women's Press.

Nestle, J. (1981) 'Butch-fem relationships: sexual courage in the 1950's,' *Heresies,* 12: 21–4.

Newman, L. (ed.) (1995) *The Femme Mystique,* Boston: Alyson.

Nichols, J., Pagano, D. and Rossoff, M. (1982) 'Is sadomasochism feminist? A critique of the Samois position,' in R.R. Linden, D.R. Pagano, D.E.H. Russell and S.L. Star (eds) *Against Sadomasochism: a radical feminist analysis,* San Francisco: Frog in the Well.

Nightwind, A. (1997) 'The new femininity.' Available: http://www.zy.net/elektra/femmeworld/NEWFEM.html (accessed 11 April 1997).

Nogle, V. (1981) 'Lesbianfeminist rhetoric as a social movement,' in J.W. Chesebro (ed.) *GaySpeak: gay male and lesbian communication,* New York: Pilgrim Press.

Olson, J. (1994) 'Butch icons of the silver screen,' in L. Burana, Roxxie and L. Due (eds) *Dagger: on butch women,* Pittsburgh: Cleis Press.

Onlywomen Press (eds) (1981) *Love Your Enemy? The debate between heterosexual feminism and political lesbianism,* London: Onlywomen Press.

Orwell, G. (1945/1987) *Animal Farm: a fairy story,* London: Penguin.

O'Sullivan, S. (1994) 'Girls who kiss girls and who cares?,' in: D. Hamer and B. Budge (eds) *The Good, the Bad, and the Gorgeous: popular culture's romance with lesbianism,* London: Pandora.

Paglia, C. (2001) 'The energy mess and fascist gays,' *Salon.com,* 23 May. Available: <http://dir.salon.com/people/col/pagl/2001/05.23/oil.index.html?pn=3> (accessed 25 March 2005).

——. (2002) 'The gay inquisition,' *FrontPageMagazine.com,* 19 July. Available: <http://www.frontpagemagazine.com/Articles/Printable.asp?ID=1975> (accessed 25 March 2005).

Penelope, J. (1975) 'Prescribed passivity: the language of sexism,' in R. Ourdouba-dian (ed.) *Views on Language,* Murfreesboro: Inter-University Publishing.

——. (1978) 'Sexist grammar,' *College English,* March: 800–11.

——. (1983) 'Whose past are we reclaiming?,' *Common Lives, Lesbian Lives,* 9: 18.

——. (1990) *Speaking Freely: unlearning the lies of the father tongue,* New York: Pergamon.

——. (1996): 'Passing lesbians: the high cost of femininity,' in L. Mohin (ed.) *An Intimacy of Equals: lesbian feminist ethics,* London: Onlywomen Press.

Phelan, S. (1993) '(Be)Coming out: lesbian identity and politics,' *Signs: Journal of Women in Culture,* 18(4): 765–90.

——. (1998) 'Public discourse and the closeting of butch lesbians,' in S.R. Munt and C. Smyth (eds) *Butch/Femme: inside lesbian gender,* London: Cassell.

Pointing, L. (1997) 'Arena Three: trailblazing lesbian magazine,' *Brighton Ourstory Project Newsletter,* 3. Online. Available: <http://www.brightonourstory.co.uk/newsletters/winter97/arena.htm> (accessed 12 August 2007).

Ponse, B. (1978) *Identities in the Lesbian World: the social construction of self* (Contributions in Sociology 28), London: Greenwood.

Queen, R.M. (1997) '"I don't speak spritch": locating lesbian language,' in A. Livia and K. Hall (eds) *Queerly Phrased: language, gender, and sexuality,* New York: Oxford University Press.

——. (2004) '"I am a woman, hear me roar": the importance of linguistic stereotype for lesbian identity performance,' in R.T. Lakoff, *Language and Woman's Place,* 2nd revised and expanded edn, ed. M. Bucholtz, Oxford: Oxford University Press.

Quim (1991) 'Hello again,' *Quim,* 2: n.pag.

Radicalesbians 'The woman identified woman,' paper presented at the Second Conference to Unite Women, New York, May 1970; reprinted in A. Koedt and S. Firestone (eds) (1971) *Notes from the Third Year: women's liberation,* New York: Notes from the Second Year; and also in S.L. Hoagland and J. Penelope (eds) (1988) *For Lesbians Only: a separatist anthology,* London: Onlywomen Press.

Raymond, J. (1979) *The Transsexual Empire: the making of a she-male,* Boston: Beacon.

——. (1989) 'Putting the politics back into lesbianism,' *Women's Studies International Forum,* 12(2): 149–56.

Rednour, S (2000) *The Femme's Guide to the Universe,* Los Angeles: Alyson.

Reicher, S. and Hopkins, N. (2001) *Self and Nation: categorization, contestation and mobilization,* London: Sage.

Reisigl, M. 'How to name a discourse,' paper presented at Symposium on Critical Discourse Analysis, Birmingham/UK, June 2007.

Reisigl, M. and Wodak, R. (2001) *Discourse and Discrimination,* London: Routledge.

Rich, A. (1980) 'Compulsory heterosexuality and lesbian existence,' *Signs: Journal of Women in Culture,* 5(4): 631–60.

Richardson, D. (1996) '"Misguided, dangerous and wrong": on the maligning of radical feminism,' in D. Bell and R. Klein (eds) *Radically Speaking: feminism reclaimed,* London: Zed Books.

Robertson, D. (1985) *The Penguin Dictionary of Politics,* London: Penguin.

Robinson, P. (2005) *Queer Wars: the new gay right and its critics,* Chicago: University of Chicago Press.

Rodgers, B. (1979) *Gay Talk: a dictionary of gay slang,* New York: Putnam.

Roof, J. (1998) '1970s lesbian feminism meets 1990s butch-femme,' in S.R. Munt and C. Smyth (eds) *Butch/Femme: inside lesbian gender,* London: Cassell.

Rosenduft, R. (2005) 'Now it's our party,' *Velvetpark,* 8: 18–27.

Rostow, A. (2004) 'Marriage of inconvenience,' *Girlfriends*, May: 14–15.

Rothbart, M. and Taylor, M (1992) 'Category labels and social reality: do we view social categories as natural kinds?,' in G.R. Semin and K. Fiedler (eds) *Language, Interaction and Social Cognition*, London: Sage.

Rubin, G. (1981) 'The leather menace: comments on politics and S/M,' in Samois (eds) *Coming to Power: writings and graphics on lesbian S/M*, Boston: Alyson.

Ryder, M.E. 'Tweaking transitivity,' paper presented at the Pragmatics and Stylistics Research Group, Lancaster University/UK, April 2007.

Sacha-Savannah (1983) 'Message to readers,' *Sequel*, 33: 3.

Samois (eds) (1981) *Coming to Power: writings and graphics on lesbian S/M*, Boston: Alyson.

Sauntson, H. (2006) 'Education, culture and the construction of sexual identity: an APPRAISAL analysis of lesbian coming out narratives,' in H. Sauntson and S. Kyratzis (eds) *Language, Sexualities and Desires: cross-cultural perspectives*, Basingstoke: Palgrave.

——. and Kyratzis, S. (2006a) 'Introduction: language, sexualities and desires,' in H. Sauntson and S. Kyratzis (eds) *Language, Sexualities and Desires: cross-cultural perspectives*, Basingstoke: Palgrave.

——. and Kyratzis, S. (2006b) (eds) *Language, Sexualities and Desires: cross-cultural perspectives*, Basingstoke: Palgrave.

Schmidt, S.M. (2005) *Lesbenlust und Kinoliebe* [Lesbian Lust and Cinematic Love], Kirchlinteln/Germany: Hoffmann und Hoyer.

Scott, N. (2005) 'The trouble with the Gay Left.' Available: <http://www.homocon.com/archives/2005/04/the_trouble_wit.html> (accessed 12 August 2007).

Searle, J.R. (1969) *Speech Acts: an essay in the philosophy of language*, Cambridge: Cambridge University Press.

Sedgwick, E.K. (1990) *Epistemology of the Closet*, Berkeley: University of California Press.

Seif, H. (1999) 'To love women, or to not love men: chronicles of lesbian identification,' in D. Atkins (ed.) *Lesbian Sex Scandals: sexual practices, identities, and politics*, New York: Harrington Park Press.

Shugar, D.R. (1995) *Separatism and Women's Community*, Lincoln: University of Nebraska Press.

Shulman, S. (1983) 'When lesbians came out in the movement,' *Trouble & Strife*, 1: 51–6.

Simmons, T. (1997) 'British lesbian magazines from feminism to commercialism,' unpublished BA dissertation, De Montfort University.

Smyth, C. (1992) *Lesbians Talk Queer Notions*, London: Scarlet.

Snyder, K. (2003) *Lavender Road to Success: the career guide for the gay community*, Berkeley: Ten Speed Press.

Solanas, J. (1993) 'Well frankly . . . ', *Shebang*, 5: 5.

Sontag, S. (1964) 'Notes on "camp"', in S. Sontag (1994) *Against Interpretation*, London: Vintage.

Spears, R. A. (1985) 'On the etymology of dike,' *American Speech*, 60: 318–27.

Spender, D. (1980) *Man Made Language*, London: Pandora.

Stanley, J.P. (1970) 'Homosexual slang,' *American Speech*, 45: 45–9.

Stein, Ar. (1992) 'Sisters and queers: the decentering of lesbian feminism,' *Socialist Review*, 22(1): 33–55.

——. (1997) *Sex and Sensibility: stories of a lesbian generation*, Berkeley: University of California Press.

Stein, At. (1999) '"Without contraries is no progression": S/M, binary thinking, and the lesbian purity test,' in D. Atkins (ed.) *Lesbian Sex Scandals: sexual practices, identities, and politics*, New York: Harrington Park Press.

Steinberg, A. (2005): 'The lesbians behind Cable TV,' *Curve*, October: 42–3.

Steinem, G. (1978) 'The politics of supporting lesbianism,' in G. Vida (ed.) *Our Right to Love: a lesbian resource book,* Englewood Cliffs, NJ: Prentice-Hall.

Stone, D. (1988) 'A selfish kind of giving,' in I. Rieder and P. Ruppelt (eds) *AIDS: the women,* San Francisco: Cleis Press.

Stryker, S. (2001) *Queer Pulp: perverted passions from the golden age of the paperback,* Vancouver: Chronicle Books.

Suhr, S. and Johnson, S. (2003) 'Revisiting "PC": introduction to special issue on "political correctness"', *Discourse & Society,* 14(1): 5–16.

Sutton, L.A. (1999) 'All media are created equal: do-it-yourself identity in alternative publishing,' in M. Bucholtz, A.C. Liang and L. Sutton (eds) *Reinventing Identities: the gendered self in discourse,* New York: Oxford University Press.

Swaim, K.M. (1993) *Pilgrim's Progress, Puritan Progress: discourses and contexts,* Chicago: University of Illinois Press.

Swales, R. (1990) *Genre Analysis: English in academic and research settings,* Cambridge: Cambridge University Press.

Swan, L. (2005) 'Working out,' *Pride 05:* 47–49.

Talbot, M. (1995) 'A synthetic sisterhood: false friends in a teenage magazine,' in K. Hall and M. Bucholtz (eds) *Gender Articulated: language and the socially constructed self,* New York: Routledge.

Talmy, L. (1988) 'Force dynamics in language and thought,' *Cognitive Science,* 12: 49–100.

Tennant, L. and Cripps, C. (1994) 'Sappho so good,' *Harpers and Queen,* June: 123–7.

Teo, P. (2000) 'Racism in the news: a critical discourse analysis of news reporting in two Australian newspapers,' *Discourse & Society,* 11(1): 7–49.

Thompson, D. (1993) 'Against the dividing of women: lesbian feminism and heterosexuality,' in S. Wilkinson and C. Kitzinger (eds) *Heterosexuality: a feminism and psychology reader,* London: Sage.

Thompson, G. (1996) *Introduction to Functional Grammar,* London: Arnold.

Tiklicorect, P. (1982) 'Smokers protest healthism,' in R.R. Linden, D.R. Pagano, D.E.H. Russell and S.L. Star (eds) *Against Sadomasochism: a radical feminist analysis,* San Francisco: Frog in the Well.

Trebilcot, J. (1986) 'In partial response to those who worry that separatism may be a political cop-out: an expanded definition of activism,' *off our backs,* May: 13.

Triandafyllidou, A. and Wodak, R. (2003) 'Conceptual and methodological questions in the study of collective identity,' *Journal of Language and Politics,* 2(2): 205–23.

Uszkurat, C.A. (1994) 'The lesbian heresy,' *Lip,* Spring: 14.

Valeska, L. (1975) 'The future of female separatism,' *Quest* 2: 2; reprinted in C. Bunch (eds) (1981) *Building Feminist Theory: essays from Quest, a feminist quarterly,* New York: Longman.

Valocchi, S. (1999) 'Riding the crest of a protest wave? Collective action frames in the gay liberation movement, 1969–1973,' *Mobilization,* 4(1): 59–73.

Vanasco, J. (2001): 'Richard Goldstein's heresy hunt,' *Chicago Free Press,* 14 November. Available: <http://www.indegayforum.org/news/show/26976.html> (accessed 12 August 2007).

———. (2005) 'I am a gay American,' *Independent Gay Forum.* Available: <http://www.indegayforum.org/news/show/26970.html> (accessed 12 August 2007).

Vance, C.S. 'Social construction theory: problems in the history of sexuality,' paper presented at the Homosexuality, Which Homosexuality? conference, Amsterdam, December 1987.

Van Dijk, T.A. (1993) 'Principles of critical discourse analysis,' *Discourse & Society,* 4(2): 249–83.

———. (1995) 'Discourse analysis as ideology analysis,' in C. Schäffner and A. Wenden (eds) *Language and Peace,* Aldershot: Dartmouth.

———. (2003) 'The discourse-knowledge interface,' in G. Weiss and R. Wodak (eds), *Critical Discourse Analysis: theory and interdisciplinarity,* Basingstoke: Palgrave.

———. (2006a) 'Discourse, context and cognition,' *Discourse Studies,* 8(1): 159–77.

———. (2006b) 'Text and context: 30 years later,' lecture and workshop given at Lancaster University/UK, June 2006.

—— and Kintsch, W. (1983) *Strategies of Discourse Comprehension,* New York: Academic Press.

Van Eemeren, F.H., Grootendorst, R., Johnson, R.H., Plantin, C. and Willard, C.A. (1996) *Fundamentals of Argumentation Theory: a handbook of historical backgrounds and contemporary developments,* London: Routledge.

Van Leeuwen, T. (1996) 'The representation of social actors,' in C.R. Caldas-Coulthard and M. Coulthard (eds) *Text and Practices: readings in critical discourse analysis,* London: Routledge.

———. (2008) 'News genres,' in R. Wodak and V. Koller (eds) *Communication in the Public Sphere* (Handbook of Applied Linguistics 4), Berlin: de Gruyter.

Vincent, N. (1996): 'Beyond lesbian,' *The New Republic,* 8 January. Available: <http://www.indegayforum.org/news/show/27165.html> (accessed 12 August 2007).

———. (2002) Blog entry 18 August. Available: <http://norahvincent.blogspot.com/2002_08_18_norahvincent_archive.html> (accessed 28 March 2005).

Wakeford, N. (2000) 'Cyberqueer,' in D. Bell and B.M. Kennedy (eds) *The Cybercultures Reader,* London: Routledge.

Walker, L.M. (1993) 'How to recognize a lesbian: the cultural politics of looking like what you are,' *Signs: Journal of Women in Culture,* 18(4): 866–90.

Walters, S. (1996) 'From here to queer: radical feminism, postmodernism and the lesbian menace (or, why can't a woman be more like a fag?),' *Signs: Journal of Women in Culture,* 21(4): 830–69.

Warn, S. (2005) 'Too butch for TV?,' *Curve,* 15(6): 51.

Weber, M. (1920) *The Protestant Ethic and the Spirit of Capitalism;* trans. T. Parsons (1930), London: Unwin University Books.

Weiss, A. (1992) *Vampires and Violets,* London: Jonathan Cape.

'Welcome to Aphrodite' (n.d.) Available: <http://www.zynet.co.uk/elektra/aphrodite> (accessed 11 April 1997).

Whitelaw, L. (1996) 'Lesbians on the mainscreen,' in L. Mohin (ed.) *An Intimacy of Equals: lesbian feminist ethics,* London: Onlywomen Press.

Wilchins, R.A. (1997a) 'Interview with a menace,' in R.A. Wilchins *Read My Lips: sexual subversion and the end of gender,* Ithaca, NY: Firebrand.

———. (1997b) *Read My Lips: sexual subversion and the end of gender,* Ithaca, NY: Firebrand.

Wilkinson, S. and Kitzinger, C. (1996) 'The queer backlash,' in D. Bell and R. Klein (eds) *Radically Speaking: feminism reclaimed,* London: Zed Books.

Wodak, R. (1996) *Disorders of Discourse,* Harlow: Longman.

———. (2001) 'The discourse-historical approach,' in R. Wodak and M. Meyer (eds) *Methods of Critical Discourse Analysis,* London: Sage.

———. (2006) 'Discourse-analytic and socio-linguistic approaches to the study of nation(alism),' in G. Delanty and K. Kumar (eds) *The Sage Handbook of Nations and Nationalism,* London: Sage.

—— and Krzyżanowski, M. (2008) 'Discourse studies: important concepts and terms,' in R. Wodak and M. Krzyżanowski (eds) *Qualitative Discourse Analysis in the Social Sciences,* Basingstoke: Palgrave.

—— and Schulz, M. (1986) *The Language of Love and Guilt: mother–daughter relationships from a cross-cultural perspective,* Amsterdam: Benjamins.

Wolf, D.G. (1979) *The Lesbian Community,* Berkeley: University of California Press.

Wolfson, D. (1993) 'The way we live now,' *Vogue,* September: 93–6.

Worden, D. and Andrews, I. (1981) 'In defense of lesbian separatism: a response to the Combahee River Collective statement on lesbian separatism,' in S.L. Hoagland and J. Penelope (eds) (1988) *For Lesbians Only: a separatist anthology,* London: Onlywomen Press.

Yescavage, K. and Alexander, J. (1999) 'What do you call a lesbian who's only slept with men? Answer: Ellen Morgan. Deconstructing the lesbian identities of Ellen Morgan and Ellen DeGeneres,' in D. Atkins (ed.) *Lesbian Sex Scandals: sexual practices, identities, and politics,* New York: Harrington Park Press.

*Ziggy (n.d.) 'Radical dyke rant,' *Raging Dykes,* no issue number given: n.pag.

Zimet, J. (1999) *Strange Sisters: the art of lesbian pulp fiction 1949–1969,* New York: Viking Studio.

Index

Note: Titles of books, films and magazines are set in italics; metaphor source domains are set in small capitals. References to persons do not include bibliographical references.

For Product Safety Concerns and Information please contact our EU
representative GPSR@taylorandfrancis.com
Taylor & Francis Verlag GmbH, Kaufingerstraße 24, 80331 München, Germany